Some Spirits Heal, Others Only Dance

Some Spirits Heal, Others Only Dance: A Journey into Human Selfhood in an African Village

Roy Willis

with K.B.S. Chisanga, H.M.K. Sikazwe, Kapembwa B. Sikazwe and Sylvia Nanyangwe

Oxford • New York

First published in 1999 by
Berg
Editorial offices:
150 Cowley Road, Oxford, OX4 1JJ, UK
70 Washington Square South, New York, NY 10012, USA

Berg is an imprint of Oxford International Publishers Ltd.

Library of Congress Cataloging-in-Publication Data
A catalogue record for this book is available from the Library of Congress.

British Library Cataloguing-in-Publication Data
A catalogue record for this book is available from the British Library.

ISBN 1 85973 283 6 (Cloth)
1 85973 288 7 (Paper)

Typeset by JS Typesetting, Wellingborough, Northants.
Printed in the United Kingdom by WBC Book Manufacturers, Bridgend,
Mid Glamorgan.

For Mary, who did so much

Contents

Illustrations

Preface

This is about gratitude, about recognizing the contributions of some of those many people in Ulungu, in Zambia and Tanzania and in Britain, without whom this book could never have taken shape. I'll begin by mentioning the University of Edinburgh, my academic home for more than three eventful decades. Within the university I want particularly to thank Tony Cohen, our Augustinian head of department, for his staunch support of this project, and especially for his remarkable book *Self Consciousness* (1994), which has proved such a splendid launching pad for my own speculations on human selfhood; Jane Palglaise and Frank Bechhofer for their very practical help in constructing the most recent research proposal; Eric Hanley for his good work as anchorman in 1990; and Mary Noble for wise counsel. I am also of course deeply grateful to the Economic and Social Research Council for their generosity in funding field research in Ulungu in 1990 and 1996.

In Zambia I particularly want to thank Ilse Mwanza, of the Institute for African Studies (now the Institute of Economic and Social Research) of the University of Zambia, and Jacob Mwanza; Mr Japhter Nkunika, Dr John Nghesha and Professor Oliver Saasa, all of whom did wonders in helping me through the tangled realm of Zambian bureaucracy in 1990. In Mbala special thanks are due to the former District Governor, Mr Samuel Wamuwi, Mr Manyando Mukela, who in 1990 was Director of the Moto Moto Museum, and Mike and Liz Lovett; in Tanzanian Ulungu warm thanks to Dan and Nancy Spooner of the Livingstonia Mission at Tatanda for their generous hospitality; thanks also to Dr Daniel Ndagala for his support of my research project, to the Tanzania Commission for Science and Technology for authorizing research in Tanzanian Ulungu, to my supervisor at the University of Dar es Salaam, Professor K.I. Tambila, and to Mr A.K. Mwasajone in Sumbawanga. I must also thank the Moto Moto Museum's present Director, Mr Stanford Siachoono, and various members of his staff, particularly our friends Chipo and Webster, and Mr Alex Zulu, for their material support for the research project; special thanks also to Mr Mwila Mulengo, the Museum's chief mechanic, who worked wonders in keeping us 'on the road' in 1996. In view of the accusations of venality frequently bandied about in the context of post-colonial Africa, it seems worth recording that at no time during my temporary residence in Tanzania and Zambia in 1990, and in Zambia in 1996, did I pay a bribe to any official, nor was I ever asked to do so.

Among the Lungu people themselves I am enduringly grateful for the help and hospitality of Senior Chief Tafuna and Namwene Tafuna and various senior members of the Lungu Tribal Council, especially Mr Israel Kasomo and Mr Robert Kazimoto Sinyangwe. Others who gave us particular help included Mr Paul Kaongela, Mr Richard Mazimba, Mr Dinesh Budhia, Mr Jeffreys Sinyangwe, Mr Kessingstone Mazimba and Chiefs Chitimbwa, Chungu, Zombe and Nondo.

As to the field research itself, nothing could have been achieved without the efforts of my industrious and variously talented assistants: Mr K.B.S. Chisanga, the late and lamented Mr Herbert Sikazwe, Mr Teddy Simuzosha, Mr Kapembwa B. Sikazwe and Ms Sylvia Nanyangwe. Thanks also to our two loyal domestic helpers in 1996, Mr Friday Maliawanda and Mr James Bwalya. I am also grateful to Madam Rides Nanyangwe for graciously making her home in Mankonga available to us for the 1996 research. My wife and life companion Mary did a tremendous job as unofficial manager of the research project in 1990 and I dedicate this book to her in recognition of Mary's devotion to the project and the people of Ulungu. The book itself is offered in gratitude and admiration to those people, and particularly the traditional healers, whose remarkable lives and work constitute its heart. The indigenous doctors of Ulungu occupy a small but significant part of what Edith Turner has well described as an Africa-wide 'laboratory of traditional healing . . . a laboratory that is kept from being swamped under the domination of science by the very poverty of the continent' (1992: 178).

Here let me also thank my students in Edinburgh, and in the Universities of Virginia, the University of California Santa Cruz, Newfoundland, Göteborg and Uppsala for their enthusiasm and critical acumen, which have served to maintain my commitment to ethnographic research as a possible path to wisdom, albeit a hazardous and often lonely one.

Thanks too to Justin Kenrick for stimulating criticism in the early stages of writing this book, and to Kathryn Earle and the anonymous referee for particularly helpful comments in the final stages. I also thank the referee for bringing to my notice Steven Friedson's excitingly innovative *Dancing Prophets* (1996), a work that resonates in many ways with my recent experience in Ulungu.[1]

Finally, if there is a Great Spirit dancing in the penumbra of this investigation it is surely that of Victor Witts Turner, he who 'dreamed of a liberated anthropology' (1985a: 177) and, inspired by the work of his own chosen ancestor spirit, the nineteenth-century philosopher Wilhelm Dilthey, strove to bring to birth an anthropology of experience, of 'man and woman alive'. If, in what follows, I critically engage with the ideas of Turner in his pursuit of that project, it is with the same grand objective in mind.

Note

1. See, in particular, Chapters 4 and 8 below.

Note on Orthography and Style

The spelling of Lungu words in this book generally adheres to a convention, codified by the Bantu linguist Wilfred Whiteley (1964), under which the English *ch* sound (as in 'church') is rendered simply by the letter *c*. A conventional exception, less logical no doubt, but which I have also followed here, retains the *ch* form in personal names: thus *Chanda*, a girl's name (and a spirit's too), but *cisaka*, 'maize', and *cuuwa*, 'malign familial spirit'.

Also in conformity with established practice, the velar *n* in *sing'aanga*, 'doctor', and *ng'oma*, 'drum', is thus rendered.

I distinguish between the title of a qualified practitioner in Western bio-medicine, rendered as Dr, and the indigenous *sing'aanga*, 'master of knowledge', by spelling the English translation in full, as Doctor. Thus in this book there is reference to Dr Muziya, head of the Government Hospital in Mbala, and to his classificatory cousin Doctor Muziya, traditional healer of Sondwa Village.

Zambia observes the 24-hour system of time reckoning and this convention is reflected in field diary references to time in this book. For example, '1830 hrs' means 6.30 p.m.

N.B. Contrary to a long-standing tradition in anthropology, there are no pseudonyms in this book. All actors, both visible and invisible, are referred to by their 'real', socially ascribed names.

Introduction: The Making of This Book

The story goes like this. In 1993 I narrowly missed getting funded for a return visit to Zambian Ulungu on the basis of a rather conventional proposal to study 'spirit possession' in that corner of East-Central Africa. Under the ESRC's rules, any further application for funding had to be framed as a recognizably new project. Then, serendipitously, I had a hunch about two evident growth areas in anthropological theory, both of which had the distinction, which made them sneakily attractive to me, of seeming rather less than kosher, dangerously 'fuzzy' as topics for social-scientific enquiry. Anthony Cohen's ground-breaking book *Self Consciousness* (1994) indeed begins by recalling how an earlier anthropology had assumed that in 'primitive' society individuals lacked any sense of fundamental autonomy and thought of themselves, in line with Durkheim's classical model of 'mechanical solidarity', as so many interchangeable components of the all-encompassing social whole. Cohen's book is a powerful argument for the universality of what he calls 'the authorial self' as the foundation of human society. The extreme radicality of this proposition has, I think, yet to be fully appreciated. Cohen marshals an impressive array of ethnographic evidence in favour of his thesis, but the appeal of this remarkable book is as much to the reader's intuition as to his intellect. This has to be so, because in 'the authorial self' Cohen is concerned with the very core of humanhood, which in its nature exists before[1] society, language and rational thought: it is, as Cohen says, 'methodologically out of reach' (1994: 179). The existence of this occult entity has, therefore, to be inferred from its 'objective' reflections in social forms and actions, much as physicists infer the existence of fundamental particles from their observed tracks in cloud chambers.

In the realm of ordinary, observable reality, Cohen tells us, the hidden 'authorial' self is manifest at any particular time as the occupant of a social role. Individuals occupy distinct roles at different moments, but the authorial self 'provides experiential continuity throughout a life which would otherwise be a series of disjunctions of the kind depicted by the structural functionalist role theorists' (1994: 68). In Cohen's view the human being is thus an amalgam of opposing qualities: 'I am simultaneously an individual, and yet part of relationships; unique, but conventional; the product of my genetic endowment, but also of society' (1994: 153).

For me this enduring and ultimately mysterious 'hidden reality' behind the partial and shifting surface of disparate and changing social roles resonated with another topic of contention in current anthropology, that of 'spirit'. The matter has been posed most forcefully by Edith Turner in an article with the challenging title 'The reality of spirits: a tabooed or permittted field of study?': 'Again and again anthropologists witness spirit rituals, and again and again some indigenous exegete tries to explain that spirits are present, and furthermore that rituals are the central events of their society. And the anthropologist proceeds to interpret them differently' (1993: 11). Edith Turner's argument for the 'reality' of entities traditional anthropology has customarily dismissed as illusory arises from her reported perception of a 'spirit form' at the climax of a healing ritual among the Ndembu of north-western Zambia in 1985: 'Then I knew the Africans were right, there *is* spirit stuff, there *is* spirit affliction, it isn't a matter of metaphor and symbol, or even psychology' (ibid.: 9).

What struck me in 1995 was a sense of similarity in kind between this ordinarily hidden 'stuff' Edith Turner called 'spirit' and the invisible 'authorial' self with its transcendence of the ordinary, partial and ephemeral reality of social relations. Zambian Ulungu readily suggested itself as a locale where such a hypothesis might be tested and refined, since I knew from research there in 1990[2] that the 'traditional' religion of territorial and other 'spirit' entities remained viable, in surprising contrast to the state of affairs among the neighbouring Tabwa and Fipa peoples (Willis 1968b: Roberts 1984). Somewhat to my surprise, in view of its seemingly esoteric nature, a proposal to the ESRC to conduct research on these lines was accepted and funded.[3]

During the 1990 research my interest had been particularly excited by reports of a secretive cult called *ngulu*, concerned with the purported 'possession' of people by 'spirits' associated with the natural environment. Here then, in the case of a people with a distinctly different traditional culture from my own Western-scientific background, was a chance to test out the newly born idea that the human sense of selfhood, though arising out of and formed within a social matrix, had an inherent tendency to 'go beyond' established knowledge and experience to embrace the 'alien' and 'other'. Perhaps indeed such a project was what human intercourse with 'spirits' was about.

Then back in the 'field' in 1996 I succeeded, with the help of three enterprising Lungu research assistants, in observing, filming and participating in five *ngulu* rituals in the heartland of Ulungu, a few miles from Lake Tanganyika. Further research showed that the *ngulu* adepts were a subcategory in a wider grouping of knowledge-bearing indigenous healers. Many of these could fairly be described as 'non-ordinary' people, a significant number of whom had acquired their special status through suffering personal catastrophe. Comparison of testimonies from 208 Lungu healers, including 'herbalists', 'spirit'-aided doctors (numerically the largest category) and female experts in sexuality and reproductive problems, suggests that a dominant characteristic was their tendency to 'go beyond' social and even human boundaries in pursuit of healing knowledge and powers.

A major – and unexpected – finding in this research was the widespread significance of dreaming in healers' development and acquisition of esoteric knowledge. Further, and this discovery was equally unexpected, it appeared that the distinctive, named social roles performed by the various kinds of Lungu healer were not as mutually exclusive as I had assumed: they often overlapped, the boundaries tended to be fluid rather than fixed. I concluded that what was generally distinctive of Lungu healers was their expanded sense of selfhood, an 'expanded self' which was also a unity of plural and disparate components.[4] Seemingly, healers were able to integrate their social selves, grounded in experience of familial, tribal and village identities, with ecological selfhood, relations with the non-human domain of the 'bush', which was both the home of *ngulu* spirits and the source of healing 'medicines'. The final chapter of this book suggests parallels between these Lungu 'explorers of consciousness' and the shifting and multiple experience of selfhood being propagated in our present, rapidly changing 'Western' culture through the combined effects of global economics and a media-driven awakening of a historically new sense of global interconnectedness and nascent planetary identity.

So this 'journey into human selfhood' has led me to a considerable elaboration of Anthony Cohen's picture of the 'authorial self' as embodied in a cluster of social roles and also to a related revaluation of the concept of 'spirit' raised so pointedly by Edith Turner. In the present enquiry human selfhood emerges not just as the substantive, if elusive, entity evoked by Cohen, but also, and equally, the negation of that 'authorial' self's irreducible particularity, in the innate impulsion of self-consciousness towards expansion, towards identification with alien otherness, in that expansive process potentially taking on ecological, even cosmic attributes.[5]

The Drama of Ethnographic Discovery

My intention in this book has been to take the reader along with me in a re-creation, through relevant use of excerpts from the fieldwork diary, of the process of ethnographic enquiry which led to these conclusions: the recurrent modifications and reformulations of theory in the light of new evidence, the puzzlements, frustrations and transient ecstasies experienced along the way. In recounting this story I also draw upon the insights of the 1990 research, the moments of understanding that contributed to making what was of value in the entire field endeavour a veritable *Erlebnis* or 'lived experience' in the Diltheyan sense of a structured unit of meaning transcending the constraints of ordinary time and locality (see Turner 1985: 224, 226).

This story of anthropological adventure is interwoven with a contrasting theme. This is the development of relations between the four people primarily involved in the 1996 research: the author and his three Lungu 'research assistants', who were also his primary sources of information. Again the field diary is freely drawn upon. The reason for the occasional prominence given to this material is that, as Goulet has recently noted, 'all ethnographic data are produced or created in the context of social, dialogical interactions between ethnographer and informant' (1994: 19).[6] An account of the production of ethnographic knowledge, such as this book aims to be, has therefore also to offer some kind of history of interactions between the main actors in the drama, however partial.[7]

The story I am telling here is, then, simultaneously an exploration of a – on the face of it – strikingly alien culture, and an account of the passions, anxieties, puzzlements and conflicts peculiar to this unusual and still imperfectly understood enterprise anthropologists call field research.

The Making of the Anthropologist

The next chapter introduces the diverse personages of my Lungu research assistants. But what of Roy Willis, that other significant actor in the drama? I now outline, as 'objectively' as I can, the relevant events shaping his life and personality.[8]

I was born of white British parents near London, England, in 1927. Childhood and adolescence were unremarkable apart from frequent moves occasioned by the aerial bombardment suffered by this corner of the country during the Second World War. A conventional middle-class upbringing that included persistent exposure to the teachings of the Church of England predictably led to the Marxism and militant atheism of my teenage persona. I left school as soon as I legally could, aged sixteen, and became an apprentice reporter with a local weekly newspaper. The war had just ended when I was drafted into the army in late 1945. Eight months later my military career came to an abrupt conclusion when I succumbed to polio while serving in Egypt. There followed eight months in hospital before I was able to walk again, after a fashion.

Life-threatening illness struck a second time in 1953. Curiously enough, I was in Zambia – then known by its colonial name of Northern Rhodesia – working for a local English-language newspaper called the *Northern News*. It was an exciting time to be there. I remember meeting the young Kenneth Kaunda, later to be the first president of independent Zambia, and his mentor, that flamboyant and bibulous hero of the anticolonial struggle Harry Nkumbula. Then suddenly I was rushed to hospital suffering from a burst appendix, which in turn brought on the potentially lethal condition of peritonitis.

Lying critically ill in a hospital in Ndola (the name means 'I see'), I had what has since come to be called a near-death experience (NDE)[9]. It consisted of a vision, appearing as if on a huge television screen about five feet in front of me, of a path that became two, one branch leading steeply upwards to my right, and the other running a short distance over green and level ground to a gate. I could see through this gate, noting that the level ground continued on the other side. I knew, however, that if I passed through that gate, which would have been easy to do, there would be no returning. Suddenly I became angry: why should I die now, at the age of twenty-six, before I'd even lived? I resolved to take the other path, no matter how steep and difficult it was.

At that moment of decision I felt myself carried away by an overwhelming force – in the mind's eye it was a roaring torrent, with myself no more than a cork or a leaf floating on the surface. At the same time I was aware of a rapid upwards movement, as in a fast lift or elevator. Three days later I was out of that hospital, walking around in the African sun. I learned then that the medical prognosis had been terminal.

My experience lacked certain features which have been described as typical of NDEs in the more recent studies (see Moody 1975), notably passage through a tunnel towards a brilliant white light, meetings with departed relatives and divine or semi-divine spiritual leaders such as Jesus, Mohammed, Moses or Krishna. Nonetheless, it may seem surprising that this experience of the intervention of what a religious person would probably call a 'higher power' failed to change my 'world-view' from conventional rationalistic materialism: somehow I managed to 'bracket off' this first encounter with the paranormal as little more than a curious, if ultimately inexplicable, event.

Journalism in Africa had, however, aroused a deep curiosity about the possibility of other life-ways and in 1960 I quit my job with Reuters news agency in London and entered Oxford University as a mature student to study social anthropology at the feet of the renowned Edward Evans-Pritchard. In 1962 I returned to Africa to do field research with the Fipa people of south-west Tanganyika (later Tanzania), spending seventeen months in a village there.

My first academic job was in Daryll Forde's anthropology department at University College London. From there I took a lectureship at Edinburgh University in 1967 and was promoted to reader ten years later. Deep strangeness entered my life again in 1980 when, without knowing why I was doing it, I abandoned my secure academic post. All I knew was that I'd been seized by a force as irresistible as the one that carried me out of the shadow of death in 1953. The difference this time was that I had no idea where I was going, what lay ahead. It was as if I'd jumped off a precipice into the unimaginable. Struggling to make sense of what was happening to my life, I experimented with illicit mind-altering substances, joined the Campaign for Nuclear Disarmament (CND), searched for spiritual roots in what I could learn of ancient wisdom. The quest led me to the literature of the nineteenth-century occult revival in Britain, and thence to Aleister Crowley and neopaganism.

By this time I'd come to see that my frightening transformative experience was itself of anthropological interest and I re-entered the grove of academe in Edinburgh, albeit *sans* job. Then in early 1983 I returned to Egypt for the first time since being struck down with polio there thirty-seven years earlier, ostensibly to see my stepson Jo, who was living in Cairo. While visiting Alexandria I underwent the most powerful paranormal experience of my life while sitting near a historical monument called Pompey's Column. It happened at noon on Friday 18 March. Sitting near the imposing fourth-century obelisk erected by the Christian patriarch Theophilus, I became aware of a voice that sounded, paradoxically, as if it were coming both from immensely far away and from deep inside me. The speech was flowing, powerful and beautiful as a river of liquid silver and, although the words were English, it was being translated, by some mechanism that also looked 'silvery', from an unknown tongue. What was said was arresting. I was, it seemed, 'guiltless and free'. Then, following something about 'karmic debt', the mysterious sentence: 'After long exile the King has come home.' I then felt myself being immersed in healing water, a wonderfully liberating experience. Finally, at about fifteen degrees above the horizon to the (I think) north of where I sat, I saw the most unexpected and astonishing object: a silver-gold cylinder tapered and rounded at both ends, with two rows of nine square windows running along its central part. These windows were glowing with an amber light as if illumined from within and the whole object, which was very beautiful, was slowly turning on its axis. After a few moments this vision, which was startlingly clear, faded and I returned to ordinary reality. The whole experience probably lasted no more than a few seconds. Before it I'd been feeling depressed and disgusted with myself; but afterwards I felt as one reborn, made anew.

Several years later came the chance discovery that the site of my Alexandrian experience had been the centre of a famed solar cult of healing and fertility in late dynastic Egypt.[10]

Five months later, back in Scotland and doing research into 'alternative' medicine, I made the surprising and disturbing discovery that I could heal, through some energy that appeared to flow through the palms of my hands. This revelation came after I'd enrolled as an 'anthropological spy' in a five-day course run by a renowned healer called Bruce Macmanaway. The evening of the second day, to my surprise, a number of Bruce's clients came in for treatment and I was dismayed when Bruce, after consulting the pendulum he used for divination, assigned me to 'heal' one of them. My 'patient' was a middle-aged woman who told me she suffered from chronic back pain. Feeling thoroughly foolish I stood behind this woman as she sat in a chair and placed my hands on her shoulders as I'd seen demonstrated by Bruce. A few moments later I was surprised when the woman said she felt 'heat' in the affected part of her back and even more surprised a little later when she said the pain was gone. Though inclined to dismiss this incident as an example of the force of 'suggestion', I was sufficiently impressed by it and Bruce's evident sincerity to put my putative 'gift' to the test soon afterwards with cooperative and variously afflicted friends and neighbours, as well as some ailing domestic animals and plants. The uniformly positive results finally convinced me of the reality of this newly emerged faculty.

At Bruce's centre in 1983 I'd also had some remarkable visual and tactile experiences while sitting in a meditation group, notably a meeting with a large and friendly jaguar – my first encounter with what I later came to recognize as a shamanic 'power animal' (see Harner 1980) – and a vision of a naked young woman with long golden hair walking along a seashore.

Three years later I attended another five-day course for established healers at Bruce's centre. There I had a scarifying encounter, again while meditating under Bruce's guidance, with a powerful female entity who was naked except for a golden helmet-mask that covered her entire head. When I (mentally) asked if I could see her face the entity replied that I 'would have to wait', but indicated that she was from the 'Middle East', leaving me trembling and mystified.

The following year, weary of dependence on state welfare, I set up a healing business and for ten months made a modest living from my late-appearing gift until invited to take up a post as visiting professor in the University of Göteborg, Sweden. I also wrote and published a paper analysing the results of my healing practice and noted a success rate of around eighty-five per cent – this with patients suffering from a wide range of afflictions, most of which had proved recalcitrant to treatment by orthodox medicine. I also described the sensation of healing, the curious sense of 'standing aside' and letting the 'healing energy', which seems to have an intelligence of its own, flow through me into the patient. While this is happening I seem to be in a light and pleasant state of trance. One curious finding was that the subjective 'faith' or scepticism of clients about my mysterious 'powers' seemed to have no effect, one way or the other, on the outcome (Willis 1992a).

Looking back over the past decade, I now see it as a period when anthropology, especially the theory and practice of field research, has again become the principal focus of my life and thought, while healing work has been subsidiary and occasional, together with the organization of neo-shamanic courses and workshops (Willis 1994). I also notice a tendency for all these activities to become integrated into a coherent whole. Thus, my field research among the Lungu-speaking peoples has evolved from a general concern with the forms of a strange culture into a particular interest in the local manifestations in this corner of East-Central Africa of a theme that has emerged as the dominant and compelling issue in my own life: the metamorphoses of the self in interaction with a world of wondrous and alien powers.

I have to say finally that virtually nothing remains of the various ideological constructs successively adopted in response to the seismic psychic events briefly narrated here, and which culminated in mid-1995 in a thoroughly disconcerting connection with primitive Christianity. During a spontaneous 'altered state' lasting three days I encountered a group of three divinities who appeared as columns of light. Despite their formless identity I 'knew' that one was male, another female and the third androgynous. I also 'knew' that the female divinity was both my mysterious visitor of nine years earlier and an entity who last incarnated two thousand years ago as the biblical figure Mary Magdalene, when she became the companion and lover of Jesus the Nazarene.[11] I was unaware of the identities of the other two divinities apart from their sexuality. I have no idea how this 'knowledge' was acquired – it seemed to have been inserted into my mind surreptitiously, as it were. By the same means I suddenly 'knew' that in an incarnation about twelve millennia ago I, as a 'divine king' of Lower Egypt, had been united in 'sacred marriage' (*hieros gamos*)[12] with the same entity who later became Mary Magdalene and who was originally a golden-haired 'love goddess' from the stars. A year later, on the eve of departure for further field research in Ulungu, a fresh insight came all unbidden while in the midst of delivering an academic paper in the strictly secular milieu of the London School of Economics. It was that, although I had memories aplenty, I am finally, it seems, devoid of *post facto* 'beliefs': a bleak but oddly liberating revelation. That's the situation as of now.

Notes

1. 'Before' in a double sense: developmentally (see discussion in the final chapter of this book on neonate 'consciousness') and logically, in that, for Cohen, authentic humanhood presupposes 'authorial' selfhood.
2. Grant reference no. R000 23 1632. See Willis (1991a).
3. Grant reference no. R000 22 1793.
4. Friedson makes a similar point when he writes of the 'expansion of self' experienced by the entranced Tumbuka *nchimi* or 'prophet' (1996: 30).
5. I make no claim to originality with this idea, which has become almost commonplace in Western intellectual circles through the 'eco-philosophy' associated with the Norwegian thinker Arne Naess.
6. It was Roy Wagner who first proposed that ethnography was a joint creation of anthropologist and 'informant' in his landmark statement *The Invention of Culture* (1975). See also Michael Jackson (1989) on ethnographic 'radical empiricism'.
7. In contrast, in classical anthropology the subjectivities of the anthropologist and his indispensable local helpers are ideally invisible to the reader. For many years I adhered to this convention, even publishing a monograph on the Fipa from the position of a disembodied intelligence floating high above the landscape (Willis 1981). Ironically,

I had earlier published an article, 'Is the anthropologist human?' (Willis 1975) that anticipated by eleven years one of the central insights of that bible of 'post-modern' anthropology, *Writing Culture* (Clifford and Marcus 1986): the contradiction between the emotional intensity of first-hand field research and the distanced, third-person style in which the search results were conventionally presented in published form.

8. The need for such information has been urged on me by Kathryn Earle and by the anonymous referee of the original manuscript, and I am grateful to them for making this point.
9. The first modern scientific study of such experiences appears to be Moody (1975), who attributes their relative frequency in recent years, in part at least, to the efficacy of medical resuscitation techniques.
10. I made this discovery while browsing through the *Encyclopaedia Britannica* in Edinburgh University library in about 1988. The cult was focused on a synthetic deity called Serapis, an amalgam of Greek and Egyptian deities, including Asklepius, the mythological founder of Hellenic medicine, Hades, god of the Greek underworld, the eternally dying and reborn Egyptian god Osiris, and the solar bull Apis (see Forster 1922). In 1992, while doing research for a volume called *World Mythology*, I came across evidence in Robert Temple's book *The Sirius Mystery,* suggesting that the sacred lineage of this site in Alexandria reached back much earlier, to the remote prehistory of the Middle East. Temple also associated this part of Egypt and this specific site with ancient traditions of visitation by extraterrestrial beings (Temple 1976: 123, 166).
11. As is recorded in the Gnostic Gospels (Pagels 1979), a document discovered in Egypt in 1945 after lying buried for two millenia. It was after this experience that I read Michèle Roberts's imaginative novel *The Wild Girl*, based on this story of Jesus and Mary Magdalene (her name comes from her home village of Magdala, on the shore of the Sea of Galilee in northern Israel).
12. In the ancient, pre-patriarchal Middle East the ritual union of the King and the 'Holy Whore' symbolized the cosmic marriage of Heaven and Earth, guaranteeing the peace and prosperity of land and people (see Long 1992: 133–4).

–1–

Research Assistance

> To him [K.B.S. Chisanga] I go for information on every aspect of Lungu culture and history. He has after all grown up as a child and adolescent in the period of full-blooded anti-colonial struggle, known the pains of exile and the triumphs of victorious nationalism as well as the aftermath of slow disillusion. (Diary 8.8.96)

> He [Chisanga] is good at solving other people's problems, but can't solve his own. (Comment by Kapembwa Sikazwe, Diary 3.9.96)

> He [Chisanga] goes round and round through 360 degrees, always finishing up with – [a named relative]. (Comment by Sylvia Nanyangwe, Diary 13.12.96)

In 1990 my principal helpers in the task of gathering information about Lungu society and culture were K.B.S. Chisanga and H.M.K. Sikazwe.[1] Both were men of mature years, native speakers of ciLungu and possessed of a wide knowledge of Lungu history and social institutions. Mr Chisanga had as a young man worked for the anthropologist William Watson during his research in the 1950s with the neighbouring Mambwe people and he had also been employed for several years as an archaeological research assistant with the Rhodes–Livingstone Museum, and later as a civil servant administering agricultural loans in post-independence Zambia.

Mr Sikazwe had a history of official and commercial employment in Lusaka and the Copperbelt before returning home to farm in Ulungu in 1983. In 1990 he was running a successful practice as a traditional healer or *sing'aanga*, based on a knowledge of herbal and other remedies, which he had inherited from his father. Both men had been active in the anti-colonial political struggle: Mr Chisanga had spent time in Tanzania as a political refugee and Mr Sikazwe was twice imprisoned for 'political' offences during the late colonial period.

Mr Chisanga was particularly valuable because of his wide range of contacts at all levels of Lungu society from the paramount chief Tafuna and the various subchiefs to the indigenous priests, prophets and village headmen, many of whom he knew through his work in the then governing

United National Independence Party (UNIP). Although Mr Sikazwe had, like Mr Chisanga, been an active party worker and office-holder, his contribution to the field research lay mainly through his inside knowledge of traditional medicine and contacts associated with his work as a healer, which included other traditional doctors and female experts on sexuality and reproduction called *navimbuuza*.[2]

The personalities of these two men made a striking contrast. Mr Chisanga was quite tall and moved with a conscious elegance; he had an undeniable 'presence' and an assured way of talking, which, in public situations, could seem charismatic; his air of patrician *gravitas* was leavened by a roguish twinkle of the eye and a winning smile, both of which could seem a touch contrived. Mr Sikazwe was a mercurial little man endowed with spontaneous warmth and enormous energy, his speech readily blossoming into a torrent of rhetoric. There was also a notable difference between the domestic situations of these two men. Herbert Sikazwe had in 1983 inherited the widow of a paternal cousin, along with this woman's five children and his cousin's substantial house and estate. In 1990 we (that is, my wife Mary and myself) found Herbert Sikazwe and his extensive family enjoying a prosperous existence in the village of Mankonga, five miles from the busy Lake Tanganyika port of Mpulungu. In contrast, Mr Chisanga's home was a modest cluster of wattle-and-daub huts, which he shared with his 'mother' (actually a maternal aunt in English terms) and a 'sister' (cousin) and her two young children. He told us he had been married five times, but all these unions had ended in divorce or separation.

Sadly, we were not to see again the dynamic little man we had affectionately called 'Herbie the Herbalist'. Mr Sikazwe died in October 1993 after a long illness, which some said was acquired immune deficiency syndrome (AIDS), although others disputed this diagnosis.[3]

Mr Chisanga kept me posted with news from Ulungu. Finally I was able to return to Zambia and met him in Lusaka, looking older and thinner than I remembered, but basically still the same self-assured, remarkably well-informed individual. We spent the days of waiting for my work permit and money to come through, searching for suitable transport and reviewing the tape recordings we had made in 1990.

> He is extremely intelligent, seems to know something about everyone and everything. (Diary 19.7.96)

> Ballard [Chisanga] came in and listened with me to the Chitimbwa/Cisuungu tapes, his face registering intense interest, amusement, sometimes compassion. (Diary 23.7.96)

Archetypal Power

As the almost reverential tone of these Diary excerpts suggests, by July 1996 K.B.S. Chisanga had become something very different from the 'transparent' medium of ethnographic reality of the classical paradigm. He appeared at this time to be a uniquely qualified emissary from another world, who was also conversant with the concepts and values of my own. Beings of this kind are possessed of an archetypal power, and such were the founders of the great religions. In anthropology one of the earliest examples of this genre is Griaule's Dogon muse Ogotemmêli (Griaule 1951). More recently, the Western popular imagination has been gripped by the probably mythical figure of the shaman Don Juan, who supposedly initiated Castaneda into the 'separate reality' of the Yaqui cosmos (Castaneda 1968, 1971).

Another and more relevant comparison is with Victor Turner's principal source of esoteric information on Ndembu culture, the celebrated Muchona the Hornet. On the face of it, these two men appear to have little in common. As described by Turner, Muchona is a diminutive and somewhat comical figure, with his high-pitched voice and (in terms of his own, Ndembu, culture) odd affinity with women: 'Without being markedly effeminate in his deportment, Muchona always seemed more at ease among women than men . . . he identified himself closely with his mother, even to the extent of speaking in an alto voice' (Turner 1967).

Chisanga, on the contrary, has an almost exaggeratedly masculine, even macho bearing. He appears distrustful of women, on one occasion remarking to me that 'they are all sorcerers, including my mother'. Indeed his view of humanity in general, perhaps reflecting his long involvement in politics, tends to be cynical, whereas Turner remarks on the 'curious innocence' of Muchona, for whom 'in the balance mankind came off well' (ibid.). Muchona was a doctor-diviner who had acquired his spirit helpers and therapeutic powers after emerging from a severe psychosomatic disorder. Chisanga has no such indigenous vocation, although his natural curiosity about the esoteric aspects of his own culture has given him a wide general knowledge of Lungu religion and medicine.

A Rootless Wanderer

Despite these major differences in background and personality, however, in one crucial respect there is a remarkable similarity between these two men. They are both, as Turner says of Muchona, 'doomed to rootless wandering'. The wide range of human and social experience born of this rootlessness, says Turner, was the source of Muchona's unusual ability to compare and generalize about the institutions and ideas of his own culture. Something similar could be said of Chisanga, who is, like Muchona, 'a restless man, seldom at home anywhere for long' (Turner 1967).

In 1990 Chisanga gave me an account of his own life, beginning with his birth in Abercorn (Mbala) in 1933. After leaving secondary school he worked briefly in Tanganyika before returning home to marry his first wife in 1955. This marriage soon ended in divorce. He then worked for Posts and Telegraphs in Abercorn for a year, leaving for political reasons, because the company was brought under the control of the then Federal Government, dominated by white-supremacist Southern Rhodesia. He remained single for six years, until his parents 'forced' him to remarry. This marriage ended after two years. It was during this time he worked for the anthropologist William Watson and afterwards for the Rhodes–Livingstone Museum. Returning to Abercorn, Chisanga became involved in Kenneth Kaunda's UNIP and in 1962 fled to newly independent Tanganyika to avoid political persecution by the colonial government. There he made contact with UNIP émigrés and was made secretary of the party's regional office in Tanga. He travelled widely in Tanganyika/Tanzania for two years, becoming fluent in Swahili.

When Zambia became independent in 1964, Chisanga returned from exile and was made UNIP councillor for Isoko ward, which includes and is named after the royal village of Tafuna, the senior chief of Ulungu. In the same year he was invited to the independence celebrations of the new nation in Lusaka and recalls: 'I was given a saloon car which took me everywhere in town.'

He then found a job as loans clerk in the Land and Agricultural Bank at Kasama, the Northern Province capital. At this time, Chisanga told me, he had begun to extend his formal education by studying English, history, mathematics, civics, science and geography by correspondence. But he doesn't appear to have persevered with this enterprise to the point of acquiring any paper qualifications.

End of the Good Life

In 1967, Chisanga's narrative continued, the Zambian Parliament dissolved the Bank and created the Zambia Credit Organization (ZCO), in its place. Chisanga was given a post as district credit officer with the new body, and initially stationed in Luapula Province. It was about this time that, after another spell of nominal celibacy, a third marriage ended following his wife's adultery, although they had two children together. His new job with ZCO again came to an end with the Government's dissolution of the Organization. But once again a new institution was set up, called the Agriculture Finance Company of Zambia, and Chisanga was made provincial loans officer with responsibility for Luapula Province.

He described this period of his life as the time when he became 'rich', with a company house and car and control of an office. But this good life did not long continue, for he was dismissed in 1972. According to Chisanga, he lost his job because one of the senior managers spread 'false reports' about him. However, a man who knew him well at the time told me that Chisanga had earned dismissal because of his habit of disappearing with the company car for long periods without permission and 'living in the villages'. After that, he worked for several years selling stationery and other office goods around the country. This venture too ended in disaster, according to Chisanga's own account, when one of his sons, together with a cousin, stole all his money. In 1976 his fifth marriage, to a woman from Luapula who worked as a nurse in Mbala, ended in separation. At the time I first met Mr Chisanga in 1990 he had been single, according to his own story, for fourteen years.

Between our parting in November 1990 and the re-encounter in the Zambian capital in mid-1996, Mr Chisanga's life-course appears to have maintained its characteristically chequered pattern. In 1992 he was invited by the then director of the Moto Moto Museum to address a conference at Siavonga in southern Zambia on the problem of 'witchcraft' in Ulungu. About the same time, he launched a cooperative, called the Northern Beekeepers' Association, which was dissolved a couple of years later amidst allegations of corruption against several leading members, leaving Chisanga with creditors, who eventually caught up with him near the end of the 1996 field research. He also set up a building business, called Kalambo Falls Investments, and was appointed agent for a Lusaka firm marketing agricultural machinery, although this enterprise had still to 'get off the ground' at the end of 1996.

Detachment

Soon after the two of us arrived in Mbala in August 1996 to begin the new period of research, Mr Chisanga introduced me in the street to a handsome middle-aged woman he described as his 'new wife'. She barely returned his greeting and I never saw her or, indeed, any other woman with him in circumstances suggesting intimacy during the five months we shared a house in the village of Mankonga.

What makes a man with such a questionable track record in terms of his native ethnic values a superb interpreter of his own culture? Vic Turner has already suggested part of the answer in the similar case of Muchona, whose very 'rootlessness' endowed him with a detached view of his culture, akin, it would seem, to that of the anthropologist himself. Like Muchona, Kafula Ballard Simuyemba Chisanga is patently endowed with high intelligence, conceivably also a factor in creating his endemically 'rootless' condition.[4]

However, I think we must look deeper for the motivation that made Chisanga not just a marvellous interpreter of his own culture, which he was and is, but also, as will be made evident in this book, a veritable impressario of Lungudom. For not only is he endowed with the objective vision born, like Muchona's, of the vicissitudes of his many-faceted life, but he must surely also be painfully aware, at some level of his being, of his drastic failure to measure up to the normative values of his fellows: in particular, his manifest inability to found and maintain the stable domestic establishment which Lungu conventionally expect of mature males. It was, I feel reasonably certain, out of an inner need to compensate for his perceived social deficiencies that Chisanga worked devotedly, during most of our close professional association in 1996, towards two particular ends: firstly, to build up relations with the scattered members of his family (and, no doubt, to be seen by me to be doing so); and secondly, and even more conveniently for this anthropologist, to present Lungu culture to the world through the media of published print and film.

A More than Ordinary Man

In early May 1990, I was sitting in a large circle of people outside the *musuumba* or 'palace' of the Lungu senior chief Tafuna. This was a special meeting of the *Kamata* or Council of Elders,[5] called to welcome the visiting anthropologist and his party, consisting of his wife Mary Taylor Willis and two Lungu research assistants: K.B.S. Chisanga and Herbert Sikazwe.

The meeting began with an address on behalf of the chief and council by the council's chair, a shortish man in a yellow corduroy suit with a strikingly resonant baritone voice. This was Mr Kapembwa Sikazwe. The message he delivered amounted to a deal: in return for making Ulungu and its peoples known to the world through the medium of the printed word (my perceived mission), I and my party would be free to go wherever we wanted in the country and be granted access to every source of information, including the spirit shrines.

Later we interviewed the chairman at his home in the royal village of Isoko, where we discovered that as well as being a local politician he was also a traditional healer or *sing'aanga* (literally, 'master of knowledge'). He had achieved that status through a personal ordeal similar to that undergone by Turner's Muchona. In Mr Sikazwe's own words at the time:

> I was born an ordinary man, up to 1985. When spirits came into me I had a lot of things, property, which got spoiled because of the spirits. I also got sick. I went to [African] doctors and they told me I had spirits like Kapembwa [the major territorial or 'guardian' spirit of Ulungu, with a special relationship with the royal dynasty], Chilundu Musi [a territorial spirit of the neighbouring Mambwe people], and so on. After that it was almost a vision to me, I started dreaming I was being shown medicines, roots and so on. It didn't take long, my brain changed and I went into the bush and started healing.

Mr Sikazwe also told me he had been a hotel manager in Ndola [a large town on the Zambian Copperbelt] for four years and then a store manager for fourteen years, before retiring in Isoko. Before leaving I photographed him at home with his wife of thirty years and several of their eleven children. In 1996 I was looking for a research assistant with special expertise in 'spirit' healing and was delighted when Mr Sikazwe, generally known as 'Uncle', agreed to take on the job. He had by then resigned his chairmanship of the Lungu Tribal Council but was now chair of the Mpulungu Constituency Development Committee, a Government-sponsored body. He also temporarily moved from his home in Isoko to Kafukula, within walking distance of our village base. In 1996 Mr Sikazwe gave me a much more detailed account of his initiation into spiritual healing (see below, Chapter 6).

During this period Uncle's wife, who came across as a good-humoured but strong-minded woman, also stayed with him several times, occasionally visiting us as well. What convinced me of Kapembwa Sikazwe's suitability for the job of research assistant was not just his qualifications as a practising 'spirit' healer but also his lively intellectual curiosity about the nature and workings of 'spirit' agencies.

Soon after arriving in Mankonga in early August 1996, I recruited a third member of our research team in Sylvia Nanyangwe, a daughter of our landlady Madam Rides Nanyangwe. Sylvia, a young woman of twenty-eight years, was born and grew up in the village. She told me her father had worked as a 'houseboy' in Mbala during the colonial period and she had been named after an admired employer, a missionary nurse called Sister Sylvia. Later her father became a successful farmer in Mankonga. (I remember interviewing this man, John Lamek Sinyangwe, during the

1990 research. He told us he had married four wives, but only the third (Rides Nanyangwe) remained with him. Sylvia was the sixth of nine children he'd had with her).[6] When I met Ms Nanyangwe in Mankonga Village in 1996, she had the status of *musiimbe*, a divorced or separated female with her own household.[7] Talking with this self-possessed young woman, I soon realized that she, like the two other already established members of the team, was endowed with a remarkable independence of mind:

> My father had a friend Mr P*** [a Greek businessman of Mpulungu] and he wanted to marry me, but I refused. Then one day I went to a party at Mr P***'s house and stayed the night. Then Father told me I now belonged to this man and had to marry him. I did so, but immediately afterwards ran away to stay with a relative in Lusaka [1000 kilometres away]. After a while Mr P*** followed me there and begged me to return home with him. But after I had done that I ran away again, to Kafukula [adjacent to Mankonga, her natal village] and got a teaching job there, against my husband's wishes. However, he forgave me and we had two children together. I kept the teaching job for three years.

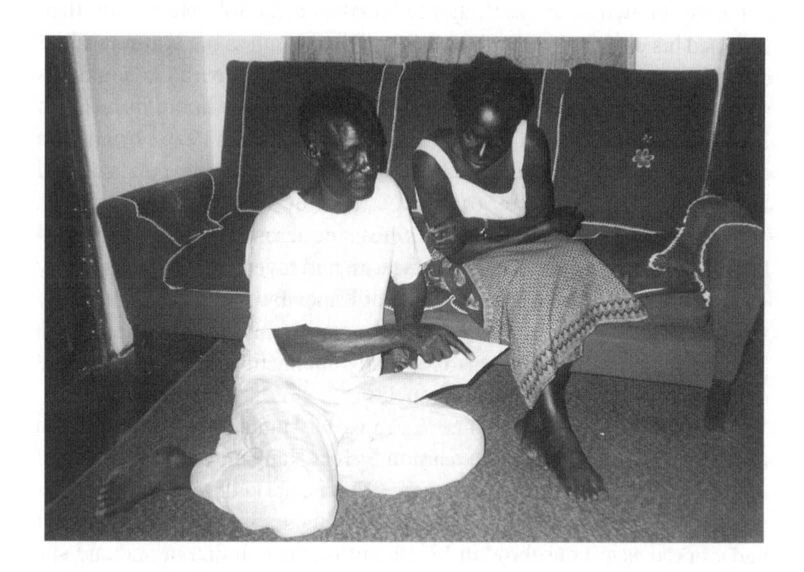

Figure 1. K.B.S. Chisanga showing Sylvia Nanyangwe how to 'write ethnography'. The book is a Zambian text on the Lunda *Mutomboko* ceremony. Photo: Roy Willis.)

Ms Nanyangwe told me her husband had returned to Greece the previous year and was not expected to reappear in Zambia. He had been, she said, a kind and considerate man, though 'too playful' [fond of other women]. She also said she was determined to remain single and did not want any more children, partly because of the expense of bringing up and educating them in present-day Zambia: 'Other women get married, have a couple of children, get divorced, remarry and have more children, and so on. I want none of that.'

Since her husband left, she'd been earning a living making and selling popcorn in Mpulungu market. She envisaged a future in commerce, adding, surprisingly and rather shockingly: 'I want to die when I can still look after myself.'

What should We Call Them?

How do people involved in this peculiar kind of enterprise anthropologists call fieldwork think of and feel about each other? Regrettably little is known on how our indigenous colleagues view the matter,[8] but, since the loss of the illusion of the 'transparent', virtually invisible, indigenous interpreter, anthropologists have been agonizing about their relationship with their local intermediaries in the business of understanding an alien culture. The still-unresolved question of what to call these indispensable agents is itself symptomatic of a deeper problem to do with the nature of anthropology and its encounter with what is fashionably called 'the other'.

I suspect that one reason for our difficulty in putting a category name to our primary indigenous sources of knowledge is that the relationship has no exact parallel in the social experience of either Western or non-Western cultures. In my own case, I resolved the issue as best I could by calling my principal local helpers 'research assistants' and enrolling them in the 'Ulungu Research Project' as salaried staff, complete with written contracts. Chisanga, by reason of his primacy on the scene and his long-maintained contact with me, was dignified with the title of senior research assistant. We had periodic 'staff meetings' over which I presided as 'director'. In a culture which is both profoundly hierarchical and attuned to consensus-seeking group discussion, these arrangements worked well as far as my primary objective was concerned: the production of ethnographic knowledge.

That process was also inextricably part of a social drama (to borrow Vic Turner's useful expression) arising from the sometimes problematic relationships between the four of us. In what follows, I make frequent use of initials to represent these various actors – a labour-saving practice originating in my field diary: thus BC for Mr Chisanga, KS for Mr Kapembwa Sikazwe, SN for Ms Nanyangwe, RW for myself and MTW for my wife Mary Taylor Willis, who played a catalytic role in the later stages of that drama.

Notes

1. In Tanzanian Ulungu I was ably assisted by Mr Teddy Simuzosha, a young married farmer of Tatanda Village.
2. Nowadays often called traditional birth attendants, but this term is misleading in that the range of their competence includes authority over sexuality as well as childbearing.
3. Another traditional doctor who had attended him during his illness told me that Mr Sikazwe's symptoms had not been those typical of an AIDS patient. This doctor held that Mr Sikazwe's death was due to attack by evil spirits called *majini*. However, these two diagnoses are not necessarily mutually exclusive.
4. Cf. Turner's speculation on the socially alienating consequences of Muchona's 'mental brilliance' (Turner 1967: 145–6). Turner seems to hint at something comparable in the 'curious quirk of fate' that brought Muchona 'an audience . . . of a kind he could never have encountered in the villages' (ibid.).
5. Also known in English as the Lungu Tribal Council, this body is charged with advising Senior Chief Tafuna on all matters of policy.
6. Mr Sinyangwe died before our return in 1996 (I forgot to ascertain the year of his death).
7. Typically, as in Ms Nanyangwe's case, such a woman returns to her natal village. Surveys of two plateau and two valley villages in 1990 showed that households headed by divorced or separated females, and excluding single widows, ranged from one in six to one in eight of the total number of households. In Mankonga/Kafukula, with a population of 1218 distributed among 290 households, 35 of those household heads were females of marriageable age.
8. The subject is beginning to be investigated in the new 'reflexive' climate in anthropology: see, for example, Crick (1992).

–2–

Homeland and Familihood

The native land of my Lungu colleagues is vast and varied. Ulungu (the name of the country) covers an area of more than 11,000 square kilometres around the southern extremity of Lake Tanganyika. Most of the terrain is a high plateau, rising to more than 2000 metres above sea level at its highest points in north-eastern Ulungu. The plateau is patchily covered with *Brachystegia* scrub forest, apart from the north-east, which is largely grassland. The plateau falls precipitately to the lake shore at 800 metres above sea level, except for the hinterland of the port of Mpulungu in the east, where a low-lying fertile region is watered by the river Lunzua and its tributaries, and in the far west, where the valley of the Lufubu river is similarly productive.

Geographical differences are reflected in differing ecologies. Outside Mbala, the local administrative centre, the plateau dwellers live by the cultivation of an array of subsistence and cash crops, principally maize, finger millet, cassava and lima beans.[1] In the low-lying valley region, the main crops are maize and cassava, with rice grown in irrigated gardens beside rivers and by the lake.[2]

On the plateau, human habitations are sparsely scattered, with distances of fifteen to twenty kilometres between villages. The same goes for the inhabitants, where a population of 300 can be strung out over several kilometres, with members of extended households occupying clusters of dwellings separated from the next cluster by several hundred metres of cultivated land. Things are different in the fertile lowlands between Mpulungu and the escarpment and in the Yendwe valley in western Ulungu. Here villages are found every few kilometres and houses are often quite densely packed together, reflecting the superior fertility of the soils in comparison with the relatively infertile plateau. In one particularly sought-after part of the Lunzua valley region, where rich soil is combined with access to the busy Mpulungu–Mbala road and the perennial waters of the Lunzua river, what were once spatially separate villages have expanded to become a single conglomerate settlement, as in the case of Mankonga/Kafukula.[3]

Outside the two major townships of Mbala and Mpulungu, the most densely concentrated populations occur in the lake-shore fishing villages, where pockets of cultivable land exist between stretches of rocky and precipitous coast.

These ecologically determined differences of lifestyle not withstanding, it would, I think, be true to say that for most Lungu people, and indeed most Africans apart from the Westernized élite, the world of shared kinship provides their most complex, all-enveloping and emotionally engrossing social experience.

The Familial Universe

To be honest, I didn't become fully aware of the likely effects of the Project car on Mr Chisanga (BC) until after my return to Britain. In the 'field', I'd merely felt irritated by the overly frequent stops and often prolonged verbal exchanges with people encountered in the street (like any Muzungu (white person), for me the main purpose of travelling was to get as rapidly as possible from A to B). Noticing my own annoyance, I tended to feel guilty, for was it not through the daily input of 'gossip' that my senior research assistant managed to accumulate the huge fund of social knowledge I so admired in him? And he was always ready to explain, whenever his passing interlocutor was unfamiliar to me, the precise nature of their relationship. Usually it was a kinsman or kinswoman, the family link specified in terms of blood relation or in-lawship; or it was someone involved in one of Mr Chisanga's several ongoing business ventures; and frequently these two categories – kin and business partner – coincided. Of course, I knew that these 'brothers', 'uncles', 'mothers' and so on were almost always what anthropologists call 'classificatory' relatives, what in English terms would rank as some vague and distanced cousinhood, if the kin link were recognized at all. Only once in five months did BC admit, in the case of a certain Mr Bowa encountered in Mbala high street, that there were 'just too many links in the chain' to say exactly what the family relationship was.

Our vehicle was an ancient Peugeot 403, acquired in Lusaka on long-term loan. Almost daily we moved from our base in the village of Mankonga to see people in or near Mpulungu, the teeming lakeside port ten kilometres away, or drove thirty kilometres up the escarpment to visit the district's commercial and administrative centre of Mbala. Just outside Mbala, the Moto Moto Museum was a frequent destination.[4] It was in the crowded streets of these two urban centres that the interruptions to our motorized progress that I've just mentioned were most common. The experience reminded me of one of those instructional films where the viewer's understanding of the growth process of a plant, say, is strikingly heightened by accelerating the succession of frames; similarly, from the perspective of the moving vehicle, the seemingly endless ramifications of Lungu familihood (a neologism of my own coining) were being displayed in dramatically rapid order. The effect on Mr Chisanga must, I now think, have been no less profound as he sat, visibly powerful behind the wheel (he did most of the driving), talking, shouting and gesticulating his way through town. Nor were these momentary activations of family links confined to the two local urban centres of Mbala and Mpulungu: even walking down busy Cairo Road in the middle of distant Lusaka we had, I recalled, met several of his relatives.

Nor was familihood (as I am here wanting to call it) less of a pervasive theme of conversation in the car between Mr Chisanga and our other two research assistants as we drove through the villages and farmsteads distributed either side of the road between Mankonga and these two townships. The sight of a house, a garden under cultivation, a group of women washing clothes in the river or a boy herding goats was enough to provoke in any of them a discussion of marriages, deaths, inheritance and, almost always, the related business of sorcery. These two – inheritance and sorcery – were indeed the topics most commonly discussed by my travelling companions. To understand why requires a grasp of the principles structuring the primordial social universe that is Lungu familihood.

As already noted, Lungu kinship terminology, along with most other terminologies in Africa and, indeed, elsewhere in the non-Western world, is defined by anthropology as 'classificatory'. This is something of a misnomer, since several English terms, for example, 'uncle', 'daughter', 'cousin', 'brother', can refer to classes of people as well as single individuals. However, in the Lungu system of kin terms this device of gathering a whole collection of individuals under the umbrella of one term is carried to much greater lengths.

How this works can be seen if we consider the parental terms 'father' and 'mother', which, in the English terminology (and similar, related terminologies in many Indo-European languages), refer to single, specific individuals: a person knows only one of either in the strict, genealogical sense. In ciLungu (the name of the Lungu language),[5] the word *taata*, which we might want to translate as 'father', means something more like 'male authority figure of the immediately senior generation', while *maayo* is a similarly respectful term that refers to women of the same genealogical rank. So all the male siblings of, in English terms, my 'real' father are all *taata* to me, and all the female siblings of my 'real' mother are likewise *maayo*. This does not of course mean that, if I am Lungu, I cannot distinguish, in speech as well as thought, between my 'real' father and mother and all these other people in the kinship universe who for me belong to the same category. If necessary, I can add a qualifying term, *mukulu*, meaning 'big' or 'senior', to distinguish my legal begetter from his 'brothers', and likewise with the woman who bore me. (The other 'fathers' and 'mothers' can similarly be distinguished with the qualifier *munono*, 'little' or 'junior' – irrespective, incidentally, of their age ranking in relation to my 'big' father or mother.)

Constraint and Inequality

There are further and important consequences of this slotting of parents and parental siblings into the same general categories. In Lungu society everyone is given a name which identifies that person as a member of a particular descent category, of which there are at least forty in Ulungu. These descent categories are sometimes called 'clans' but the term is misleading because these 'clans' have no corporate identity: there is no 'clan head' nor are there any 'clan meetings'. What these descent categories importantly do is determine who the person with a particular name may or may not marry. This is because members of the same descent category, with two partial exceptions (I shall have more to say about these categories later), cannot intermarry: in anthropological jargon each category is exogamous. Membership of each descent category is transmitted in the male line, 'patrilineally', as anthropologists say. This means that, if I am a Lungu man, I inherit my descent name from my *taata* ('father'), a name which he in turn inherited from his *taata*, and so on; and the same name will be inherited by my 'son' (*mwaana monsi*) and also by my 'daughter' (*mwaana kaci*). (I am putting 'son' and 'daughter' in quotation marks to emphasize that these kin terms in Lungu refer to categories that are far broader than their rough equivalents in English.) However, because these descent names are transmitted patrilineally, only my 'son' will transmit the same name to his legal progeny; the legal offspring of my 'daughter' will bear the descent name of her husband.

Putting together the lines of patrilineal descent formed by these non-corporate name categories with the male and female *taata* and *maayo* classes of 'parent like' relatives, we can see that all the offspring of people I call *taata* or *maayo* will be 'siblings' to me (in ciLungu *ainane* (sing., *mwinane*)). We are all 'brothers' and 'sisters' to each other, and in Lungu culture that means we are subject to certain behavioural constraints: most importantly sexual relations between us are prohibited – a prohibition called *isiku*. The closer we are in day-to-day living, the more rigorous this prohibition is felt to be. A similar cultural constraint imposes a hierarchical order on us, most affecting those who live together in a single household. Here the eldest 'brother' is called *taata lenzi*, meaning something like 'father who stays', and has quasi-parental authority over his younger siblings. A similar authority is vested in the elder 'sister', who is called *maangu lenzi*, 'mother who stays'.

Ainane ('siblings') are not the only class of kin relation subject to these constraints governing sexuality and status. The same rules apply to all those I call *taata* or *maayo* and, reciprocally, all those I call *aana*, 'children' – an extensive class that includes not merely those whom I have personally borne or begotten, but also the offspring of all my *ainane* ('siblings'). A further and important class of relatives with the same characteristics are those of the immediately senior and immediately junior generations who are linked to me by marriage: those in a parental relation to my husband *(iya)* or wife (*uwane*) and called, according to gender, *taata vyaala* or *maangu vyaala* ('father' or 'mother' 'who brings forth') and those married to my 'son' or 'daughter' and who are called by the same names as the 'parents-in-law'. Looking at it from the point of view of one who is part of the kinship system, these four classes of relative, belonging to my own and to the immediately senior and immediately junior generations will be seen and experienced as a distinctive kind of person, primarily associated with obligations of respect, what in ciLungu is called *mucinzi*, together with behavioural constraint and recognition of status hierarchy.

Untranslatable Terms

Not all kin relationships are as clear-cut as this kind in regard to behaviour and feelings. Two relatives of the parental generation have characteristics and powers which mark them out as special. Unlike those relatives I have roughly translated as 'father', 'mother' , 'brother', etc., albeit with qualifying quotation marks, there is no relation in English kinship even vaguely corresponding to them. Their extraordinary quality, even for Lungu, is signalled by the cross-gender meaning of their names *nyiinaluume*, 'male mother', and *maanguseenje*, 'mother of the father kind'. *Nyiinaluume*, more commonly called *yama* in ciLungu, is a male of my immediately senior generation who stands in a relation of siblingship to those women I call *maayo*, 'mother. The closest *yama* to me is, of course, the senior male natal sibling to the woman who legally bore me. As a Lungu male, I would have hopes of eventually inheriting his status and property. The eldest 'son' of my natal 'sister', my *mwiipwa*, will, again if I am male, have similar hopes in relation to me. This is also a relationship which is peculiarly liable, because of the jealousies and fears intrinsic to it, to give rise to sorcery accusations. In Lungu traditional history, the origin of the central political institution, the *Tafuna*-ship, is ascribed to a conflict between a particular *mwiipwa* and his mother's brothers. Some versions of the story say that the nephew, whose name was Ngoolwe, was accused of bewitching his maternal uncle, or uncles; other versions say he was accused of adultery with his uncle's wives.

Eventually, Ngoolwe was either obliged to submit to the poison oracle (to determine his guilt or innocence of the charges against him) or he demanded to be put to the oracular test. He took a leaf of the *musangati* tree *Pseudolachnostylus maprouneifolia*, and chewed it (probably to induce vomiting) before taking the poison. Ngoolwe duly vomited, thus proving his innocence according to custom. As compensation for the wrongful accusation, Ngoolwe demanded and obtained the chiefship of Isoko, the premier royal village of Ulungu, and told the people his title, and that of his successors in office, would be *Mweene Tafuna Musangati*, meaning the chief who chewed (*-tafuna*) the *musangati* tree.

Joking and Fellowship

On the other side of the family, the eldest natal sister, *maanguseenje*, also has a special status and significance. She has powers over her brother's children, including a right to a portion of the bridewealth received for a 'daughter'. But the most important general attribute of these two 'cross-gender' relatives is that their children compose the kind of kinsfolk with characteristics opposite to those of hierarchy and constraint: these are the *avyaala* (sing., *muvyaala*), literally, 'those who procreate'. These are also the people with whom sexual relations, joking and play are permissible, indeed encouraged. Because this class of relations has no equivalent in English though common in non-Western kinship, anthropologists have invented a special term, 'cross-cousins', to denote them. Like the classes of 'mothers', 'siblings', etc., their numbers are virtually infinite, because uncountable. They are usually called, inaccurately, 'cousins' in the ethnography. Similarly egalitarian and relaxed relations are customary between Ego (in anthropological conventions, the name given to the imaginary person from whose viewpoint the kinship system is described) and his/her affines of the same generation: my husband's or wife's siblings, who are all called *walamu* (sing. *mulamu*). Two other classes of relations of a similar kind are the reciprocals 'grandparents' (distinguished as *isikulu* or *kuku*, 'grandfather', and *nyiinakulu* or *maama*, 'grandmother') and 'grandchildren', generalized as *yizikulu* (sing., *mwizikulu*). As a Lungu male or female, I customarily enjoy easygoing relations with both these 'alternate' generations, as anthropologists call them. Typically, when I am with kin classified as either 'grandparents' or 'grandchildren', the atmosphere is one of equality, jocularity and fellowship.

One further addition to the set of 'easygoing' relatives is the class of what are sometimes, though again inaccurately, called 'clan cousins'. As mentioned earlier, every Lungu person is born into a descent category, which, if the child is the offspring of a legal marriage in which bridewealth (*impango*) has been paid by the father's to the mother's family, is that of the male parent. Each of these patrilineal descent categories, which are called *imiiko* (sing., *umwiiko*), has a distinctive name, sometimes denoting an occupation, sometimes an animal or plant.[6] Each name category is supposed to be paired with another, and the members of both linked categories call each other *ayombo*, meaning something like 'cousins' (*avyaala*), with the connotations of jocular fellowship associated with that kind of kinship. The linked names themselves may suggest a special connection, as between the descent category *Kasote* ('Grass') and the category *Ulupya* ('Grass burners') or between *Lwamba* 'Elephant') and *Ulapwa* ('Bow', referring to the weapons formerly used by elephant hunters). Sometimes more than two name categories are linked in this way. For example, the *Muyemba* ('Green Beans') category is linked with both *Chilima* ('Farmers') and *Uluta* ('Cultivation Ridges').[7] Two of the numerous Lungu patrilineal descent categories are so widely distributed that they are divided into two segments, the members of which, unlike the members of other descent categories, are permitted to intermarry. These are the *Kazwe* and *Nyangwe* categories, both of which are intimately connected historically with the royal dynasty of Ulungu.[8]

It may seem to the reader from this brief account that Lungu kinship is a densely complex matter, and, in the sense that familihood is an all-pervasive preoccupation in Ulungu, this impression is correct. However, and as this analysis has sought to suggest, the day-to-day experience of kin relations by a participant in the system has a structured simplicity derived from reduction of the variegated array of relationships to three types or sets, each set defined by contrasting behavioural norms, expectations and emotions.

Basically, then, there are two diametrically opposed kinds of relationship, one characterized by hierarchic values and behavioural constraint, particularly sexual constraint, and the other by norms of equality, fellowship and sexual licence. Each of these opposed sets comprises several nominally distinct but behaviourally similar relationship pairs. The relationships of hierarchy and constraint are those of parent and child, siblingship, and those linking Ego to his/her spouse's parents and Ego to his/her child's spouse. In contrast, the relationships of equality and fellowship include 'cross-cousins', the children of 'real' and classificatory maternal uncles and paternal aunts, the relationship of grandparents and grandchildren, and that between 'in-laws' of the same generation.

There is also a third and crucial set of relations in the Lungu kinship universe, a set which, unlike the nominally varied relationship pairs comprising the two opposed sets, consists of two pairs only: these are the 'cross-gender' relatives *maanguluume* (or *yama*) and *maanguseenje*, who, as already noted, function as mediators or 'transformers' between the two opposed sets. In the same way that their names combine cultural gender categories – male and female – which are otherwise rigorously separated, these two figures join peculiar power with provision of access to the most desired relationships, those of *uvyaala*, or cousinhood. When using English, Lungu regularly translate '*yama*' as 'uncle' and '*maanguseenje*' as 'aunt'.[9]

Conflicts and Crises

So far we have been talking about the basic grammar, as it were, of Lungu familihood. Now we need to look at how this 'grammar' is used to construct the 'language' of daily life in Ulungu. To understand that, we must consider the structure and functioning of the concrete 'family', called in Lungu *ulupwa*. This is a collectivity of people linked by shared recognition of common descent or affinity ('in-law' relationship). The first thing to notice is a division of this familial collectivity into two opposed categories called *mutwe* (literally, 'head') and *musana* ('loins' or 'lower back').

In the conceptual opposition of 'head' and 'loins', Lungu-speaking people are invoking a symbolic duality to refer to a fundamental division between a set of familial relations which we have already seen to be largely resistant to direct translation into English. And we have not yet exhausted the meanings of the head/loins contrast. Looking at the form of the symbolism, it seems apparent that the Lungu *ulupwa* or 'family' is being implicitly compared to a human body, to a corporeal unity: but it is a unity of opposed parts, parts with contrasted statuses and functions. The human head, for Lungu-speaking people as for us, is the centre of intelligence (ciLungu: *amaano*), authority and control. The fact that the head is positioned above the lower body, including the loins, also implies both superiority and seniority. However, though inferior and junior, the loins are seen by Lungu as pre-eminently endowed with 'meat', unlike the 'bony' head. A saying or *vwangilo* commonly invoked in debates over marriage or inheritance is *kwa musana kwene kuli nyama*, 'in the loins there is meat'. This means that the maternal kin, the receivers of bridewealth, are also, through the incoming wives, the source of children, the future 'wealth' of the family. There is a 'rule' that inheritance should alternate between 'head' and 'loins' sides of the family. I was told that the alternation should also go in that order: first 'head', then 'loins', and so on. But this would also seem to be a 'symbolic' statement, expressing in the idiom of temporal sequence the priority in status of the established 'head' side of the family in relation to the incoming women and their kin. I was also told that the representatives of the 'loins' side were most likely to quote the adage 'in the loins is meat' if they felt in danger of being overlooked in inheritance negotiations, of being deprived of their 'turn'.

A rough translation of the contrast between 'head' and 'loins' in this context would be, respectively, 'father's side' and 'mother's side' of the family. But here we must remember that 'father' and 'mother' (and other basic kin terms in English) are far from accurate renderings of the Lungu *taata* and *maayo*. Moreover, *pali taata* and *pali maayo* ('on the "father's" side' and 'on "mother's" side') refer to only one element in the complex of meanings associated in Lungu with symbolic 'head' and 'loins'. The contrast is also between 'male' and 'female' and, most importantly of all, between 'those who give bridewealth' and 'those who receive bridewealth'.

Boundary Rituals

> Thinking again today how alien, incomprehensible, our compressed little families must seem to Africans. How many relatives do I encounter on a typical day's journeying between Linlithgow and Edinburgh? None: everyone is a stranger, apart from the occasional friend/acquaintance. The equivalent African experience would mean meeting three to four relatives in every railway compartment, all of whom would have to be greeted and information exchanged on births, marriages, deaths (especially deaths) and inheritance meetings. And these matters would, almost inevitably, lead to the topic of *uloozi* [sorcery]. (Diary 2.9.96)

The accession of new members to the family in birth and marriage, and the departure of others in death raises the question of the boundaries between the *ulupwa* and the external, non-familial world. In the management of childbirth, an acknowledged expert, called *nacimbuuza* ('mistress of sacred things'), is customarily brought in. Usually the *nacimbuuza* is a senior relative of one or other of the parents but her status and special knowledge (typically she learns her craft through several years of apprenticeship to an already established *nacimbuuza*) makes her a privileged intermediary between the family and the wider world of society and the 'bush' (*mpanga*), the source of medicines.

A difficult labour is held to be caused by the adultery of one or other of the parents. If the foetus is carried high, it points to the husband as the guilty partner.

> This condition is called *ncila*. The husband has to confess and pay compensation to his wife, otherwise both mother and unborn child can die.
>
> But if the woman's eyes go all over the place, her hands are twitching and she bites her lips, those are signs she has been unfaithful. There is a medicine called Kalongwe for this, made from tree roots. The woman drinks this medicine and also has it smeared on her abdomen.[10]

After the birth, the *nacimbuuza* remains in charge of the mother and the newborn child. When the infant is about a week old, the *nacimbuuza* accompanies the child and its mother to a specialist in herbal medicines, called a *sing'aanga* (literally, 'master of knowledge'). After the infant has been bathed in specially medicated water; the mother's breasts are also washed. After this ritual the newborn can be slung on its mother's back and for the first time be touched by people other than its two parents and the *nacimbuuza*. Another symbolic act affecting the status of the newborn is the first cutting of its hair. Again the child has to be taken to a traditional doctor, who applies an ointment made from the same ingredients as in the ritual washing (from the roots of three trees and a shrub) to the child's head. Then he cuts the hair from four corners of its head,[11] allowing the mother to do the rest. The hair cuttings and remains of the medicine are then thrown into a latrine or into a hole in an ant hill.

These and other life-cycle rituals, to be discussed, suggest a seemingly obsessive preoccupation with the management of boundaries – between individuals, between groups and between the living and the dead. The social and physical union of two individuals in marriage (*icuupo*) initiates a potentially long-enduring relationship between two families and is typically preceded by some months of negotiations over the amount of the bridewealth (*mpango*) to be transferred from the wife-receiving to the wife-giving family. If the marriage turns out to be infertile, the husband's kin may properly ask for repayment of two-thirds of the bridewealth.[12]

Testing the Wedding

The aspirant husband also has to work for his prospective wife's father, cultivating his fields for up to a month, although the period can be shorter if the young man is assisted, as often happens, by his brothers and friends. This work is called *nsuumba* and in return the prospective father-in-law provides his helper, or helpers, with food and beer. The young man is also expected to prove his ability to support a wife by building a house and clearing a stretch of bush for cultivation.

Before the wedding ceremony (*uwiinga*), the couple undergo a ritual called *kukuzya uwiinga*, 'testing of the wedding'.

> It happens after the groom has taken food to his father-in-law, a gift called *kupaula.* Four elder 'grandparents', a man and a woman from both the *mutwe* [bride-receiving] and *musana* [bride giving] groups gather secretly in a hut.
>
> The couple to be married lie naked on a mat in front of the four witnesses. Beforehand the two are given instructions (*masuunde*) by *Nacimbuuza*. They lie facing each other, the woman lies on her left side and uses her right hand to touch the man's private parts and help him to enter her. The man lies on his right side and uses his left hand to prepare the young woman before entering through her legs. If the couple fail to achieve union, the wedding can be cancelled.[13]

I was told that this 'testing' used to take place on the wedding eve but nowadays it usually happens several days earlier because, if the date and location are known, 'jealous people can spoil it with medicines that make *Siwiinga* [the bridegroom] impotent'.

Passionate Debate

> 'The idea that human spirits go up to heaven is wrong They stay on earth, with the family'. – K.B.S. Chisanga to Roy Willis, 23.7.96

The death of a kinsperson precipitates another round of intense familial negotiations punctuated by ritual:

> this evening, a passionate discussion over the *indoosya* [funeral] problem between SN [Sylvia Nanyangwe] and a kinsman, with BC interposing some comments. For the past century and a half anthropologists have been trying

> to get across to Europeans the kinship-pervaded universe of other peoples. But concepts like 'extended family', 'community of the living and the dead' are but pale reflections, partial at that, of the impassioning, utterly engrossing mix of intellectual challenge and emotional whirlpool that family death and inheritance mean for these people. They also have no idea that the issues they are so totally involved in are, at base, incomprehensible to Europeans, any more than they can grasp the nature of the European experience of 'family'. (Diary 21.9.96)

The same evening that I made that Diary entry Sylvia explained to me that the burial of her maternal aunt Dorothy Nanyangwe could not take place in Mbala, where she had died (in hospital). This was because divination had revealed that her aunt's recent death, and the earlier deaths of her 'mother' and 'mother's brother', were caused by the *cuuwa* (malign spirit) of Sylvia's dead maternal grandfather. This meant that the corpse of Dorothy Nanyangwe had to be buried in the family graveyard at Posa (a village near Mpulungu), where all the graves could be properly 'medicated' to protect their spirits against the offensive *cuuwa* (which had the ability, Dracula-like, to transform them in turn into monstrous *vyuuwa*).

Purification and Separation

The funeral of a family member is replete with symbolic acts of purification, clearly designed to separate the persona of the dead from the community of the living. A key role in the ritual drama is played by a female cross-cousin (*muvyaala*) of the deceased. This woman is known as *Kambula*, 'the one who throws away'.

It is *Kambula*'s duty to accompany the other mourners and the corpse to the place of burial while carrying a plate loaded with an item of the dead person's clothing – a shirt if the deceased was male, a dress if female. This material is called *nsambala*, 'cloth'. After the interment, *Kambula* returns with the funeral party to the home of the dead person, still carrying the *nsambala*. She lays her burden in the centre of a mat placed in front of the house and sprinkles the piece of clothing with medicated water. This act is part of the process of cleansing of objects and people associated with the dead person, a process called *ku-sangulula.*

The ritual purification continues with the making and 'cooking' of cleansing 'medicine' by a mourner who was not present at the death. This has to be done inside the house so as to rid it of the ghost (*mafwiila muntu*) of the deceased. After the medicine has been boiled, the *afunda muntu*, the witnesses of the death, smear it on their hands and legs. What remains is smeared on the hoes or other tools used in the burial. The person who made the fire then collects the three small stones used to support the pot and throws them towards the west, 'the direction of the setting sun', as Herbert Sikazwe explained it.

Mr Sikazwe said the next task was the selection of an acting or provisional heir. This is called *ku-samika nsambala*, 'the hanging-up of the cloth': 'An elder person of the deceased's family addresses the group of mourners, saying '*Mutuloosya, mukwaai!*', 'Help us bereaved people!' The audience respond by asking how many have so far died in the house. For the first dead person should be inherited by the father's side (*mutwe*), the second by the mother's side (*musana*), and so on.

The elder invites a representative of the side which is to inherit to come forward. (This 'acting heir' is usually a child, to make things easier when the definitive heir is chosen.) The elder picks up the *nsambala* from the plate and places or drapes it on the shoulder or breast of the acting heir. This person must not touch the cloth but should let it fall to the ground on its own, after which anyone can pick it up, for it is now 'clean'.

The acting heir has to be the last of the mourners to leave the house. Early the next morning, *Kambula* sweeps the courtyard clean – her last duty. She is given a small amount in cash, the plate and a quarter-bag of maize flour, called *icituundu ca usu*.[14]

On Sunday, 22 September 1996, I spent the day at the *indoosya* (funeral gathering) in Posa, a convivial occasion for which the Ulungu Research Project (URP) supplied maize flour and *kapenta* (Lake Tanganyika sardines). The mortal remains of Dorothy Nanyangwe arrived in early evening by chartered lorry from Mbala, to be interred in the family plot as decided. Before the burial, the *nsambala* was briefly draped around the frail shoulders of a female *musana*-side (matrilateral) relative of the dead woman, the acting heir, before she shrugged it to the ground in the customary fashion. It was then given to a female *muyombo*, or 'clan cousin'.[15] I was told that the eventual, definitive heir would be chosen from among the dead woman's *mutwe* (patrilateral) kin.

Cleansing and Inheritance

The inheritance meeting is usually held several months after the funeral, partly to allow time for all members of the family to be informed, but mainly to enable the typically long list of potential heirs to be reduced to a manageable number, ideally one person.

There are usually three stages. First, there is a meeting called *ukwamba imfwa*, 'discussing the dead', attended by the deceased's closest kin. The purpose is to make sure there is no unseemly wrangling at the later and larger meeting by narrowing down the number of candidates to the succession. A series of such meetings may be necessary before agreement is reached. The person selected is informed and, in the case of the death of a married man, is asked whether he wishes to inherit the widow (*mukamfwiilwa*) or widows of the deceased. Other arrangements are made, including the raising of money for transport of people to the general meeting and for provision of food during the gathering.

Second, on the eve of the day of the big meeting, the widow(s) and children are told of the decisions reached. The widow has an opportunity to declare her own wishes if these are contrary to those of the heir – e.g. she may elect not to be inherited and to live as a single householder (*musiïmbe*).

Third, the general meeting, held the following morning, is informed and the property (*ivizwaalo,* literally, 'clothing') of the deceased is distributed among those present.

Inheritance in Ulungu, as among other neighbouring peoples of East-Central Africa, means that the chosen heir, called *mupyaani* or *kapyaana,* assumes the social personality of the dead (rather like royal or aristocratic succession in England). He or she takes on the social responsibilities of the deceased. When a man dies leaving one or more widows, a major concern of the family is the 'cleansing', *ku-sangulula*, of the bereaved woman or women. It is held that marital relations have so fused the spirits of the wife or wives and the dead man that his spirit *(mupasi* or *muzimu)* remains with the bereaved and can only be released by an act of ritual copulation between the widow and a kinsman of her dead husband.[16]

As described by Herbert Sikazwe, this ritual is supervised by *Nacimbuuza*:

> Late that night the heir should have sex with the widow to 'cleanse' her. *Nacimbuuza* goes outside the room while this is done. Once the 'cleansing' has been achieved the heir knocks on the door to signal the fact, and *Nacimbuuza* then announces to the people outside that the heir is innocent of adultery with the widow during her husband's lifetime: if guilty he would not have been able to achieve the 'cleansing' – the ghost of the dead man would have returned to prevent it.
>
> After the 'cleansing', *Nacimbuuza* goes back into the room and the three have to wait, without sleeping, until near dawn. When they get up from the bed, the couple do so with little fingers intertwined.

> The three go to the river, where the couple wash each other's backs, with clothes on, and return quickly to the house, before the break of dawn.

Senior members of the family will by this time have gathered at the house. Heir and widow have to remain silent, communicating by signs until *Nacimbuuza* gives them permission to speak. They are then given fresh clothes and anoint (*-pakala*) each other with *mpemba* (white clay) on the forehead. 'This', says Mr Sikazwe, 'is the sign that you have done nothing bad to your fellow.'

> The couple are taken outside the house, and are seated on chairs. Then everyone related to the heir is allowed to tell him, very freely, what he or she thinks of him, even sons and daughters, brothers and sisters. These frank comments are called *amasiizo* (singular, *isiizo*). After speaking thus, each person lays some money in a plate. The heir is not allowed to reply.
>
> The eldest person present then takes both heir and widow by the hand and leads them inside the house, where they stay for at least ten minutes. Then the heir can say he doesn't want to live with the widow, and gives her money to support herself. She is free because the heir has 'cleansed' her. Otherwise she would not be free of the *muzilo*, 'prohibition' [against having sex with anyone outside the family of her dead husband].[17]

If the heir has not managed to 'cleanse' the widow during the night, divination (*kusaapola*) has to be done to find out the cause, whether witchcraft or the heir's adultery.

Afterwards, the couple eat food prepared by *Nacimbuuza*. The remains of the meal are thrown into trees that bear edible fruits, such as *masuku* (*Uapaca kirkiana*), *mweembe* (mango) or *muula* (unidentified).[18]

'Go Free and May God Care for You'

Monday, 30 September 1996 This morning I sit crammed together with about thirty other people, men, women, children, in a house in our village of Mankonga. Business begins with an address by the *ad hoc* chairman, a matrilateral cousin of the dead man, whose name was Lwamfwe Arnold, a 'Coloured'.[19] The chairman summarizes the events and decisions of the previous day, when the meeting was disturbed, and nearly abandoned, because of a suspected *majini* (evil spirit) attack on the infant son of one of their members. A local traditional healer successfully dealt with the problem and the meeting continued.

The speaker goes on to name the chosen heir, who is sitting to my half-left and whose name is Zombe Chisanga Simuyemba, a maternal grandson of the deceased (and a 'son' of our senior research assistant

K.B.S. Chisanga, who is also present). The chairman tells us that one of the widows of the dead man has chosen to remain behind in Kasama (the provincial capital), where she has illicitly 'married' another man. The other widow, the dead man's second wife, is present but had also been a 'problem'. The heir had decided not to inherit her (I was told afterwards that this was because the heir was already married and his church forbade polygyny). Seemingly, the widow had accepted this decision but insisted on her 'right' to be 'cleansed' in the traditional manner. The meeting had decided against observing this custom because of the AIDS risk, but a compromise had been worked out: the widow would be given the sum of 5000 kwacha (£2.50), which she could use to obtain the services of a *cisonsololwa* or 'firebrand', a distant kinsman of the deceased, to 'cleanse' her.

Now the heir turns to a young girl sitting beside him, the granddaughter of the dead man. This twelve-year-old child is the acting heir, who received the *nsambala* (cloth) after the burial several months earlier. Now *Kapyaana* (the heir) kneels before the girl and gives her a K500 note (25 pence sterling). In return, she hands him the 'cloth', which I now see is a pink-striped shirt. The heir, a youngish man of thirty-seven years, gravely pulls this garment over the plain white shirt he's already wearing. In some sense that, I feel, is as mysteriously ambiguous for these others as it is for me, this pink-shirted man has become the dead Lwamfwe Arnold. I reflect that actually being here, at this event, is, in comparison with being told about it afterwards, like watching a film compared with looking at a bunch of snapshots. Now the heir dips his hand into a grip and extracts a plastic bag, which turns out to contain three pairs of shoes, which he gives to relatives sitting nearby. He does the same with a cap, a jacket and several shirts and pairs of trousers, all of which appear to have been freshly laundered. He keeps for himself a suit, a pair of trousers, another shirt and a cap.

The distribution completed, the heir turns his attention to this woman seated in front of him, a reddish cloth coiled round her head.[20] She is the widow, seems young and self-contained and, I suspect, is enjoying her starring role in this social drama. Among the large group of women and children to her right is her aged mother.

Again the heir kneels. From the plate before him he takes a bracelet bearing a single white bead and gently ties it round the widow's left wrist. Then he takes a small piece of white maize meal[21] and daubs it on the middle of her forehead. Now he seems almost like a priest as he speaks the words that end her connection with the family: '*Mukwaai, katwaalwe kuli wensi, wapeelw' insambu na Leza kusunge!*' ('Madam, take over yourself, you are given authority and may God care for you!'). With these words, the heir reaches forward and unties from her head the *mupango* cloth, emblem of her widowhood. She is now free.

Now we are at the stage of *kusiiza*, the addressing to the newly appointed heir of words of advice, encouragement and criticism. The chairman begins by reminding the heir that instead of two children he now has twelve. He also advises him to look after the widow until she is 'settled'. Another man tells him to keep to his 'spiritual path' in order to care for his new and enlarged family. A succession of people, male and female, follow, some ending their address by placing a banknote in the central plate. Others contribute notes without speaking. The heir's grandmother sits beside him, apparently overseeing the collection.[22]

The heir's father sounds the most severe note, warning his son to be more respectful towards him. All through, the heir remains silent, his face expressionless. Now BC stands up to speak and, in his characteristically grand manner, informs the heir that 'from today I give you the task of being humble'. He also asks the widow if she has any questions. She replies by asking for two metres of cloth for her newly born child and transport money back to Kasama.

The *masiizo* over, there follow practical discussions about disposal of some beds and bedding belonging to the deceased. It was agreed that these and other items of property should be sold and the proceeds used to help the younger children produced by both wives. Discussion then turned to the provision of schooling for the two eldest children, Arnold and Agnes, who were sitting to my left. After half an hour of inconclusive debate, I leave with Kapembwa Sikazwe (KS) and SN, B C remaining behind for 'private talks' with the family.

Afterwards, KS tells me that the diagnosis of a *majini* attack on the baby the day before had been a mistake: he had learned through his helping spirits that the actual cause had been the disturbed spirit of a dead member of the family, a *cuuwa*. Back home, a discussion starts up between KS and SN about BC, who has played a leading role in organizing the inheritance meeting, including provision of food (courtesy of URP). They describe BC as 'movious', a useful and amusing word in Zambian English implying inability or unwillingness to form stable relationships. In his defence, I suggest that BC is 'married' to his work with URP. KS agrees.

A Day in the Field

Wednesday, 11 September 1996 The Camcorder battery has to be recharged so it's off to Moto Moto Museum. While waiting in the *nsaka* (open-plan hut of the kind used mainly by men for meetings and informal conversations) I ask Sylvia if she is enjoying the work and she replies enthusiastically in the affirmative. Especially yesterday, she adds (we had interviewed and filmed a traditional healer in trance). Had she seen *kusaapola* (divination) before? Yes, when her elder sister Mary was taken ill. Mary was born in 1956, educated in Kampala (Uganda) because their father found her 'too demanding financially', where she reached Grade 12. She found a job as secretary in the magistrate's court in Ndola (on the Zambian Copperbelt). She was unmarried, with one child (a girl now at boarding school in Mbala).

When Mary was barely thirty, she began to get sick. Said she felt a snake at her fingertips and it would crawl towards her head and when it reached there she would fall down unconscious. She was taken to several hospitals but they could find no identifiable disease. Three or four times a day she would start crying, shout and collapse. She got thin.

Then their father began taking her to African doctor-diviners in distant places including Zaire (Congo), Tanzania and Kazembe (north-west Zambia). He sold goats, sheep, a sewing machine, bicycles and dresses to pay them. Most said Mary's sickness was caused by a close male relative (identified) in the village. Since then relations with this man had been 'difficult'. Mary died on 16 June 1986.

When their father died, he asked to be buried 'peacefully', i.e. without sorcery investigations.

After these revelations, we go into Mbala with Mr Mulengo (chief mechanic at the museum) in search of superglue to repair the broken horn (Zambian English 'hooter') lever on the Peugeot. The bookshop has no glue, but outside BC meets the *umwipwa* (sister's 'son') of Jeffreys Sinyangwe and BC gives him a letter for his *yama* (mother's 'brother') about our proposed interview in a few weeks' time.[23] We find some glue and I think of the complicated interconnections of the car's mechanism as a metaphor of the complex connections between individuals in society. At the same time, it is moving in the car that particularly activates these social connections. While I am musing thus, BC interestingly observes that the Moto Moto research staff can never go on combined operations because they can't agree on who is to occupy the 'first class' seat next to the driver: a transposition of the African sensitivity to the hierarchic implications of seating levels to the horizontal mode of vehicular transport.

At lunchtime, BC suddenly remarks that when we were in Kasama recently he ran into a man who said he knew his (BC's) face from somewhere. BC recognized him as the man who had 'committed adultery' with his (BC's) wife but replied he didn't know him. Next time, he added, he would tell him.

Earlier, at the market, BC had lectured a group of bystanders, vague relatives, on the proper procedure at inheritance. The complex calculation of rights and duties between father's (*mutwe*) and mother's (*musana*) sides. A bit like a chess game? 'I am her father, I have the power to reject (a proposed heir to a recently dead female relative),' he said.

In the afternoon, we visit Jenera (the prophetess) at sixteen hours (4 p.m.) as arranged. She is drunk and amusingly aggressive.

Back home again, a young male relative informs SN of a new *indoosya* (funeral). A new round of intrigue over inheritance, coupled with sorcery allegations, has begun.

Notes

1. The higher elevation of the almost treeless plateau in Tanzanian Ulungu and the consequent absence of tsetse-fly infestation allows the keeping of cattle – impracticable in most parts of Zambian Ulungu, where tsetse-borne trypanosomiasis is endemic. The bovine basis of the domestic economy in Tanzanian Ulungu may be connected with an apparent shift from cognatic to patrilineal inheritance in this part of Ulungu.
2. These gardens are called *matiimba* in ciLungu and *mianda* in the Mambwe language (see Pottier 1988). A large-scale switch from cassava to maize cultivation between 1990 and 1996 was evident, particularly in the Lunzua valley region, apparently a response to 'free market' measures instituted by the Chiluba administration.
3. Where the research team was based in 1996. Kafukula is the older settlement, mentioned in traditional history, and the seat of the 'junior' queen mother with the hereditary title of Namailye, but it is now overshadowed by Mankonga, which is the site of an important government primary school and the residence of a renowned tribal elder, Mr Kazimoto Sinyangwe.
4. Now government-owned, this ethnographic museum was founded in 1974 by Fr. Jean-Jaques Corbeil, a Roman Catholic missionary of the White Fathers' society. In 1996, I arranged with the director to make use of the museum's four-wheel-drive vehicles for journeys to the more inaccessible 'bush' villages. I also, with the director's kind permission, used the museum's electrical supply to recharge the camcorder batteries.

5. CiLungu is a Bantu language, most closely related to the languages of the neighbouring Fipa and Mambwe peoples (Guthrie 1971). Grammatically, it also shows close affinities with Bemba (Doke 1945). The only scholarly study of the Lungu language is Kagaya (1987). The Mporokoso enclave of Lungu territory in the south-west (see Figure 3, p. 62) was overrun by the expansionist Bemba in the late nineteenth century but the territory was restored to Lungu control by the British colonial administration. It is now almost entirely Bemba-speaking. The reigning *Tafuna,* Robinson Chishimba Kapumpe, began his chiefly career as *Mukupa Kaoma*, chief of the Mporokoso enclave.
6. Many of these descent names also occur among the Mambwe and Nyamwanga and some other groups, occupying territory to the east of Ulungu (Willis 1966: 42, where the Lungu descent categories are incorrectly described as 'patrilineal clans'). Male and female members of Lungu descent categories are differentiated by the prefix *Si*, connoting fatherhood, or *Na,* connoting motherhood, respectively. Thus *Sinyangwe* denotes a male member of the *Nyangwe* descent category, *Nakazwe* a female member of the *Kazwe* category.
7. Similar 'cousin-like' relationships, linking two or more descent categories, have been recorded among the neighbouring, matrilineal Bemba (Richards 1937).
8. According to some versions of Lungu traditional history, the senior chiefship originally belonged to the *Nyangwe* descent category but was improperly appropriated by members of the *Kazwe* category after the mid-nineteenth century dispute referred to earlier (p. 26).
9. In conversation, the patrilateral cross-cousin is readily assimilated to the parent – the intermediate relation with Ego. Thus a man who married a classificatory father's sister's daughter may say in English, 'I married my aunt.'
10. From statements by *Nacimbuuza* Roda Namfukwe and two colleagues at a meeting in Mankonga Village on 27.9.90. The 'mystical' affliction the Lungu call *ncila* appears to be widespread in East-Central Africa. Parkin (1978), writing of the linguistically related disease called *chira* by the Nilotic Luo- speaking people of Kenya, observes that '[t]he disease arises from an improper mixing of categories which are normally kept distinct'. See Willis (1972) on *ncila* among the Fipa.
11. Probably a reference to the quadripartite Lungu cosmos (see Chapter 3).
12. In Zambian Ulungu in 1990, the typical amount in cash transferred for an 'educated' young woman was the equivalent of between £50 and £60. In addition, the groom's family could expect to hand over

up to a dozen chickens, a goat and quantities of rice, beans, paraffin, charcoal and firewood. For a woman without formal education, the cash transferred could have been as little as £12. The value of bridewealth in Tanzanian Ulungu in 1990, seemingly reflecting differences in ecology and social structure in comparison with Zambian Ulungu, was roughly twenty times as much.

13. Statement by *Nacimbuuza* Roda Namfukwe, 11.10.90.
14. Statement by H.M.K. Sikazwe, 28.10.90.
15. Contrary to Mr Herbert Sikazwe's information, I was told that the cloth would have to be 'medicated' before it could be safely worn.
16. See Hinfelaar (1989) on a similar Bemba custom. Although little studied, this custom of 'cleansing' widows appears to be widely practised in Zambia. It is also part of the traditional practice of the Fipa of Tanzania, ethnic relatives and neighbours of the Lungu (see Willis 1972, where I wrongly supposed it to be peculiar to the Fipa).
17. Although less is made of it, because the inheritance of a widow is a public matter concerning the whole family group, a man whose wife dies is subject to similar 'spirit' problems. According to BC, 'a widower who goes with another woman after his wife's death can fall sick because of the ghost of his dead wife remaining with him. Only a woman from the same family as the dead woman can cleanse him.'
18. Statement by H.M.K. Sikazwe, 26.10.90.
19. Zambian English for a person of mixed European and African descent.
20. This cloth, called *mupango*, should properly have been black or white, I was told later. She had worn it since her husband's death.
21. Maize meal was a substitute for *mpemba*, the white clay used in religious rituals to symbolize 'spirit' and purity.
22. I was told the money would be used to assist members with transport back to their homes.
23. The Revd Jeffreys Sinyangwe leads a faction that disputes the title of the present *Tafuna* to the senior chiefship of Ulungu (see pp. 40n8).

–3–

Managing Time and Space

> Last evening observed BC [K.B.S. Chisanga] examining my little piece on Lungu cosmology (Willis 1992b) with the same minute attention, focusing on all the structural features and interconnections, which he had earlier devoted to the taking down and re-assembly of the [Peugeot's] carburettor. As though he were divining the hidden threads linking the social-scientific heritage all the way back to Vico.
>
> Diary 20.8.96

This chapter begins by considering Lungu perceptions of time and space as inferred from field experience. At a broader and more abstract level, the collective selfhood that is Lungu ethnic identity conceives time and space as structured by the uneasy interaction of two sources of extrafamilial authority: chiefship and priesthood. The history of chiefship is a record of time-driven development, differentiation and progressive emergence of hierarchic control over people and land. In contrast, the priesthood expounds a cosmology of perpetual re-creation of an eternally unchanging male–female duality within the overarching spatial image of the 'cosmic egg'. These contrasting 'official' world-views are problematically reconciled in two major rituals: chiefly initiation and the supposedly annual pilgrimage of the living incarnation of the chiefly ancestress Mwenya Mukulu to the shrine of the dominant Lake divinity, Kapembwa.

In 1962, when I first saw Mbala, it was a spruce township of well-maintained buildings and tree-lined streets, a miniature garden city set beside lovely Lake Chila with its golf and sailing clubs. It was then known as Abercorn but reverted soon after Independence in 1963 to its original name. Today Mbala ('Bushbuck') is dusty and dilapidated, a result of two decades of financial deprivation following the collapse of the world market in copper, then, as now, Zambia's major source of foreign exchange, in the late 1970s. In 1996, it conspicuously lacked the commercial buzz that has animated Lusaka in the wake of economic liberalization. Just off Mbala high street there is a modest eating place called the Old Soldiers' Restaurant, originally another initiative of Mr Chisanga's, which offers a daily menu of *insima* (maize porridge) with beans, meat or fish. Inconspicuously located behind the counter is an object the like of which never existed in the superficially prosperous colonial days: a fax machine in working order, a means of exchanging information with sources all over the developed and developing world.

When I think of the vast sea-change that has overtaken anthropology in recent years, I remember the first substantial work of my revered teacher, the late Sir Edward Evans-Pritchard, entitled *Witchcraft, Oracles and Magic among the Azande.* Published in 1937, some years before its author's famous conversion to the Church of Rome, the book was written from the standpoint of rational materialism. It won a deserved reputation, not only for its limpid prose style, but more importantly for its sympathetic and believable portrayal of a radically alien African culture.

University students of anthropology are taught that Evans-Pritchard's magisterial work on the Azande showed that, although this people's belief in the existence of occult forces, including witchcraft, was illusory, the reasoning they deployed on the basis of this mistaken premise was thoroughly logical and so readily understandable, once he had mastered the language, by the white rationalist ethnographer.

Evans-Pritchard succinctly states his reason for rejecting the reality of the Zande world-view: whatever is not perceptible to the senses (including, presumably, phenomena mediated by scientific instruments), does not exist. In his own words, 'mystical notions' (such as those held by the Zande people) 'attribute to phenomena supra-sensible qualities which, or part of which, are not derived from observation or cannot be logically inferred from it, and which they do not possess' (1937: 12). This is the Enlightenment-derived cosmology that posits an objective world of material objects, including human and other animate bodies, governed by laws that operate with the predictable regularity of a machine. To the Evans-Pritchard of that epoch, the reality of this world-view was transparently obvious. Today, instead of being a solid and unassailable bedrock of knowledge, the mechanistic model of the universe is increasingly seen as a product of a particular phase in the socio-economic history of Western civilization. There is irony in the fact that Evans-Pritchard, while pointing to the 'irrational' unexamined premise underlying Zande thought, was unaware that his own thinking reposed on just such a premise.

Forty years after the publication of Evans-Pritchard's masterpiece, Favret-Saada could write of her study of occult action in rural France: 'The aim of my book . . . is to take magic force seriously, and not to be content to describe it as a logical error, or someone else's belief' (1980: 195).[1]

The difference is between an anthropology ensconced in a position of taken-for-granted superiority to ways of perceiving the world which violate the principles of rationalistic materialism, and one devoted to investigation without exclusions or preconceptions. Those forty years have seen a radical change in the images conjured up to represent the entire scientific enterprise, natural as well as social. During that time, the modernist picture of the scientist as detached and superior observer facing a machine-like universe devoid of consciousness has been succeeded by a conception of the universe as 'an interconnected web of relations', a web which includes the 'observer' and is, moreover, 'alive' (see Capra 1982: 77–9). Such a picture can make the 'irrational' presuppositions of the Zande and other 'primitive' peoples seem notably less absurd than they did to Evans-Pritchard.[2]

The ascendance of this image of the universe as a dynamic web of interconnections has been mirrored in the 'real world' by the rapid growth in recent years of electronic communications in a global network. The fax machine in the Old Soldiers' Restaurant is one instance of this process of 'globalization'. In this fluid and rapidly changing situation, how should anthropology conceive its mission?

Modes of the Ethnographic Present

> BC has spent the entire afternoon working on the recalcitrant driver-side front door lock [of the Peugeot]. [He] seems to enjoy taking machinery to pieces and reassembling it.
>
> Diary 23.8.96

Among the plethora of 'post-modern' critiques of classical anthropology, one of the most interestingly controversial has been Johannes Fabian's impassioned denunciation of traditional anthropology's use of the so-called ethnographic present as a mode of description. In *Time and the Other* (1983), Fabian argues that the conventional use of the present tense in anthropological accounts of 'primitive' societies has, paradoxically, served to create temporal distance between the colonizing and colonized by situating the latter in a 'timeless' state outside the movement of history, or, at any rate, in an inferior position in the social-evolutionary stream of time. For Fabian, this narrative device denies what he calls the 'coevality' of the anthropologist and the object of study – the fact, made increasingly apparent by the process of globalization, that we are living in the same time.

More recently, another anthropologist, no less 'post-modern' in approach, has taken up Fabian's concern with narrative style to advocate the ethnographic present as 'the sole narrative construct of time which can preserve the reality of the ethnographic encounter'. For Kirsten Hastrup,

> Fieldwork defies our ordinary historical categories . . . The dialogue was 'then', but the discourse is 'now'. There is no choice of tense at this level: the ethnographic present is the only construction of time which renders the truth about the 'absent' reality (Hastrup 1992).

Hastrup associates her advocacy of the ethnographic present with her perception of the fieldwork situation as 'ecstatic': in it the subject–object boundaries of the ethnographer's own culture are transcended or 'collapsed'.[3] Fabian, on the contrary, links the ethnographic present with the construction of a false objectivity and 'the obstinate use of the nonperson "third person" in ethnographic accounts' (1983: 85).

Hastrup is aware of the contradiction between her and Fabian's reading of the ethnographic present (Hastrup 1992: 117), but does not attempt to overcome it. It was while listening to Lungu conversation in 1990 that the solution occurred to me. There are not one but two modes of the ethnographic present tense, which exist in ciLungu as they do in English. They could be called the ethnographic present objective (the target of Fabian's polemic) and the ethnographic present interactive (Hastrup's version). I also noticed a difference between the use of these modes in the two languages. In English there is a strict division between the two narrative modes. Thus, a a statement such as

> Nuer do not think of the relation of man to God as one of soul, as a separate entity, to Spirit but as one of the whole man to Spirit (Evans-Pritchard 1956: 177) [ethnographic present objective]

cannot be directly connected with, for example,

> 'Soul?', says I.
> 'No,' says he, 'it's more.'
> 'What?' says I.
> 'Body and estate', says he. [ethnographic present interactive]

In ciLungu, however, seamless transitions between these two modes constantly occur, so that the passage above could be directly followed by some such statement as 'A person's body, soul and property are all related to God.'

The Lungu narratives I'm talking about are oral statements and they are not delivered in a vacuum, as it were, but in a specific social context: the re-encounter after a substantial interval of time (several weeks, months, even years) of two family members. There then ensues an exchange of narratives in which both persons recount their lives as experienced from the moment of parting to their present re-encounter.

Listening to such narratives, I had the sense that the speakers were constructing an unbroken chain bridging the period of absence, constructing 'total coverage' of the temporal gap. What I have called the 'interactive' ethnographic present features prominently, as all significant meetings with other family members during the same period are reported. Another thing I've noticed about these bursts of present-tense direct speech is the frequent appearance of the negative, 'S/he[4] says No' (*Aati 'Aawe'*), often repeated several times in a single interchange. I reckoned, indeed, just by listening, that this simple phrase occurred more often than any other in Lungu speech. Its effect is to describe, in what I am calling the ethnographic present interactive, successive modifications in the shared perception of a particular situation. This is Hastrup's peculiarly ethnographic mixture of dialogue and discourse, where the dialogue was 'then' but the discourse is 'now' (1992: 125–6, 127). I am also reminded of Popper's account of the scientific approach to truth through repeated falsification of hypotheses.

> Had what seemed like an important insight today while preparing the new URP [Ulungu Research Project] programme. Highlighting the days when the Moto Moto Land Rover will be needed I saw that the first line was orange, then there were three non-LR dates, followed by a solid block down to the end – all orange. Looking over my shoulder to help me in this task, BC insisted on reading out each line, including those comprising the solid orange block, and so on through each of three (identical) photocopies. It was as though I , for the purposes of this exercise, saw the signs on this piece of paper as constituting several blocks, whereas he saw only the chains linking smaller blocks of letters that made up words.
>
> Diary 14.10.96

Something similar happened whenever we went shopping in the stores of Mbala or Mpulungu. The impression I got was that the essential exchange of money for one or more commodities (essential, that is, as seen from the *Muzungu* point of view) was being encapsulated in a chain of transactions involving words and body language, all of which were seen and felt as being of equal importance.

More, the unspoken 'message' seemed to be that the point or 'essence' of the whole business lay in the process of interaction itself, in the sequence of exchanges of words and things, beginning with initial greetings, and proceeding to enquiries about family and friends before moving into more commercial matters. Towards the end Mr Chisanga would ask for, or, rather, demand, a receipt, which further prolonged matters. Again my impression was that the cultural drive was towards elongating such social encounters (or, in the *Muzungu* optic, dragging them out).

I had a similar impression, of being involved in a chain of connections, all of equal value and without any overriding principle, when it came to navigating Lungu space. *Amanzila* , pathways between villages and, often, between segments of villages, form intricately branching networks. If unfamiliar with the country or neighbourhood, you need a guide. Returning through such unfamiliar terrain would often be a trial for me, even though I had just travelled the same way, though in the opposite direction, not long before. But I noticed that my Lungu companions, even when the place was as unfamiliar to them as it was to me, were never in any doubt as to which of two or more paths to take at a crossing or intersection. In contrast, my frequent hesitations were, I saw, causes for surprise and, indeed, incredulity. How could I not recall what I had that very day already experienced? The sense of inadequacy I felt on those occasions forced me to examine what it was that I was doing, and not doing. The conclusion I came to was that, as with the URP programme, I was conceptualizing the object as an abstract schema. In the case of the programme, this cultural habit was advantageous when it came to performing simple operations on it, like using a highlighting pencil. But, when dealing with a complex network of paths, a simplified mental map of relations between villages was often not enough to keep me from getting lost. My companions, I eventually realized, focused their attention on each connection, each point of pathway intersection, as a link in a chain of such connections, which they remembered in the same way that they could recall the chain of events since their last encounter with a 'significant other'. They had, I suspected, no overall mental map of the terrain, nor did they need one.

From Chaos to Order

> It is high time that we also have proper records, because other tribes in the country have people to stand on their behalf.
>
> Senior Chief *Tafuna*, 4.5.90

> A major consequence of the historical and theoretical movements traced in this Introduction has been to dislodge the ground from which persons and groups securely represent others.
>
> James Clifford, *Writing Culture*, 1986

In 1990, as yet innocent of 'writing culture', I came to Ulungu with a brief to carry out the first reasonably comprehensive survey ever made of Lungu sociocultural institutions. It was a mapping operation, in the 'top-down' mode typical of modernist anthropology. In 1990, I spent many hours working to uncover what could be called the official ideology of Ulungu on such matters as the creation of the world and what has happened since. My sources were mainly royal or priestly. In 1996 I had only occasional converse with king or priest, and the work was largely of the 'ground-level' kind, more congenial to the post-modern sensibility. As is hardly surprising, however, there is much in common between these different levels and perspectives in Ulungu.

I've already mentioned the explicit 'deal' agreed in 1990 between this anthropologist and the Lungu authorities: basically, it was information in exchange for publication. On 4 May 1990, the same day that this 'deal' was arranged, we were given a long 'lecture' (his term) on Lungu history by Israel Kasomo, then, and still, Ulungu's senior elder.[5] Born in 1904, he told us his great-great-grandfather Nyenye Simpungwe was called upon by Mwenya Mukulu, the mythological founder of Lungu chiefship, to be her commoner consort or *lumbwe*.[6] A quasi-legendary leader of the independence struggle, Mr Kasomo also told us he began collecting traditional history in 1923, while listening to the tribal elders talking in the *nsaka* (men's meeting hut) in the royal village of Chinakila, one of the subchiefdoms under the paramount Tafuna.

Mr Kasomo's story began in a country called Uzao or Uzabu, said to lie to the north-west of Lake Tanganyika. In that country, there was a great spirit called Muleza wa ku Zimu[7] and from that spirit descended two beings, a man and a woman. The man was called Muwalanzi Nkunda (whose first name appears to mean 'Person of the Sun' (*ilanzi*), and the woman was called Mwenyami (whose name appears to mean 'Owner of Femininity'). Originally, these two lived underground, unable to distinguish night from day and separated by a lake, the man living on the right and the woman on the left of this lake. Eventually, after emerging into the light, they met and Mwenyami produced a daughter by her brother Muwalanzi. This daughter was called Chilobwe, but she died. The couple produced a second daughter, who was called Mwenya Mukulu ('Owner of Seniority'). At this time, these people lived in a state of sexual promiscuity, lacking custom or law. The mothers acted as midwives (*yanavimbuuza*).

Already in this narrative of Mr Kasomo's we can recognize the beginning of a dominant theme in the traditional histories recounted by the Lungu royalists: what I want to call 'time-driven development'. From an initial state of primal chaos, in which the two potential actors Muwalanzi and Mwenyami exist in darkness, unable to distinguish night from day and lacking, it would seem, any sense of self-awareness, they emerge into the differentiated world of daylight and the new sense of identity brought about by mutual confrontation with each other.

For 'centuries', according to Mr Kasomo, the primal pair and their offspring lived in a 'lawless' state of sexual promiscuity. Then, the experience of time was introduced into this 'timeless' situation with the deaths of the primal parents Muwalanzi and Mwenyami, followed by the death of their first child and daughter Chilobwe. Mr Kasomo's narrative becomes increasingly specific as he introduces the event that, for Lungu royalty, signals the beginning of history: the migration of Mwenya Mukulu.

> After population growth in Uzabu [Uzao] and the deaths of the first two people there was conflict among seven of their children. The elder [surviving] sister Mwenya Mukulu went to Malungu country [south-eastern Congo] with two younger sisters, Mwenya Muche ('the Younger') and Mwenya Musato ('Python'), and built a fortified village at Mulumbi. The other two went to Sumbu [west of the Lufubu estuary on Lake Tanganyika]. At each place they made all sorts of things: basketry, weaving, canoe building, fishing nets. At Masumbu one man started work as an iron smith (*sikasula*).

Mwenya Mukulu resumed her eastward journey, according to Mr Kasomo, and there then ensued an event which was to prove crucial for the development of Lungu society. The narrative makes clear that the encounter with Kapembwa is one with a different order of being with whom there are problems of communication: 'While passing the promontory of Polombwe in north-west Ulungu, Mwenya Mukulu encountered the spirit Kapembwa. He was then in the form of a man, and he had come to Ulungu from the north-east, from Ng'amba mountain overlooking the Rukwa valley in what is now south-west Tanzania.' As Mwenya Mukulu and her party were passing by, Kapembwa coughed and they looked up and saw him. The Azao party spent the night at the foot of the cliff and the next morning Mwenya asked her first-born son, who was called Musika, to ascend the cliff and investigate. Kapembwa was also wondering what the noise was about down below. He started to descend and met his visitor halfway. But they couldn't understand each other and were obliged to communicate through signs.

Kapembwa, it is said, was attracted by Mwenya Mukulu's classificatory daughter Mangala, child of her dead sister Chilobwe, and a marriage was arranged. So Kapembwa became the son-in-law of Mwenya Mukulu, the 'Great Mother' of Lungu chiefship.[8]

Continuing eastwards to Mbete, Mwenya Mukulu found there a minor chief or headman called Muzombwe, a 'brother' of the chief of the Mambwe people, who live further east. Muzombwe was frightened when he saw Mwenya Mukulu and, giving up his chiefly stool to the visitor, sat down on a log, signifying he had sunk to the rank of a commoner.

Another senior elder, Mr Kazimoto Sinyangwe, said of this episode: 'Mwenya Mukulu was a brilliant woman wearing necklaces, with beads on her head and anklets called *nsambo*. Muzombwe was frightened of this "heavy lady" and gave up his stool of office to her and sat down on a log.'[9]

Mr Kasomo records that at Mbete the Azao immigrants also met 'short people', called *Tunkulungu*, from whom they obtained meat in exchange for craft goods.[10]

What Mr Kasomo is talking about in the episodes of Kapembwa and Muzombwe is a social development that appears to have occurred in a similar form over much of central and south-eastern Africa. What seems to have triggered this development in many indigenous communities across this vast region is a crucial encounter, which in most cases occurred some centuries ago, between groups embodying two radically different forms of authority: one derived from descent from a deified ancestor, an authority legitimized by a supposedly unbroken line of descent through time, and one derived from a parahuman entity or 'spirit' identified with the land or territory, an authority in and over space. Typically, the original encounters between these two forms of authority are remembered in local tradition as a meeting between incoming 'royals', bearers of the time-based ancestral line (or 'lineage') and the already established 'priestly' representatives of the territorial spirit. That the coming together of these two forms of authority should be thought of in this way is hardly surprising: how else could it be imagined? The outcome has been a cluster of indigenous societies, of which Ulungu is one, which are based on a complex and potentially unstable resolution of the inherent contradiction between the two concepts of authority and power: lineage and land (Mitchell 1956; Ranger 1973; Werbner 1977; Schoffeleers 1979; Lan 1985). Typically, both parties, royal and priestly, gain something substantial from the 'deal': the incomers 'borrow' the idea of territorial authority to establish administrative control over settled populations, a development symbolized in the Lungu narratives in the episode of Muzombwe's humiliation and subjugation by Mwenya Mukulu. The priestly bearers of spiritual authority over the land, symbolized by Kapembwa, obtain political and, in many cases, military protection from their royal patrons (see Willis (1981) on the case of the Fipa, where the outcome was the creation of an indigenous 'state').

Mr Kasomo's rendering of Lungu royal tradition fits the model of social development proposed by Africanist scholars, down to the order of events: establishment of territorial[11] cults, advent of intrusive 'royals', accommodation between the two types of authority and extension of royal rule over local communities. Mr Kasomo's narrative, like all royalist narratives, is time-dominated, in that it is the progressive unfolding of events in time that determines the no less progressive demarcation and control of space. In both dimensions – temporal and spatial – the driving processes can be described as increasing differentiation and hierarchization, or distinction of social 'levels' and statuses. In the Lungu origin myth, as recounted by Mr Kasomo, there is a movement from an initial state of total non-differentiation, which is followed by a condition of minimal social differentiation without incest prohibition or distinctions of generation or gender status. According to Mr Kasomo, it was only after the deaths of the primal couple Muwalanzi and Mwenyami that the former was honoured with the title *Mweene,* meaning 'chief' or 'monarch' in ciLungu, and the latter was called *Namweene*, 'queen mother'. Then ensued the historic migration of the Azao under the newly recognized queen mother Mwenya Mukulu. In the newly established communities, there is now a social division of labour, including craft industries.

Then the encounter with Kapembwa, followed by that with Muzombwe, inaugurates the bipolar structure of Lungu society and culture as it exists to this day, epitomized in the complementary opposition of priesthood and royalty, spiritual and secular authority.

Mr Kasomo's narrative continues by describing how, after the conquering Azao had established themselves at Muzombwe's village of Mbete, twelve of them went off, with Mwenya Mukulu's permission, in various directions:

> Mwenya Mukulu's younger sister Mwenya Muche went south and established herself in Malaila country [the present Lungu subchiefdom of Mukupa Kaoma]. Her sister Mwenya Musato went west and became mother of the Tabwa people. Mwati, another elder sister, Chikwati and their brother Fukingala went north

to Kasanga [on the lake shore in south-west Tanzania]. There they found a certain chief called Tombwe but when he died the two women remained and founded the Chamukolechi branch.[12]

A second branch was started in the same direction.[13] Other sisters and brothers, namely Bunda and Namukale, Mwasi and Kabwe, all women, together with their brothers Chungu and Nkuba, went to establish another fortified village, in Lyangalile, Ufipa. It was founded together with Chief Milansi of Nkansi [northern Ufipa]. There another woman, Kabwe, branched from Lyangalile and established a *musuumba* [royal village] in Pimbwe country. The Lungu 'survey' ended at Ukonongo. A son of Kabwe started a chiefship called Chindo.[14]

With this specification of names and places, Mr Kasomo evidently seeks to connect the Lungu royal line, the incomers from Uzao, with the history and geography of the southern Lake Tanganyika region. He now returns to the crucial relationship between the Azao royals and the spiritual lordship of Kapembwa, the source of Lungu society and culture. His account concerns a conflict in the house of Kapembwa, and its resolution illuminates the problematic nature of that fundamental relationship.

A Wandering Spirit

According to Mr Kasomo, Kapembwa had found some tiny mushrooms, called *nsamfwe*, which grow on or under anthills. He told his wife Katai to go and collect them but she delayed doing so and the lord (Kapembwa) sent Mangala instead. But Katai followed Mangala and attacked her as she was bending down to pick the mushrooms. In the fight that followed Katai was beaten because she was old, while Mangala was young and strong. However, Katai managed to pull the crown of feathers (*ngala*), which the people of Ulungu had given Mangala, from the young woman's head. She then tore it up and threw the pieces away in the bush. Mangala returned home without her crown while Katai disappeared to avoid punishment, never to return.[15]

About this same time, according to Mr Kasomo's information, the Azao elders appealed to their leader Mwenya Mukulu to send a delegation to Kapembwa, asking his permission to catch and eat fish from the lake. When Mangala looked down from the cliff top and saw this delegation of her kinsfolk coming, she was frightened and hid, because of the conflict in the family caused by her fight with Katai.

Kapembwa explained to the Azao what had happened, and apologized to them for his first wife's bad behaviour. The delegation returned to

Mwenya Mukulu and a subsequent meeting of the Azao community decided that Kapembwa must pay compensation for the insult to Mangala. Kapembwa then agreed that the lake fish would thenceforth belong to all the Lungu people who lived on the lake shore. Kapembwa then made another, second promise: every November[16] he would persuade his brother-in-law Chisya, who lives on the plateau, to cause the clouds on the lake to ascend the sky and bring rain to the plateau, so that the people there could cultivate their crops.[17] 'The Queen Mother [Mwenya Mukulu] and the Azao people accepted these promises, and Kapembwa and Mangala returned home.'

What appears to be celebrated in this rather involved episode in Lungu royalist tradition is a degree of social and political development qualitatively different from, and more problematic than, that symbolically represented in Mwenya Mukulu's domination of the chiefling Muzombwe. For Muzombwe and his following belong to the same circum-Tanganyika lake-shore economic community, with its abundant resources of fish and its fertile and well-watered valleys, of which Kapembwa is the acknowledged spiritual overlord. But the high plateau, 1500 metres above the humid lake shore, with its perennial fields of rice, cassava and sweet potato, is a distinctly different ecological zone. Here, the relatively dessicated soils, still largely covered with the scrub forest of *Brachystegia* , are farmed by a method of shifting cultivation generally known by its Bemba name *citemene*.[18]

This upland zone of Ulungu has its principal guardian spirit in Chisya, who rules the area administered by the chief with the hereditary title of *Chinakila*. The story of Kapembwa and his quarrelling wives and the way the quarrel is resolved addresses a complex problem involving two kinds of hierarchic authority. At issue is the paramount Tafuna's control, from his royal village of Isoko in the eastern lake hinterland, over the distant plateau. There is also, in the same narrative, an assertion of the lake god Kapembwa's influence, and possibly authority, over the same region. It was not surprising to find that the resident royals and priests of Chinakila had different views on both matters.[19] In 1990, I learned of a four-year dispute over the succession to the Chinakila-ship, which had followed the death of the previous chief, Jim Chitumba, in 1986. The Tafuna's nominee, Mr Frank Chilanzi, had been rejected by the local people in favour of Mr Edington Chinakila, supposedly a descendant of a brother of Mwenya Mukulu, called Lyapa Kasonso, who had first settled the Chinakila area.

At Chinakila's I was informed that the guardian spirit Chisya, speaking through the shrine prophet Ponkwe, had expressed disapproval of the

Tafuna's choice. I also heard a different account from Mr Kasomo's of the relation between Chisya and Kapembwa. Instead of being a brother-in-law, a relationship implying equality, Kapembwa had, I was told, married Chisya's daughter Chilingala and was thus his son-in-law and social inferior. All these stories from different chiefly courts and priesthoods offer varying perspectives on a single and all-pervasive sociocultural reality: the complementary opposition of royal and spiritual authority.

In 1996 the dispute over the Chinakila succession was still unresolved.

Tradition and Scholarship

How do the data provided by Mr Kasomo and other recognized tradition-bearers in Ulungu square with the findings of world scholarship on the historical formation of the Lungu-speaking ethnicity? Not at all badly. Archaeological evidence suggests there was a fairly continuous process of migration of peoples into north-eastern Zambia from the eleventh century of the Christian era. These peoples brought with them a novel technique of working with iron as well as new forms of government (A.D. Roberts 1976: 38). Both these innovations are featured in Lungu indigenous histories; indeed, it seems possible that the name *aLungu* (the plural form) originally meant 'people of the kiln *(ilungu)*'. Although Roberts is properly cautious about the provenance of these immigrant peoples, he does suggest that the archaeological data point to a source in the Shaba region of south-east Zaïre (Congo).

There is some disagreement among the various Lungu traditions as to the place of origin of the legendary Mwenya Mukulu and her followers. Some say that the people called Azao came from a place called 'Kola', now generally identified with the mythological place of origin of the Lunda peoples of north-west Zambia, southern Congo and northern Angola. Many other peoples in northern and central Zambia also claim 'Kola' as their place of origin, including chiefly elements among the Bemba, Lala, Bisa, and Mambwe peoples (Brelsford 1956).

But where is or was 'Kola'? Earlier scholarship, mistakenly it seems, saw 'Kola' as a corruption of 'Angola' (Brelsford 1956: 31, 71). More recently, A.D. Roberts has placed 'Kola' considerably further east, in the heartland of the chiefship of Mwata Yamvo between the Kasai and Lulua rivers (Roberts 1973: 50). Since then, however, the first-hand field research of Filip de Boeck (1992) has identified the Shaba region, still further east, as the original 'Kola' and the mythological place of origin of Lunda (Luund) chiefship, which nicely coincides with the archaeological evidence invoked by Roberts.

The most circumstantial version of the 'Kola' theory was given to me by the elders of the Chinakila chiefdom of Ulungu. They said that 'the origin of Ulungu is from Kola, from Chief Tendwelesa. This chief found his land was too small and there was not enough food for the people. So he asked his eldest daughter Mwenya Mukulu and his son Lyapa and others to find another country where they could settle.'[20] Another source told me: 'The Lungu came from Kola, led by a spirit called Mwansa Leza. They walked over swamp grass (*vizao vyavwa*). The leading humans were Mwenya Mukulu and Chilombo, both female. At Mbete they met Muzombwe.'[21]

The story of Uzao (or Uzabu) as the place of origin of Mwenya Mukulu and her followers seems to have a respectable ancestry, being cited by J. Gibson Hall in an account of Lungu traditional history included in the Abercorn (Mbala) District Book in 1905.[22] The Uzao story was collected by Watson in the 1950s and included in Brelsford (1956). I recorded a similar version of Lungu origins and the epic journey of Mwenya Mukulu at the Tafuna's court in 1964 (Willis 1966: 42–3). Werner encountered the story again during his research in Ulungu in the early 1970s (Werner 1979). Most of these accounts situate Uzao to the north-west of Ulungu, in what is now Congo. An exception is an account by Mr Frank Chilanzi, a classificatory son of the Senior Chief Tafuna, who said the migrating people of Uzabu (Uzao) moved northwards to Ulungu. Mr Chilanzi's narrative was also the most detailed I have recorded on the lineage of these people:

> Long ago there was a country called Uzabu in the eastern Congo where a chief called Chibabwa lived. He produced nine sons and two daughters and their clan was Mazimba, meaning Leopard. While in Uzabu the tribe became very big and they became short of land. So the sons and daughters, led by Chomba the first-born son, left their father and settled at a place called Lupale.
>
> After some centuries Chomba Chibabwa and his brothers and sisters left that country and went to the north, passing Lake Mweru and reaching the country called Malungu, then going through what is now the country of the Tabwa people until they reached Lake Tanganyika at Nsumbu.[23]

Unfortunately, no such country as Uzao, or Uzabu, has ever been located. Werner, referring to the frequent statements in the traditional accounts that the Azao used canoes in their journeys around the lake shore, suggests a connection between Azao (or 'Azau', as he spells it) and an ancient Bantu linguistic root meaning 'net' (1979: 108).[24]

Can the Uzao/Kola dispute be resolved? Several of the Lungu sources, including the seemingly ancient Chinakila tradition, assert that the Azao originated in Kola. I was even assured at a major meeting of Lungu indigenous priests at Musende in 1990 that Uzao and Kola 'are the same place'! However, this 'resolution' of the problem conflicts with our present knowledge that 'Kola' is located in Shaba, which lies several hundred kilometres to the south-west of Ulungu, whereas most of the Azao narratives insist they came from the north-west, travelling down the western shore of Lake Tanganyika.

Common sense suggests a slightly more complex solution to the Azao problem than that proposed by the Lungu priests in 1990. Conceivably, a group of migrants from 'Kola' could have headed northwards into the rain forests of Congo some centuries ago, taking with them memories of their ancestral homeland, as well as knowledge of ironworking techniques and a body of political and administrative practice. They hit the western shore of Lake Tanganyika, acquired the ability to fish and make canoes and became known as 'the people of the net' (Azao). Then they travelled down the lake, finally settling in Ulungu.

Can scholarship suggest anything about the dating of the Azao advent in Ulungu? The Africanist historian A.D. Roberts has made a careful comparative study of the various oral traditions of chiefly groups claiming to originate in 'Kola' who apparently founded dynasties in north-eastern

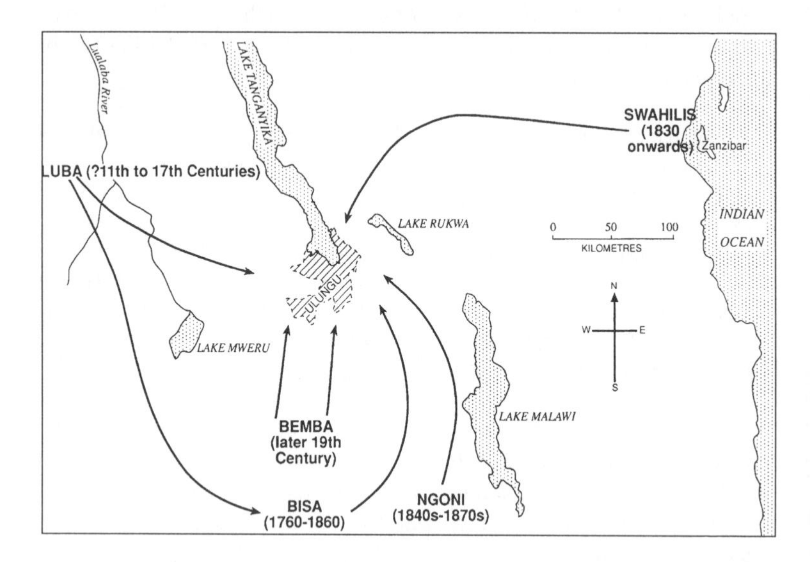

Figure 2. Precolonial influences on the formation of the Lungu ethnicity. (Cartography: Department of Geography, University of Edinburgh.)

Zambia. His conclusion is that 'there is good reason to suppose that at least the older chiefly dynasties now established in north-eastern Zambia were founded by about 1700' (Roberts 1973: 64). Again according to Roberts, it also seems likely on the basis of archaeological and linguistic evidence that the early part of the second millennium of the Christian era witnessed the intrusion of new groups, 'probably from the general direction of Katanga (Shaba)', into north-eastern as well as southern Zambia (ibid.: 67). This implies that, at the time of the arrival of the politically dominating groups directly or indirectly (like the Azao) from 'Kola', there already existed in north-eastern Zambia ethnic groups which had also originated in the Shaba region. In Ulungu, according to the testimony of Mr Kasomo and other traditional sources, these Shaban groups coexisted with 'Sukuma' from the north-east and small-statured people belonging to a Late Stone Age culture widely distributed through southern Africa.[25]

Inside the Cosmic Egg

Engrossing as the work of recording Ulungu's rich traditional history certainly was, nothing in my experience as an anthropologist was quite as exciting as the first interview with *Simapepo* ('Master of Prayers') Paul Kaongela at his lakeside home at Kapoko, near Mpulungu, on 12 July 1990. As I listened to this master fisherman, who was also a senior priest of the lake god Kapembwa, I was conscious of being in a world radically different from the world of Lungu royal tradition I had come to know with Mr Kasomo and others. That was a world, as I've already described it, of linear development, social differentiation and hierarchy, of the demarcation and control of territory: a world, as I've also said, in which time is the dominant modality; and a world, finally, with recognizable affinities to Western cultural notions of 'progress' and 'evolution'.

In the world-view of Lungu indigenous priesthood, as it was unfolded during that first meeting and in subsequent conversations with Mr Kaongela and fellow priests, I encountered a way of seeing and being which was radically other in its seeming defiance of Western principles of logic. This was also a world, as I also came to see, where the dominant image was one of space, where time was a subordinate dimension controlled by the rhythmic punctuation of recurrent ritual.

The excitement of that morning by the lake was the excitement of being the lone explorer of the anthropological myth, one with Griaule (1951), with the Lévi-Strauss of *Tristes Tropiques* (1955) and *The Anthropologist as Hero* (Hayes and Hayes 1970), and indeed with Castaneda (1968, 1971), part (at last!) of what Judith Okely has called the 'Great White

Man' tradition in anthropology. This, Okely says, is a tradition in which the anthropologist appears as a 'lone achiever', constructing and representing his uniqueness as a being outside historical and social conditioning (Okely 1992: 7). The paradox, as Okely also notes, is that this very self-representation of being outside of, indeed superior to, society and history is itself a cultural construction, part of the illusory sense of anthropological objectivity denounced by Fabian in *Time and the Other* (1983).

But so it was that morning beside the lake in 1990 We knew that word had gone out from Senior Chief Tafuna, following our enthusiastic reception in early May, authorizing the priests of the country to reveal to us their long-concealed 'secret' knowledge.[26] From the senior priest's opening words, *'Mpanga zyapalanyile n'iyaai'* ('The country was curved like an egg'), I knew I was in a different world from the one portrayed by Mr Kasomo and the other royalist tradition-bearers. Where the royalists had presented a picture of emergence from a particular place, with the complex world of the present the outcome of a long developmental process, the priest immediately summoned up an inclusive vision of a world structured from the very beginning according to principles which serial history serves perpetually to recreate.

> The world was curved like an egg. Then there was a Word, and the Word was there for a long time. And from that the Word turned into a man from the east and that person came to be known as Muwalanzi. And after some years that same Word made Mwenyami, a female from the west. Muwalanzi did not know there was another person, and Mwenyami, she also thought she was alone. Muwalanzi's house was a stone, and Mwenyami's house was also a stone. Mwenyami stayed there for three thousand years. Then he started moving, following the right hand.
>
> By that time so many things were created, like animals and birds and other moving creatures And he, Muwalanzi, observed them all. And so he reached the centre of that curved thing and decided to go back. He was then moving west. He rested for three days and resumed his walking journey. Then he saw one moving creature, which was a human being. When he realized what it was, he was unable to move. So he decided to return to his stony home. And all the thoughts he had, about naming those moving creatures, he put aside because he wanted to return again to see that strange thing (*icintu*).
>
> After another three days he did return, and when he saw again that person he had seen before, he realized she was a woman called Mwenyami. She wore an *mpande* [*Conus*] shell on her mouth and another covering her genitalia. Muwalanzi wore only one *mpande* shell, on his mouth.
>
> Muwalanzi could not return home. He realized he had to stay with that woman, and he did so. He could not even think of going back east to his home. He stayed in the west with the woman.

Mr Kaongela went on to describe how the primal pair produced six children, the eldest a son called Mpulungu, 'Give Ulungu to Me'. Altogether there were six children and, with their parents, eight people in total, each having a stool of office (*ciliimba*). 'That was the beginning of Ulungu having eight parts, the priest added in a comment I initially found mysterious, like much else in his narrative.

> All powers were given by the spirits to Mpulungu. Muwalanzi and Mwenyami returned to a small lake where they remained, with three of their children, for a thousand years. Then Muwalanzi changed his name to Mangochimikwa and Mwenyami changed hers to Mwenya Mukulu. Then that man to whom all powers were given, Mpulungu, married the second-born child Mwenya Chamukolechi and they had six children, three boys and three girls. And the same with their two brothers, Nsanza and Chilaonyi, and their two sisters, Mwenya Chitewa and Mwenya Luwemba: they all married each other and produced three boys and three girls.
>
> When they grew up, all these children also married among themselves. And that was the beginning of the people of Ulungu and all the other tribes, just from one mother and one father.

Then Mangochimikwa and Mwenya Mukulu came to Kabwe Nsolo near the cliff of Polombwe, which is the site of the Kapembwa shrine. They stayed there for three thousand years. It was then that Mwenya Mukulu saw Kapembwa in a thick bush, and 'picked' him from there. That, Mr Kaongela said, was in the month of February (*Koolo*) when they went to gather mushrooms.[27]

> She could not leave Kapembwa in the bush alone so Mwenya Mukulu carried him back to her home, because by then Kapembwa was a young boy. She took him home and made him stand near a big tree where there was some shade. Then they tried to bring Kapembwa into the house, but failed. He stood there for three days.

Mpulungu meanwhile, according to Mr Kaongela's narrative, swam to the island called Mbita (Nkumbula island off the port of Mpulungu, locus of the Mbita spirit shrine) and stayed there for two days. He returned to Musende (a village outside Mpulungu), then left for Kafukula, where he stayed for a day, then went to Chitongo, where he stayed for three years, then went down to Isokola (now called Isoko (now and for many years the official residence (*musuumba*) of Senior Chief *Tafuna*).

This narrative by Simapepo Kaongela set off a train of questions which I was to pursue with him and other priestly sources for several months.

His long and complex story, of which I have reproduced only a portion here, seemed to have little in common with the royalist narratives, apart from the names of the primal couple, Muwalanzi and Mwenyami. With the Lungu priests I was in a world of symbolic meanings quite distinct from the ostensibly factual histories of Mr Kasomo and his colleagues. With the royalist traditions, it was a matter of checking the narratives against the historical picture built up by scholarly expertise. With the different 'discourse' of Lungu priesthood, it was the more challenging and exciting business, as I then saw it, of 'cracking the code' of indigenous symbolic statement. Structural analysis in the tradition of Lévi-Strauss was the obvious way to reveal the hidden order behind this semantic puzzle, with the first 'binary oppositions' present in the contrasts, embodied in the genesis of the primal pair, between male east and female west. The name Muwalanzi, 'Person of the Sun', fitted with his prior emergence, as the sun rising in the east. His westerly movement also made sense as the apparent daily motion of the sun across the sky; and his final 'settling' in the west also fitted with the solar trajectory.[28]

Muwalanzi's decision to stay with his new partner in 'her' direction, the west, conceivably represented an ancient tradition of husbands going to live in their wives' villages on marriage.[29] It also seemed to me that Muwalanzi's decision, by putting himself in a position of residential dependence on his female partner, served to change initial superiority, by virtue of his prior creation, into a relationship of equality. But what of the frequent iteration of the number three as a measure of time? In Lungu symbolism, 'three' appears to stand for totality and completion, as the three symbolic colours white, red and black have a cosmic resonance, spanning and pervading all life and experience.[30] And what of the *Conus* (*mpande*) shells- worn by the primal pair? These are recognized symbols of authority throughout East-Central Africa, usually chiefly or royal authority (Shorter 1972: 102). They are also symbols or measures of wealth and Mwenyami's possession of two shells, in contrast to her partner's single shell,[31] may again be a reference to matrilineal inheritance. In the association of this woman with the west, there may also be a connection with the tradition of the matrllineal Azao arriving in Ulungu from that direction. That both wear a shell over the mouth suggests a mutual inability to communicate, which recalls the problems attending the first encounter between Kapembwa and Mwenya Mukulu in the Kasomo narrative.

All these points of contact with or unconscious reference to material in the royalist traditions are no more than incidental details in the priestly narratives, which are primarily not about serial events leading to the present, as in the royalist traditions, but about the encompassing or binding of seriality, of time, in the enduring symbolism of space. This is evident in the very beginning of Mr Kaongela's narrative, in the presentation of the cosmos as an enclosed space initially defined by its east–west axis. The primal couple do not die, thus precipitating a continual process of development through time, as in Mr Kasomo's history, but endure, though with different names or social personae: Muwalanzi, the first man, becomes Mangochimikwa, his representative in the world of historical time; Mwenyami, the primal female, becomes the Great Mother of Lungu royalty, Mwenya Mukulu. And who is Mpulungu, the first-born son of the primal pair, the man on whom 'all powers' are bestowed by the spirits? That Mpulungu is the Tafuna, the Senior Chief of Ulungu, is apparent from the recital of his actions beginning with his two-day stay on the island of 'Mbita' and his subsequent journeys to, and sojourns in, the ancient villages of Musende, Kafukula and Chitongo before finally taking up residence in 'Isokola', the present-day Isoko. For this narrative passage recapitulates the series of ritual acts incumbent on a newly chosen paramount chief, beginning with the *Kwalama* 'swimming' ordeal, in which he submits himself to the god of the lake, Kapembwa, before receiving initiatory instruction on Nkumbula island from the priest of Mbita. Having returned successfully from the island, he then has to go through the lengthy itinerary described in Kaongela's narrative and culminating in his installation as *Tafuna* in Isoko.[32]

Here Mr Kaongela made two more connections with the royalist historical tradition. Mpulungu, he told us, beqeathed his powers as chief of Ulungu to his son by Mwenya Mukulu's sister Chamukolechi, a man called Ntenda Mukote. Chamukolechi was also his (Mpulungu's) sister, so Ntinda Mukote was also Mpulungu's uterine nephew or *umwiipwa*. Then Mpulungu returned to his home in Uzao, leaving his nephew and heir as paramount chief in Isoko.

Mr Kaongela had here legitimized, as it were, both the royalist lineal connection with Uzao and the accepted story of the foundation of the *Tafuna*-ship in a transaction between mother's brother and sister's son. But the effect was to reinforce, not the royalist ideology of development in time, but his own priestly vision of cyclical rather than serial time. For, as Mpulungu's heir, Ntinda Mukote became his mother's brother Mpulungu, the son of Muwalanzi and Mwenyami. In discussion that followed Mr Kaongela's narrative, the same structuralist point was made when he explained that he, Paul Kaongela, was Muwalanzi, since Mangochimikwa was one of his (Kaongela's) several titles.[33] That meant the Tafuna, as Mpulungu, was his son.

All this was dizzying enough. The sense of structuralist vertigo was further heightened by Kaongela's response to my question on his relationship with Mwenya Mukulu: 'I was the husband of Mwenya Mukulu long ago, but now she is a sister to me.'

I needed to know more about Kaongela's, and the Lungu priesthood's, ideas about the mythological ancestress of Lungu chiefship. This enquiry led back to Kapembwa and eventually to a fairly detailed picture of the structure of the Lungu cosmos. Things began to come together, in my understanding at least, at a major gathering of Lungu priests at Musende in late September 1990.

The twelve priestly title-holders at this meeting, which included Paul Kaongela, also laid great emphasis on the necessity of strict adherence to the traditional procedure of choosing and installing a senior chief of Ulungu. A candidate chief had to be a son of Chamukolechi, hereditary sister of Mwenya Mukulu, and had to go through the full series of *kwalama* initiation, especially the central 'swimming ordeal'.[34] Unfortunately, the Zambian Government had rejected the choice of the Council of Elders following the death of the previous Tafuna in 1967. The Council had

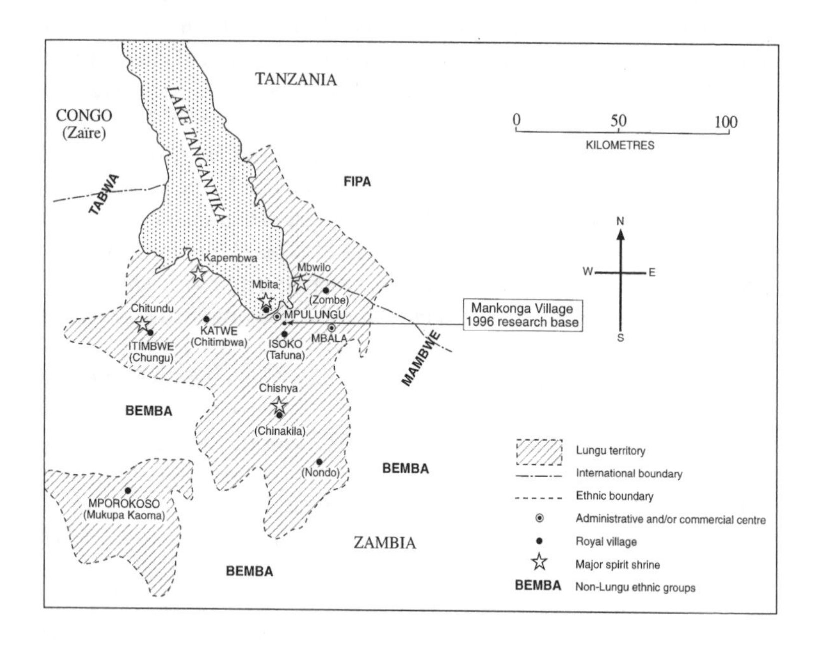

Figure 3. Centres of power – royal, priestly, political and commerical – in traditional and modern Ulungu. (Cartography: Department of Geography, University of Edinburgh.)

elected Chief Chanza, son of Chamukolechi, but the Government had forcibly installed the present office-holder, Robinson Chishimba Kapumpe, in 1968. The present Tafuna had refused to 'swim', and that was why the spirits refused to bless the country,[35] which had consequently been afflicted with economic disaster and AIDS.

The aspirant Tafuna is not the only Lungu royal noviciate who is required to submit to the will of the local guardian spirit before being recognized as a legitimate office-holder. The senior queen mother, who has the title of Mombo and resides at Kaizya Village, has to swim across the deep pool at the foot of Kalambo Falls. If Namukale, the female guardian spirit of the Falls, approves of the candidate, 'it will be easy for her – if not, she will die'.[36] This ritual is held on the same day as the candidate Tafuna undergoes the 'swimming' ordeal.[37] Likewise, the man nominated to the plateau chiefship of *Chinakila* has to submit to a test to ascertain the verdict of the guardian spirit Chisya on his suitability for office. Again we find the same theme of chiefly submission to the power of spirit, even to death.

The candidate chief enters a cave with a narrow entrance at the foot of a cliff called Chisya (after the spirit) in company with the the priest Ponkwe and elders of the Chinakila court. The elders instruct the candidate in his duties and he swears by the spirit Chisya to follow these instructions. 'They then all leave the cave, but if the Spirit decided the Chief was bad for the country he would not be able to re-emerge through the narrow entrance: he would remain inside and "disappear"'.[38]

Journey to Kapembwa

Although all the Lungu chiefdoms have their local guardian spirits, not all require their chosen chiefs to submit themselves to approval or rejection by spirit in the explicit fashion mandatory on candidates for the titles of *Tafuna*, *Chinakila* and *Mombo*. There is no Kwalama initiation ritual for the chiefs *Chungu*, *Zombe*, *Nondo*, *Mukupa Kaoma* or *Chitoshi*. But the Tafuna and his deputy (*Musika wa Kalamba*) *Chitimbwa* are involved in an annual ritual celebration of the uneasy alliance between the regionally dominant guardian spirit Kapembwa and the mythological ancestress of Lungu royalty, Mwenya Mukulu.[39]

The *Mapepo* ('Prayers') ritual has the form of a pilgrimage to the shrine of Kapembwa atop the promontory of Polombwe. Both royalty and the priesthood are represented among the small group of pilgrims, which includes two senior priests – *Mangochimikwa* and a man with the title of *Kaazengula,* meaning 'One who reports or instructs', the senior wife of

Mangochimikwa, who has the title of *Mukumbo*, the chief Chitimbwa and a young prepubertal girl, described as 'the wife of Kapembwa' and who bears the title of Mwenya Mukulu. This girl is escorted by an older woman, who is the previous bearer of the title, by her *Musika* or executive, and by a man with the hereditary title of *Chipapa* who has the duty of carrying the 'wife of Kapembwa' on his shoulders during the journey to and from the shrine.

During the 1990 research, I learned about the Mapepo ritual from both royalist and priestly sources. There were significant differences between their respective accounts. The royalists presented the ritual as a means of procuring 'blessings' for the country and people of Ulungu: tribute is taken by Chitimbwa to the shrine, and in return Kapembwa bestows fertility and prosperity on Ulungu and its inhabitants. The priests saw the ritual as a re-enactment of the prime creative event by which Ulungu came into being, an event which was itself a reaffirmation of the cosmic union of the primal couple Muwalanzi and Mwenyami. Where the royalist version of the relationship between Mwenya Mukulu and Kapembwa saw the god as the son-in-law and social subordinate of Mwenya Mukulu, the priests told me that Mwenya Mukulu and Kapembwa were married and equal partners.[40]

Lake Tanganyika, 27.10.90 Out into the lake, with Paul Kaongela on board. Passing Mbete, the remnant of primal rain forest that serves as the burial grove of the chiefs of Ulungu, from Mwenya Mukulu onwards. From the lake, the grove is a thick dark line at the base of the great escarpment, appearing as if balanced between lake and sky. Earlier we were introduced to Kawamba, hereditary guardian of the sacred grove, who has the duty of burying the chiefs. Now we are heading for Kombe, home to a spirit of the same name and an important 'station' on the Mapepo pilgrimage route. Mango (Paul Kaongela) prays to the spirit beneath a huge tree, commenting afterwards: 'We pray not just for Ulungu but for the whole world.' He explains that during the Mapepo 'pilgrimage' he stops here and meets with Chitimbwa and his party. They exchange seeds of all the crops planted in Ulungu, including millet, maize, groundnut, beans and pumpkin (symbolic of the common interest of priests and royals in the prosperity of Ulungu?). Also they collect perfumed oil called *vinunkilo*, made by an old woman, to be offered at the Kapembwa shrine. Mango says that if he allows even a drop of rain to fall into the cup of perfume it will be a disaster, the whole ritual will fail. Then the two parties proceed separately to their common destination, Chitimbwa and his party resuming their journey by land, and the priests, Mwenya Mukulu *et al.*

continuing along the lake by canoe. Mango mentions that Kombe is not the only resting place on the way to Kapembwa. They also stop at places along the lake-shore owned by the spirits Mweela, Soonga, Tongwa and Namulukilwa, and a little of the tribute of seeds and perfume is given to each. Namulukilwa is called the 'last gate' (*impoongolo lya cisila),* because this is the pilgrims' last stop before they reach *musuumba Kapembwa* at Polombwe.

The Shrine as Cosmic Symbol

What did the shrine (*mucisi)* of Kapembwa look like? I asked Paul Kaongela on another occasion. He told me it was round and had two doors. One faced east and the other west.

> At Mapepo, when we reach the shrine, only Kaazengula [the other senior priest] , Mwenya Mukulu and her escort [mother] and myself enter the shrine. We enter through the eastern door. We pray for two hours, and Kapembwa tells us what is good for the country. Then we go outside, leaving by the western door, and inform Chitimbwa, who is waiting, of the lord's [Kapembwa's] instructions for the coming year and he transmits them to his father, Tafuna.[41]

I liked the two doors, which immediately suggested a connection with the 'cosmic egg' and Muwalanzi's solar journey. But soon after recording these details from Mr Kaongela I again came across the senior priest Kaazengula at the house of Katoposya, the priest responsible for the *kwalama* 'swimming' ritual of the queen mother Mombo. Kaazengula explained that there were two Kapembwa shrines:

> There is the shrine made by men, round with two doors. And there is another shrine, made by Spirit and visible only to those who are pure, without the taint of *uloozi* [sorcery].
>
> That other shrine is a shining thing, and square. It shines with all the colours of the rainbow (*mulalanfuti).* Kapembwa is inside that square house. To the east he is guarded by Songola, his *musika* [chief executive]. To the west he is guarded by Chaifika. Both these spirits are male. To the north he is guarded by Kamimbi, who is female, and to the south by Chilingala, a female spirit who is also his wife.[42]

From another source, Mr Godfrey Ngoolwe Sikazwe, I learned that the *musika* Songola had the privilege of greeting his lord Kapembwa standing, by striking two reeds together, whereas the other three guardians had to greet kneeling and clapping their hands.[43] They say of Songola,

Songola akulye, 'Songola can kill you,' because if anyone offends Kapembwa or his priests Songola is the one who punishes. According to Mr Kaongela, it sufficed for an aggrieved priest to make an offering to Songola of red *nkula* powder (made from the bark of the camwood tree), accompanied by a suitable prayer, for the offender to die forthwith.

Questioned on cosmic architecture, Mr Kaongela was explicit on its quadrilateral form. There were four winds, one from each cardinal direction, which he said were the 'four pillars (or props) that shape the world' *(mpaanda ziini zya ntungilila*). When he prayed, he asked 'for good from the four corners, to be given to good and bad people alike'.

It wasn't hard to find other references to quadrilaterality in my field notes. Two objects were kept at the Kapembwa shrine, according to Mr Kaongela: a large round drum called *Maangu* ('Mother'), a symbol of royalty, and a square basket called *Salakata* and made from palm leaves. This basket was sent by Tafuna and used to carry beads and perfumes offered to the spirit. In 1964 I was informed that, when a young man was about to take a hoe and cash as the first instalment of bridewealth to his prospective wife, the father asked the mother to bring white clay (*umuula*):

> She puts a piece in her [left] hand, spits on it, then works it into a paste with her right forefinger; she then dabs a little of this paste on the throat and forehead of her son. The rest of it she uses to anoint the hoe in the form of a *cross*. The father then says: 'I call upon the spirits of *east, west, north* and *south* to go before you and behind you on your errand.[44]

More than thirty years later, in 1996, I watched a Lungu *ngulu* doctor waving her fly-whisk in 'the four directions' in invitation to the spirits.[45]

Katoto, 20.9.90 This is an encounter for which the priest (Paul Kaongela) has long prepared us: we are going to meet the child-wife of Kapembwa, the little girl who bears the title of Mwenya Mukulu. Katoto is a tiny settlement along the rocky lake shore, about twenty kilometres west of Mpulungu, perhaps half a dozen huts and a hectare or so of cultivable land.

The wife of the god is a girl of about seven years old, chosen by Kapembwa speaking through the mouth of one of his prophets.[46] She is a pretty little thing, slightly disfigured by a dark circle around the top of her head, which Mary says is ringworm. Paul (Kaongela) earnestly warns BC, Herbie and myself not to touch the girl, on pain of death. However, it's OK for Mary, and to prove it I take a photograph of her shaking the little wife's hand. Apparently only three men are allowed to lay hands on the girl: Mr Timpa Flotia, the *Chipapa*, who carries her on the annual pilgrimage to Polombwe and back; her father; and Paul Kaongela. She is not allowed to attend school. Kaongela explains that the little girl, whose secular name I was not told, will remain 'married' to Kapembwa until she reaches puberty (*cisuungu*). Then the spirit will divorce her and in due course will choose another 'wife'.[47] The divorced 'wife' is then free to marry a mortal man. The little girl's mother and father are here. The mother is also called Mwenya Mukulu and held the office some time before her daughter was chosen.[48] She now has the title of *Namweene* or Queen Mother. She tells us:

> I became Mwenya Mukulu as a small child. My main duty is to take the wife of the Chief (i.e. Kapembwa) to him. This happens in November [at the Mapepo pilgrimage].
>
> All the Lungu chiefs, including Tafuna, are small ones. I am the mother of them all. When Chief Chitimbwa comes here he has to kneel down and clap his hands before me, then he gives the tribute he has brought for Mother Mwenya Mukulu.
>
> Paul Kaongela is my brother. He gives me food, and money to buy soap and cigarettes.
>
> I am the greatest.[49]

James Sichinsambwe, the mortal husband of Kapembwa's former wife, demonstrated how he knelt and clapped before being allowed to enter the marital home and told us, 'I am happy with my life: I am being kept by the Queen.'

Sacred Symbols of Time and Space

There was a round house at Katoto, said to contain wooden stools (*viliimba*) used by successive holders of the Mwenya Mukulu title. Neither I nor my research assistants were allowed to look inside this house, which was called *miziingwa*.[50] This word is widely used to refer to houses used to contain the stools of office of departed chiefs. It is also used of spirit shrines. The word appears to be a passive and plural form of a root *-ziinga*, meaning to 'drive away' or 'separate', for example, a divorced wife from her former husband. *Miziingwa* thus appears to mean 'things which are kept separate', recalling Durkheim's classical definition of the sacred as 'things set apart and forbidden.[51] A peculiar feature of a *miziingwa* house, also signalling its special, sacred character, is that it supposedly has to be constructed during the daylight hours of a single day. For that reason, it is sometimes called *muntaalala*, meaning that those who build it do not sleep (*-lala*) during its construction.

These special houses contain, or are held to contain, the sacred symbols of the two dominant forms of social authority and power in traditional Lungu culture: royalty and priesthood. The sacred collection of *viliimba* (royal stools) symbolizes the unbroken succession of Lungu chiefs, extending back in time to the founding ancestress Mwenya Mukulu.[52] The characteristic symbolic objects placed in the priestly *miziingwa* are pieces of white cloth, known by the special name of *myaala*. ''Whiteness' in Lungu cosmology symbolizes benign spirit power and, in this particular context, these pieces of cloth stand for the territorial dominion of the *myaao* spirits. These two categories of sacred object – the one (*viliimba*) signifying authority over time, the other (*myaala*) signifying authority over space – are never mixed. So it would seem. Yet there are central episodes in the rituals of Lungu kingship and Lungu priesthood that appear to derive their peculiar power from just such an 'unthinkable' conjunction.

I return to that morning beside the lake in 1990, our introduction to the unexpected concept of the 'cosmic egg'.[53] Herbie's balding head assumes an appropriately egglike patina as he sweats to render each surprising phrase in Paul Kaongela's throatily authoritative delivery into intelligible English. It's the first of many sessions with Kaongela, who invariably comes on with the same confident air, eyes shining with what seems like amusement at our – to him – naïve questions. He is transparently delighted to be able to answer my question on why, if Muwalanzi and Mwenyami had six children, that was the beginning of Ulungu being divided into eight parts, each with a stool of office (*ciliimba*). Didn't he mean six parts? No, he replies, I'd forgotten that Muwalanzi and Mwenyami each had their part too, so eight was the correct total!

They become something like an addiction, these question-and-answer sessions with this most articulate of Lungu priests. The trouble, which is also a peculiar pleasure, is that while every session resolves certain questions, at the same time new ambiguities, calling for further enquiry, emerge from our Talmudic discussions. There is always an enticing direction to follow inside the 'cosmic egg', but eventually our curved path leads us, as in the hypothetical journey of a traveller round the Einsteinian universe, back to our point of departure: the ultimate nemesis of the anthropological structuralist.

The goal I'm working towards, not always clearly or consciously, is to understand the place of the Mwenya Mukulu myth in the priestly world-view. As far as Israel Kasomo and the other royalist historians are concerned, her role as founder and legitimizer of chiefly rule in Ulungu is readily comprehensible, as is her symbolic role in the annual celebration of the alliance between secular and spiritual authorities. But with Kaongela and the other priests of Kapembwa I am in a thought-world that's different in fascinating and disturbing ways. It began with Kaongela's statement, 'I was married to Mwenya Mukulu long ago, but now we are like brother and sister.'

Who were the 'I' and the 'we' in that statement? Gradually it became clear that, in this and similar formulations, Paul Kaongela was condensing and combining symbolic concepts concerning what in 'Western' terms could be called the structure of the universe and the nature of time. Muwalanzi and Mwenyami name primal agencies or forces that continue to act and exist in various forms throughout history. Time itself is cyclical and recurrent, qualities captured in the rituals of *Kwalama* and *Mapepo*.

Where the ideology of Lungu chiefship is driven by ideas of separation, hierarchy, us against them, 'putting Ulungu on the map',[54] etc., Paul Kaongela and the other senior indigenous priests project notions of inclusion and equality. After addressing the spirits of Kombe, Mr Kaongela remarks: 'We pray not just for Ulungu but for the whole world.' It seems to me, indeed, that the notion of Ulungu as divided into eight equal parts is as much a statement of wholeness, analogous to the eightfold division of the Celtic calendar, as of separation and differentiation. In that abstract sense Ulungu is the world. I realize this after our first meeting with Mr Kaongela, at the end of which he countered our questions with one of his own: where had we (my wife Mary and myself) come from? Later I learn from our two research assistants that Kaongela's intention in asking this question had been to locate us, as presumptive children of Muwalanzi and Mwenyami, on his eightfold world 'map'.

I press my enquiries into the arcane business of the relationship between Paul Kaongela and his protean other selves as Mangochimikwa, Muwalanzi, Kapembwa *et al.,* and Mwenya Mukulu. His response is to elide the temporal distinction in his earlier remark, that Mwenya Mukulu had been his wife (in the past) but was now his sister (present), into the 'timeless' statement, 'Mwenya Mukulu is my wife and my sister'. He amplifies it thus: 'That means we have close marriages, you have to marry your sister. In our language we say, *Ukandi, kukandana*.'[55] This expression *ukandi* was one I'd already learned at the meeting with the Lungu priests in June, when they'd explained it as referring to the type of intersibling marriage traditionally associated with chiefly families. 'Chiefs', they said, were not allowed to marry outside – it was the policy that a chief marry a sister to produce a proper chief.' Yet here was Kaongela using the word 'we' as if he, a commoner, were also a royal – another instance of conceptual inclusion!

At our next meeting I ask Kaongela to explain the meaning of this phrase *Ukandi, kukandana*. His response:

> The Chief [*Tafuna*] before he becomes Chief, he has to make his full [uterine] sister his wife. Otherwise he can't 'swim'. The house he uses is like a *miziingwa*, being built in one day, but it is made of grass [only]. It is not a real house. It has to be made at Kasakalawe.[56] After this exercise, which is done at night, between 22 and 24 hours [midnight], the grass house is completely destroyed. This is a great secret (*inkama*). After that they bring *Cizaka* [the Chief's senior wife] to the Chief.
>
> In the morning they make *Muntaalala* [one-day house], also at Kasakalawe. They bring *viliimba* [chiefly stools], which are afterwards returned to Isoko. At midnight they start beating the drums and everyone knows the Chief has come through his ordeals at that place and it is his country.[57]

These priestly narratives and comments play, in terms of ritual and symbolic statement, with an impossible ideal: the union of brother and sister. Such a union, forbidden to commoners by the prohibition against incest *(isiku)*, is expressly enjoined on aspirants to chiefship. What does such a union, or rather the idea of such a union, mean against the background of Lungu cosmology? Here the anthropologist cannot shirk his duty as interpreter, the onus of his privileged status as one who is both outside and inside the Lungu cultural universe. As I see it, this fantasized ideal of incestuous siblingship is also an image of a posited unifying reality behind the disparate appearance of things, a permanent, unchanging reality beyond the flux of time. The union of uterine brother and sister dissolves the endlessly ramifying network of family relations and the conflict of head and loins, patrilateral and matrilateral interests, givers and receivers of bride and bridewealth. Re-creating the primal union of Muwalanzi and Mwenyami, the sacred marriage of brother and sister also obliterates temporal succession and all conflictual concerns with descent and inheritance.

The image of brother–sister union is one of total inclusion and equality, dissolving all division, all separation, all hierarchy. This is, according to my reading of the priestly narratives and discourse, a statement of the conceptual ideal animating the Lungu priestly world-view. According to those same sources,[58] the ritual of royal initiation briefly includes at its heart the 'acting out' of this image of timeless inclusion and equality, before the *viliimba*, the chiefly stools, symbolic of royalist concern with temporal succession and status, are brought on to the ritual stage.

But it's in the annual pilgrimage of *Mapepo,* according to the priestly reading of this ritual, that the cosmic fantasy of cross-sex sibling union is most elaborately played out. For, as Kaongela repeatedly affirmed, he was Kapembwa, and Mangochimikwa, and Muwalanzi, and Mwenya Mukulu was Mwenyami, and his sister and his wife.

In 1990, I was, I now see, unduly impressed by the rhetorical style of Paul Kaongela and others, including royalists, who magisterially delivered statements about the *Mapepo* ritual in the ethnographic present. In 1996, I asked a question I'd somehow failed to put six years earlier: when was this ritual last performed? After much humming and hawing, Mr Kaongela finally conceded that there had been no *Mapepo* since 1980. It's impossible to know for certain whether this statement in its turn is true or not.[59] In a sense the question is irrelevant, since my main interest at this point is in the structure of ideas embodied in representations of the *Mapepo* ritual and its principal actors.

I now see also that, in 1990, my work was dominated by relationships with what could be called the official ideologues of Lungu culture, the royalist and priestly tradition-bearers. In 1996, I concerned myself with less exalted but no less remarkable people, who, against the background of a shared ethnic identity historically forged, as we have seen, from structurally opposed definitions of reality, were exploring for themselves the mysteries of space and time.

Notes

1. 'L'objet de mon livre est . . . de prendre la force magique au sérieux, sans qu'il ne suffise de la désigner comme une erreur de logique ou comme croyance de l'autre' (Favret-Saada 1977: 251).
2. Besides Favret-Saada, other anthropologists who have taken Evans-Pritchard's 'supra-sensible qualities' seriously include Stoller and Olkes (1987) and Edith Turner (1992, 1993).
3. Hastrup 1992: 118. I return later to Hastrup's version of the fieldwork encounter (p. 185).
4. In ciLungu, as in other Bantu languages the pronoun, or, more accurately, the pronominal particle, is not gender- specific.
5. His full name is Israel Kasomo Chitalu Simpungwe. It was only in 1996 that I learned that this remarkable man, who was a member of the Zambian Parliament for several years, is also a traditional healer.

6. A queen mother could take a number of such commoner consorts. Hence the often quoted saying, 'Chiefs have no fathers: they come from queen-mothers.'
7. *-leza* is a root meaning 'territorial spirit' or 'god' in the languages of the central savannah region and *-zimu* is a common Bantu root meaning 'ancestor spirit'.
8. In a published version of this story, also attributed to Israel Kasomo, the ethnohistorian Douglas Werner puzzlingly makes Kasomo say that 'through this marriage Kapembwa became the brother-in-law of Mwenya Mukulu' (Werner 1979). In Lungu kinship terms, the daughter of a woman's sister is likewise a 'daughter', so marrying this woman would make Kapembwa son-in-law to Mwenya Mukulu, which is what Mr Kasomo told me in 1990. See also Willis (1991b).
9. In ciLungu, '*Muzombwe waali umweene, lyene waasyaala uku mulando.*' This episode of an incumbent office-holder being deprived of his status by an incoming royal female is the most persistent cliché or stereotype in Lungu traditional history. It has its counterparts elsewhere in the southern Lake Tanganyika culture region, e.g. in Ufipa (see Willis 1981; see also Southall 1972). '*Muzombwe*' means 'stick insect', a creature whose hesitant movements suggest the fear attributed to the human Muzombwe at the approach of the powerful Mwenya Mukulu.
10. Conceivably these 'short people' could have been pygmoid people related to the present-day Batwa, who still live near Lake Mweru. But an earlier occupation of the southern lake region by ethnic Bushmen is suggested by the bored stones, similar to the stones used by Bushmen women to weight their digging sticks, which have been found all over the region (Fagan 1966). Another tradition, recorded at Chitimbwa's royal village of Katwe, says that Muzombwe's people 'cultivated with digging sticks because they didn't know how to make hoes'.
11. Some scholars use the term 'ecological' (van Binsbergen 1979; Schoffeleers 1979). The title of Schoffeleers' 1979 collection of essays, *Guardians of the Land,* neatly encapsulates their significance. Werbner (1977, 1989) prefers 'regional', highlighting what he sees as the cults' 'middle range' position between the local and the universal or global.
12. Chamukolechi is the name of a royal title-holder in Tanzanian Ulungu, now said to be living in the village of Chilambo or Kilambo. Other sources said that Chamukolechi was the name of the royal woman

who founded this branch of the dynasty.

13. Mr Kasomo is probably referring to another chiefship in Tanzanian Ulungu with the title of *Fwema*.
14. These statements correlate to some extent with traditional accounts collected in this region of south-west Tanzania among the Lungwa and Pimbwe peoples (Willis 1966: 63). Chindo was said to be the name of an aboriginal chief of the Mambwe people (Watson 1958). In the early 1960s, I collected a tradition from the Fipa chief Chatakwa, who lived at Milansi, associating the origin of his line with Ulungu (Willis 1964).
15. Katai, goddess of epidemics in Ulungu and Ufipa, is said to move about and, unlike the other territorial spirits, has no permanent home.
16. The six-month rainy season in this part of Africa usually begins in November.
17. Chisya is the guardian territorial spirit of the plateau subchiefdom of Chinakila, under the paramount Tafuna.
18. *Ntemele* in ciLungu. This technique was banned in colonial times, ostensibly for ecological reasons but more probably because of political and administrative concerns (see Moore and Vaughan 1994). It remains officially illegal to this day, but is employed by the majority of farmers who cannot afford the artificial fertilizers necessary to support permanent cultivation in this region.
19. It seems relevant that Israel Kasomo, today and for many years the devoted spokesman and adviser of Senior Chief Tafuna, was born and grew up in the chiefdom of Chinakila and that his father, from whom he acquired much of his knowledge of Lungu tradition, was an elder of Chinakila's court.
20. Statements by a group of elders of Chinakila, including the chief and Ponkwe, priest of the guardian spirit Chisya. Mr Kasomo also said that the reason for the migration from Uzao was 'overpopulation'. The royal village of Uzao was called Lupele, or Lupale.
21. Statement by the late Izaia Kaingene, Mankonga Village, 31.5.90. Mbete is the site of the royal burial grove. 'Swamp grass' could refer to the marshy region around Lake Mweru to the west of Ulungu.
22. Zambia National Archives, Lusaka.
23. Interviewed by K.B.S. Chisanga at Isoko on 20.11.94. Again interviewed and tape-recorded at Mankonga Village on 12.12.96.
24. The present-day Lungu word for 'fishing net' is in fact *muzao*. Unhappily I found no one in Ulungu willing to recognize a connection with 'Azao', notwithstanding the idea's seeming plausibility.

25. Roberts 1973. The earliest reference to what appear to be Late Stone Age people in Ulungu is a tradition recorded in the Abercorn (Mbala) District Book in about 1957. According to this report, 'the Azao brought the knowledge of ironworking and the making of hoes. Before that the Lungu used digging sticks (*yamunkowe*) made from hard wood (*mipangala*).' Compare also a similar tradition from Chinakila reported on p. 49 above.
26. So it was put, but the contention receives at least negative support in the total absence from the colonial records from the early twentieth century held in the Abercorn (Mbala) District Book of any texts emanating from the Lungu indigenous priesthood (Zambia National Archives, Lusaka). Werner's (1979) account of Lungu religion and associated ritual seems to be entirely based on royalist sources.
27. This detail appears to be an obscure reference to the episode in Mr Kasomo's narrative where Katai attacks Mangala while she is gathering mushrooms on Kapembwa's instructions (see comments below).
28. The matter is complicated by Muwalanzi's 'return' after his initial encounter with Mwenyami, but his overall progress is westwards. It is hard to track Muwalanzi's movements according to this narrative and a further complication is introduced by the fact that 'following the right hand' can mean movement in a southerly direction. 'Right' is also the side of masculinity in Lungu bodily symbolism.
29. Uxorilocally, in anthropological jargon. This custom is always associated with matriliny, descent and inheritance through females. The present-day custom in Ulungu is that wives go to live with their husbands, 'virilocally'.
30. White stands for priesthood, spirit and life and also for male semen. Red stands for royalty and death and also for menstrual blood. Black signifies undifferentiation, commonerhood and pubic hair. I intend to examine Lungu colour symbolism in relation to personhood in a later publication.
31. Again, the shells number a total of three.
32. Mr Kaongela's list is abbreviated. The full itinerary, according to a consensus of priestly and royalist sources, is Kasakalawe, Kaizya, Kasasa, Namukolo, Mbita (Nkumbula Island), Kafukula, Chitongo, Isoko.
33. 'My full name is Mangochimikwa Fukamila Nkombe Zyonsi Simapepo Nkandawa' (Paul Kaongela, 27.7.90).
34. According to a knowledgeable senior elder of Tafuna's court, Mr Robert Sinyangwe, the last Senior Chief of Ulungu to have been a son of Chamukolechi was Wantekwe, who died in 1920.

35. The Zambian government's action in 1968 is understandable, since accepting Chanza's nomination to the Tafuna-ship would have meant accepting the accession of a foreign national to a position of authority in a sensitive border area (Chamukolechi lives in the village of Kilambo, across the border in Tanzanian Ulungu). The last Tafuna to have undergone the 'swimming' ordeal was George Ngoolwe, known as Chivunde, in 1945. There is currently a move among Lungu traditionalists, apparently impressed by the publicity given in Zambia to the Ngoni *incwala* ritual and the annual ceremonial migration of the Lozi paramount and his court, to resuscitate the *kwalama* ritual, which should properly be held early in the dry season, in the months of May or June. The Tafuna is said to have agreed in principle to the request of the recently formed Walamo Committee that he undergo the 'swimming ordeal', suggesting he has overcome earlier reported misgivings.
36. Statement by priest of Namukale at Mwanangwa Village, 27.10.90.
37. The noviciate Tafuna swims across the quarter-mile strait to Nkumbula island between two fully-manned canoes, so he is able to hold the sides of these canoes and allow them to pull him along whenever he gets tired. However, it is said that an unpopular candidate could be stunned by a well-aimed blow from one or more of the paddles and left to drown. Hence, I was told, the long reluctance of the present Tafuna to undergo the ordeal.
38. From statement by a group of elders, including Ponkwe and three sons of the previous Chief *Chinakila*, Chinakila Village, 23.10.90.
39. I was told by Paul Kaongela that the noviciate Chitimbwa had to go through a form of *Kwalama*, walking barefoot to the Kapembwa shrine from the house of the priest in the Yendwe valley. At the shrine, he would be instructed in his duties by the priest. Because the present Chitimbwa did not do this he 'had no powers', Kaongela added. (Interview, Mpulungu, 3.9.90.)
40. The curious episode in Mr Kaongela's narrative where Mwenya Mukulu 'picks' Kapembwa from a bush and carries him until he becomes a youth can perhaps be read as recognition of the way extension of royal power over Ulungu enabled Kapembwa to 'grow up' and become the dominant spiritual power over the whole southern lake region.
41. Statement by Paul Kaongela at Mpulungu, 23.9.90.
42. Statement by Samuel William Kapembwa (Kaazengula), 4.10.90.
43. The normal manner of greeting a Lungu chief. Extreme deference is indicated by lying on the back and clapping.

44. Willis 1966: 44. Emphasis added.
45. See below, p. 101.
46. Formerly, the choice would have been made by the resident prophet, who lived near the Kapembwa shrine and who was apparently always male. According to Mr Kaongela and the resident priests at Kapembwa, this office has not been filled since the death of the last prophet, Timpa, 'several years ago' (Timpa was seemingly alive in the early 1970s, according to Werner (1979)).
47. According to Macrae (1963), there was formerly a less civilized way of disposing of these 'little wives', who were regularly thrown to their deaths from the top of the Polombwe cliff. I was not told when this custom, assuming Macrae's information is accurate, was changed to the present, markedly more humane, practice.
48. When she held office was not clear. She told us she was born in Kasakalawe and may have been the 'Mwenya Mukulu' mentioned in Werner (1979) as living in that lake-shore village. Mr Kaongela told me there had been twenty-eight holders of the title, and they all came from 'the Asikate clan'.
49. Statement by Aides Nakazwe, Katoto Village, 20.9.90.
50. Nor were we allowed to inspect other *miziingwa* houses, for example at Kapoko, residence of Paul Kaongela, where *Kawamba*, guardian of the Mbete burial grove, lives in a round house called *miziingwa* and said to contain the chiefly stools of Wantekwe, Kamata, Vikoline and Chivunde.
51. Durkheim 1912: 47. The contents of a priestly shrine are called *miziingo*, 'separated things'.
52. A late nineteenth-century chief, Kakungu, is said to have thrown the chiefly stools into Lake Tanganyika shortly before being exiled to Nyasaland (Malawi) by officials of the British South Africa Company. He is said to have died in Blantyre in about 1892. A curious story is currently circulating in Ulungu to the effect that the lost stools have been recovered from the lake by a certain fisherman.
53. I have not come across this concept anywhere else in the admittedly patchy literature on East-Central African cosmologies. Indeed, across the whole continent, I know of the 'cosmic egg' motif only among the anthropologically famous Bambara and Dogon peoples of the West African Sahel.
54. Adopted as a slogan by the Ulungu Research Project.
55. Kapoko Village, 13.9.90.
56. A reputedly ancient village a few kilometres south of Mpulungu. Kasakalawe is one of the villages on the ritual itinerary customarily

followed by aspirants to the Tafuna-ship (see above pp. 59–61).

57. Statement at Mpulungu, 23.9.90.
58. I did not obtain an account of the ritual of chiefly incest from royalist sources in Ulungu.
59. Kapembwa Sikazwe, alleging to me that the *Mapepo* ritual had not been performed for many years, cited a story that Priest Kaongela and his son had been attacked by ants and bees while hunting near the Kapembwa shrine, and forced to abandon game and weapons. This happened, he said, because they were 'not pure'. (Statement on 11.12.96.)

–4–

Making Ethnography

> BC's [K.B.S. Chisanga's] mother told him several stories about Katai. One was of a man she knew whose son had died. One day this man was visited in the fields by a Being who appeared as a column of light. The unhappy man cursed the apparition, which vanished. But when he returned to the village he found the same Being there prophesying as the goddess Katai. He offered a white cock, flour, and so on, and received blessings. BC commented: 'The missionaries have stopped these things happening.' (Diary 29.8.96)

> 'Some spirits heal, others only dance.' (Diary 15.9.96, quoting an observation that morning by Kapembwa Sikazwe)

Dancing to the *ngulu* drummers, a woman of uncertain age raises her head and sings a song of weird beauty, quite unlike the monotonous chanting of the earlier ritual and a world away from her gibbering and writhing of a few moments earlier, before the spirit in her spoke and infused her body with its rhythmic motion. Up and down the scale the song goes, and whether it has words I doubt, reminded of Siegfried Sassoon's strange and lovely poem, 'Everyone suddenly burst out singing'. For this woman's song has wings, like Sassoon's liberated bird. I curse on discovering that the camcorder battery has just gone flat, and that haunting song has gone unrecorded, except in my own memory.

Going Underground

In 1990, I'd heard about *ngulu* sessions, and been told that certain practitioners, usually women, beat drums to persuade mysterious spirits called *ngulu* to reveal themselves in their patients and, in so doing, enable those patients to be healed. I was also made aware that *ngulu* was a secretive cult, frowned on by the churches as 'primitive' and 'pagan'.[1]

In 1996, my brief to investigate the expression in ritual of 'selfhood' and 'spirit' made *ngulu* practices a prime object of research. I soon discussed the matter with Mr Chisanga, who seemed as keen as I was to get to grips with what he evidently saw as an important component of

Lungu culture. But how to obtain knowledge of what was effectively an 'underground' activity? Traditionally, anthropological field research meant sitting around waiting for significant cultural events, such as life-cycle and healing rituals, to 'happen'. Mr Chisanga had a better idea: we, the Ulungu Research Project (URP), would make it our business, in collaboration with recognized practitioners, to organize a series of *ngulu* rituals. Instead of being passive recorders of cultural activities, doing ethnography, we would actively intervene in the ritual process, we would make ethnography.

The first job was to locate an *ngulu* practitioner. Sylvia Nanyangwe (SN), who had heard of a woman with that reputation in the neighbouring village of Kafukula, was sent to investigate. She returned saying she had found the woman drunk, but willing to see us any time. Her name was Jenera Nalondwa, which I remembered as that of a prophetess *(kasesema)* who had divined for us in 1990[2] but had said her church forbade *ngulu* sessions. We called on Jenera the next day and she agreed to perform at a date to be arranged.

But an *ngulu* session needs several other ingredients besides an indigenous practitioner, notably skilled drummers and one or more patients. The English word 'patient' is used as a translation of *mulwale*, 'sick one'.

> Tuesday 3rd September, 1730 hrs. Sylvia returns, exhausted but triumphant, from her search for a drummer for the 13th. Apparently she has walked 25 miles along bush paths to run him to earth. His name is Johnston Sichone and he will visit us on Thursday at 1200 hrs to discuss terms, etc.

Eventually, three drummers, all experienced *ngulu* performers, are commissioned at K4000 (£2) each, plus beer and food. Fortuitously, a suitable patient also appears the same day. Mary Nakazwe, a young unmarried woman who is a classificatory younger sister of Sylvia's and a village resident, shows up at home and tells us she is ready to be treated. She began feeling unwell more than three months earlier. By then, she had already dreamed of snakes, a well-known portent of *ngulu* possession. In May, she began feeling cold and feverish, with heart palpitations, and then found herself persistently crying.[3] Mary tells us she feels 'something' at the back of her neck. We agree to take her for treatment.

> Wednesday, 11th September. At 1600 hrs we visit Jenera . . . Her list of requirements for Friday's session is long, and includes maize flour, *kapenta* [sardine-like fish from Lake Tanganyika], bananas, cassava, sugar cane, groundnuts, rice and *cancine* [maize spirit, officially illegal].

> Jenera told us she was born at Chitimbwa's royal village on the plateau, but didn't know when. She never went to school. She had been twice married, and had five children, of whom only one, a daughter, was still alive. She had two grandchildren and was now living alone.
>
> Jenera said she had *ngulu* spirits for a long time but only became fully aware of them after her second marriage. Her sisters and paternal grandparents also had *ngulu*. Her spirits, which included Kapembwa, had forbidden her to eat pork, hare, zebra, barbel fish *(nsinga)* or cassava leaves.

The session begins at Jenera's house at dusk on Friday 13 September, because *ngulu* spirits don't arrive until after dark. We hear the Queen Mother Namailye, the senior queen mother Mombo's lieutenant, who lives a few hundred metres away on the other side of the road, has taken offence at not receiving a personal invitation. The ritual begins with a modest offering to the *ngulu* of a small bowl of maize flour, a knob of tobacco and a K500 (25p) note. Sylvia makes the presentation, then Jenera goes inside with the offerings, accompanied by SN, Roy Willis (RW), and a mature male, who seems to be playing some sort of managerial role.[4] Jenera lies down, on her right side, and begins to breathe heavily and to utter strange cries: she is moving into a trance state. Suddenly she sits up, smiles and hugs the two people nearest to her, the 'manager' and Sylvia, and then moves outside, where a sizeable group of about fifty people, including many children, are waiting. As she does so, the three musicians, all male, set up a rapid drum rhythm, dah-di-dah, dah-di-dah, and Jenera, or rather her 'possessing' spirit, drapes a *citenge* cloth over the head and shoulders of her patient Mary Nakazwe, who is sitting upright with legs straight. She is almost completely hidden by the cloth. Nakangulu, 'the mother of Ngulu', as she is called when in trance, begins to dance, slowly and majestically, ankle bells (called *nsambo)* sharply percussive against the resonating drumbeat. There is an atmosphere of mounting excitement as the hidden form of the patient begins to shake under the cloth and to emit high-pitched cries. Now she is thrashing about on the ground as the relentless drumming continues. Sylvia quickly moves in to adjust her clothing, apparently in the interests of decency. Mary sits up again and begins to speak – or rather the *ngulu* spirits speak their names through her: Chilimanjaro (Kilimanjaro), Kapembwa, Chilingala, Katai, Mbita, Katende, Chisike, Mangala . . . This is the stuff I promised to get in my ESRC proposal, what I have come all this way to hear: the spirit declaring itself through the mouth of the possessed. Yet, I am aware almost immediately of a certain scepticism among the *cognoscenti* around me. These names, it seems, came out just too quickly and easily, as if rehearsed.

Uncle Kapembwa, in particular, is clearly unconvinced of what anthropology would call the 'authenticity' of this performance, and what happens next confirms his suspicions. As the drumming goes on with the same driving energy, I see Mary standing, her body vibrating with increasing violence. 'Hidza!' she cries repeatedly, interspersing this strange name (Hitler?) with what sounds like 'O Jesus!'. Eventually she sinks to the ground, seemingly exhausted. KS (Kapembwa Sikazwe) comments that Mary is 'not pure': she is possessed by unknown spirits called *mizyuuka* ('awakened things'), which have nothing to do with the genuine spirits of the land. As to the 'Jesus' cries, these come from her involvement with the Mutumwa Church.[5]

The uncertain outcome of the 'treatment' seems not to affect the performance as a whole, which continues throughout the night under the sway of the entranced Jenera Nalondwa, who in dancing waves her fly-whisk or *mupunga*, the symbol and instrument of her connection with the *ngulu* spirits. Sichone the drummer shows his expertise in *ngulu* ritual when he tells us the two white chickens we have contributed cannot be consumed because they would properly be shared with a 'cured' *ngulu* patient (which Mary, seemingly, is not).

Sylvia tells me that the spirit animating Jenera is called Matipa, an *ngulu* divinity from far-off Bisa country, 300 kilometres south. She definitely heard the name (I didn't) and also recognized the Bisa language spoken by the spirit. To her ear, the words sounded, as she put it, 'bent'. I'm disconcerted by this information, having expected the *ngulu* spirits to be unambiguously local, quintessential manifestations of Lungu ethnicity. Once again, ethnographic reality plays havoc with neat anthropological categories! But neither the questionable nature of the patient's spiritual affliction nor the 'foreign' provenance of the presiding divinity seems to detract from the felt success of this performance. Even Uncle, despite his reservations about Mary, seems moved by the event as a whole.

> The session ended soon after 1300 hrs. Everyone tired (esp. RW!) but the atmosphere today, building on the emotion and drama of last night, was quite extraordinary. BC was moved to make a speech, a torrent of eloquent ciLungu. He commented afterwards, only half-jokingly I felt, that the *ngulu* spirits had helped him speak. Luckily, I got it on tape.[6]
>
> There was tremendous power in the drumming and the dancing – two interdependent activities. Epecially did one sense the power in the older women, Jenera and one or two others. The attitude towards them was reverential – though the word seems odd when their work provoked so much gaiety and laughter . . .

The crowd, including many children and young people, were there all morning. The young son of the lead drummer Sichone danced with astonishing control and vivacity. A girl of perhaps twelve years from among the spectators put on a solo performance charged with confident eroticism, then rushed to hide among her child-companions, as if suddenly overcome by shyness. Sylvia surprised me by dancing with elegance and style.

The final act in the ritual drama came when the 'manager' , Mr Chisungu, returned Jenera to ordinary reality by bidding her spirit Matipa farewell, '*Mupite mukwai, tukateni!*',[7] at the same time twisting the hair on top of her head.

This experience has sharply exposed for me the inadequacies of anthropological theory in the area of 'spirit possession': the 'deprivation' idea in relationship to the predominance of women (Lewis); the entertainment aspect (Beattie); the symbolic approach (Vic Turner); and the structuralist (Lévi-Strauss, de Heusch). Here was both exorcism and adorcism, in de Heusch's terms. To be sure, all these models and theories contain part of the truth, but the whole is something else! What happened last night was an 'ethnic' display of confidence and power, a cosmic drama with the forces of Nature and the ancestors visible in the bodies of the women, audible in the rhythm of the drums. (Diary 14.9.96)

'Not Your Fault'

In retrospect, I can see that this moment during and immediately after Jenera Nalondwa's masterly performance as '*ngulu* mother' marked the emotional peak of my relationship with K.B.S. Chisanga. We both felt that something of peculiar importance had occurred. Through our joint agency, a fundamental but suppressed element in Lungu cultural identity had been brought to powerful life for a night and a day. Call it proactive ethnography, creative anthropology, whatever, the energy charge was palpable. Later, with BC's help, I transcribed his speech at the end of it, and this is an English translation:

Firstly I would like to thank all you elderly women and elderly men, young women and young men, who came to watch what was happening and especially those who assisted by beating drums from last night up to this day.

I hope and believe that you also have harvested something from all you have seen. Although you could not take part in singing or clapping, that is not your fault at all. It is the mistake of those who came here in our country and forced our ancestors and parents to stop such activities, who were told that such was a Satanic way of living.

Our ancestors followed the orders given them by white missionaries who first came here in our country, especially the London Missionary Society and the Roman Catholic missionaries based in the countries of the Bemba, Fipa and Lungu.[8]

Our parents feared and obeyed the rules and orders of the Church It was a punishable offence to be found dancing or drumming, especially for *ngulu*, *Cisuungu* [female initiation], *Uwinga* [wedding], *Imfwa* [funeral] or *Kupyaana* [inheritance meeting].

That is why you cannot even open your mouths and sing, or even clap, you cannot even understand the meaning of the songs sung here by a few elderly women. But they will go where others went and it will be the end of *ngulu* ceremonies in our country, especially where Christianity is winning the majority of people.

Some of you call such activities and ceremonies 'primitive' and unchristian and see them as overtaken by Western culture. But some of us find that Western culture is also a bad one and can be condemned in many ways.

Here we have our Project Director in our midst: Professor Roy G. Willis, a senior lecturer in the University of Edinburgh.[9] This Project is doing research on *ngulu*, prophets and traditional healers, on traditions which had been forgotten by our forefathers. This work will go on until our tribe is put on the map.

And finally I am appealing to the *ngulu* Matipa to accept our invitation to our forthcoming programme, because we are planning to hold a very important meeting in Posa Village, where the URP is going to meet the elders of the Walamo Committee on 27 August 1996.[10]

We are asking Matipa to perform in the same way on that day, which will be a remarkable day in our life. And we want Mr Sichone and his group to come and take part by beating the drums.

Video filming [English] is very important, so that all that has been happening here can be recorded, enabling us all to remember what happened, and the Person [*muntu*] who did this was Matipa through Mama Jenera Nalondwa, the possessor [*mweene*] of the *ngulu* of Matipa spirit.

The Diary says that 'I responded to this affirmation of BC's by telling him young people in Scotland were trying to recover ancient wisdom through 'DIY [do-it-yourself] spirituality'. It also records that 'both BC and RW were completely shatttered – nodding off at 7.30 p.m. and indeed I went to bed then and slept until 6 a.m.' (Diary 14.9.96).

Three days later, our plans for a series of *ngulu* performances suffered a setback with the news of Jenera Nalondwa's imminent departure for Mufulira (several hundred kilometres away on the Zambian copperbelt), to stay with her daughter. The Diary records that the URP team was unanimous that 'this tribal treasure should be prevented by some means, such as an offer of money, from leaving Ulungu . . . However, it was all in vain. When we finally got back to Kafukula we found our quarry had flown the coop that very day. Our enterprising research team immediately began looking round for replacements. Tomorrow we have two appointments, (Diary 16.9.96).

Technology of the Sacred

> BC's resourcefulness and enterprise in matters ethnographic continue to astonish: now he suggests persuading an *ngulu* expert to imitate the behaviour of a 'proper' patient, so we can get it right. (Diary 13.9.96).

Again looking back on two months of the most intense activity that followed the *ngulu* ceremony at Kafukula, I can see that the Kafukula event set us all in the Project team, each one for rather different reasons, on a path of creative experiment very different from the reproduction of objective reality as envisioned by traditional anthropology. I am sure BC saw our success in 'staging' and filming an *ngulu* performance as a major step towards his goal of bringing Lungu culture to the attention of the world. Uncle, as befitted a healer by vocation, was clearly excited by the therapeutic potential of *ngulu* ritual practice. His concern for Mary Nakazwe is evidenced in a string of Diary entries recording his suggested measures for ridding Mary of the evil spirits afflicting her. Sylvia told me she would like to experience the central *ngulu* ritual of *kutuntuula*, to which Mary had been subjected by Jenera Nalondwa. She seemed genuinely curious, in a commendable spirit of scientific enquiry. As for myself, I was struggling with a clutch of theoretical problems related to the *ngulu* phenomenon, as I then understood it. It obviously had a bounded structure, a clearly defined beginning and end which 'framed' it as a specific social activity outside and beyond the scope and rules of ordinary life. It began with the induction of spirit into the person or persons of the *ngulu* adepts, a process called *kunwama*, 'to invite', or 'invitation', and ended with the dismissal (*kuziinga*: literally, 'driving away') of spirit. This formal 'framing' of the performance met what I saw as the minimal definition of a 'ritual', in anthropological terms. It was also clearly a 'healing' ritual, since its explicit purpose was to rid one or more 'patients' of putatively spirit-induced affliction.

What puzzled me was the apparent absence of a social-structural dimension to the ritual, of the kind exemplified in Victor and Edith Turner's work on the *Ihamba* ritual of the Ndembu, where the healing of the patient also 'heals' a social conflict, with roots that can extend back through generations (Turner, V.W., 1962; Turner, E., 1992). Another difference between this Lungu healing ritual and the symbol-rich Ndembu performances was the notable paucity of symbolic material in the Lungu case. The actions involved in the *-tuntuula* rite were instrumental rather than symbolic, recalling Eliade's description of Siberian shamanic ritual as 'a technology of the sacred' (Eliade 1951), a matter of directly controlling 'spirit' forces.

As I saw it, the only way to resolve these puzzlements was to observe more *ngulu* performances at first hand.

Posa, 7 September 1996 Mr Chisanga had a big job ferrying Mr Sichone and his party and our newly recruited *ngulu* lady, Lisita Nakazwe, and two attendants to Posa. Sylvia and I spend an anxious hour hanging about Paul Nielsen's service station at Musende before the welcome sighting of the Peugeot with its distinctive roof-mounted lights. BC drives us first to the house of Nyamukolo, priest of Mbita and chairman of the Walamo Committee, where plans are being discussed for a grandiose revival of the *Tafuna*'s 'swimming' ritual. Then to the Community Hall, where BC and Uncle have arranged the second in our series of *ngulu* performances. This time it's more public than ever and we find a crowd of maybe a hundred people waiting outside the hall. This time it's Uncle's turn to speak, probably because he, as former chairman of the Lungu Tribal Council (*Kamata*), carries more clout than BC in this heavily 'traditional' village. He speaks with his usual verve and authority, introducing our research enterprise and explaining our concern with promoting Lungu culture, including the music and dance of *ngulu*. There is an atmosphere of excited expectation: in his report Uncle notes: 'The people rejoice.'

Inside, in the darkness congenial to the spirits, I am conscious that our new *Mama Ngulu* knows exactly what she's about. In short order, she dabs the centre of each of the three drums with white maize flour to attract the *ngulu* (white being the colour of 'spirit') and puts a pinch of flour in the mouth of each person present, including RW. The drumming begins, urgent and very loud in this confined space, and almost immediately Lisita slips into glossolalia, and then starts to sing. Sylvia tells me the first *ngulu* spirit says '*Neene Kapembwa*' ('I am Kapembwa') in ciLungu, but the other two, Matipa and Chama, announce themselves in the Bisa language. (Though straining my ears, I am unable to distinguish these statements.) Then Lisita stands up and sings and now, again according to SN, it's the *ngulu* Chama who is singing. I am again made aware that my initial association of the *ngulu* tradition with a territorially defined Lungu ethnicity is way off the mark. After a few minutes, Lisita and her two attendants, both said to be her daughters,[11] stand up and go out into the courtyard, where the crowd awaits. Sylvia was to write in her diary, speaking of Lisita, 'the spirit went outside and danced and sang'. And so it did, moving in that slow, almost langourous way I remembered from Jenera's performance, a smooth gliding movement, sensual too, with simultaneously gyrating hips as the human–spirit–body turns through a wide arc and then suddenly stops, perfect control, before resuming the spiralling movement through the cleared dancing space, going through this sequence of gliding, swooping movement several times before, in a grand gesture of mastery, sweeping the magisterial fly-whisk sharply down on to Mr Sichone's leading drum, abruptly extinguishing the all-enveloping and mesmerizing sound. Silence then for half a minute, while the drummers mop their brows and swig at the *cancine* bottle, then on again and *Mama Ngulu,* her two daughters moving in formation with her, begins again the spirit dance of power and desire, gliding, swaying, swooping, rolling hips, momentarily holding the movement in mid-flight, a moment of exquisite balance, caught between tension and release.

'*Kacina! Kacina!*' the people cry, praising spirit incarnate, the dance and the dancer. *Kacina* is an untranslatable word, a verb-noun based on the root *-cina*, which combines the English meanings of 'dance', 'play' and 'make love'. *Ngulu* is all these:

> There is no systematic map to be made of Lungu culture, no pattern of complementary dualisms. In *ngulu* spirit and flesh, male and female, drummer and dancer, family and territory, are one. Perhaps also the outsider, the anthropologist, and the insider, the local . . .
>
> *Ngulu*: this dangerous conjuncture between the 'spiritual' and the 'erotic' which official Christianity has sought to obscure and deny for 2000 years. (Diary 29.9.96).

By 10 p.m., I am too tired to stay and head homewards. There is also a disappointment: the several 'patients' we had hoped to obtain through two local healers fail to materialize. Fortunately, the populace seem unconcerned: for them the music and dancing are plenty. I return next morning, camcorder in hand, and film the dancers, who are still performing, to the beat of the tireless drums of Sichone and his boys. Two women: Lisita and her daughter Lonia. In the viewfinder, the energy of their bodies seems distributed between three centres of power: head, loins and feet. Much later, back in the UK, I discover that I'd forgotten to cancel the digital 'gain-up' facility on the camcorder which I'd turned on the previous night to maximize the light intake. The result was that, without autofocus, the figures of the two women drift weirdly in and out of definition – spirit forms indeed!

At the end, about midday, the two entranced women return to the same room inside the meeting hall, and the same recumbent posture, to take leave of the spirits. Lisita shakes her head as she 'comes to', wondering aloud where she was, how she got there and why she was covered in dust (she had apparently fallen several times). Her puzzlement and – I think – wry amusement ('No, not again!') look genuine but could also have been play-acting – an old problem in anthropology.

On the way home, we stop at Kaizya and give them (now bathed and clean) their goodies and fee of K10,000 (£5) – reduced by K5000 (£2.50) because of the absence of a 'patient'. We leave promising to produce at least one next time.

> 16.00 hrs. Staff Meeting. Began feeling weary and ended inspired by the enthusiasm and constructive ideas of team members. KS [Kapembwa Sikazwe] in particular demonstrated a clear and orderly mind, reminding the meeting that we had not finished with the first issue (*ngulu*) before getting into the second item (Kamcape/Mutumwa). Fortunately I recovered and came back energetically to help frame a viable programme for October.
>
> RW said the weakness of our *ngulu* sessions so far was the absence of suitable patients. SN said Mr Sichone knew of a female patient here in Kafukula.
>
> Agreed that Doctors Malonga and Muziya be approached to help in the matter.
>
> SN [Sylvia Nanyangwe] reported that the people in Kafukula wanted a *Mucape* [witch-finder] following the sudden deaths of several teachers at the local primary school. (Diary 28.9.96)

'I am Several Other People'

> . . . to Kalambo Falls, quite unnerving in its grandeur. While there with BC and SN noticed absence of KS. BC told me Uncle had started trembling violently while on the way to the Falls and he (BC) had sent him back to the Moto Moto vehicle, which Mr Mulengo was guarding. On return there I found KS who told me he had suddenly realized he had forgotten to bring white beads to offer to Namukale, *ngulu*-goddess-guardian of the 200-metre Falls, and his heart had started beating like crazy. (Diary 2.10.96)

The team begins preparations for the next *ngulu* session, planned for 18–19 October. I hear of a male practitioner called Robert Simpungwe and we go in search of him. He lives somewhere on the other side of the Lunzua river and, after a half-mile trek, we reach a (to me) perilous log bridge over the river. After initial hesitation, I decide not to be chicken and manage to negotiate it, albeit in a thoroughly ignominious crouching posture, my three companions (BC, Uncle, Sylvia) simply walking across it, grandly unperturbed by the watery tumult below. Unfortunately, although I successfully reach the other bank, I finish up with a couple of painful splinters in the second finger of my right hand. I soldier on none the less for a further kilometre, only to find a second river to be crossed, evidently a tributary of the Lunzua. Although the river, or, rather, stream, is much smaller, the bridge is even less substantial than the first – just two slender logs. This time I decide that discretion is much to be preferred to valour and remain on the near side, while BC and KS cross over and go to interview our man, no more than a few metres further on. Sylvia, who I am sure would readily have crossed on her own, kindly elects to stay behind to keep me company. Twenty minutes later, our men reappear, with the good news that Mr Simpungwe has agreed to 'perform' – he says 'work', *kuomba* for us. Back home, Sylvia deftly removes the splinters from my finger.

Later, when I see Mr Simpungwe outside his daughter's house near the main road, he looks like a frail old man, moving with evident difficulty. But he assures BC that 'when the *ngulu* are in me I don't know I'm Simpungwe – I am several other people and can do anything, even if as Simpungwe I am sick'.

A Dream of Dead Snakes

> On the way back from our mammoth shopping expedition BC remarked jokingly that he too was going to have *ngulu* so that he could receive kapenta, flour, cassava, chicken, etc. (Diary 17.10.96)

It's the, by now customary business of slogging around in the broiling sun in Mpulungu, collecting the stack of provisions needed to lay on a full-scale *ngulu* ceremony. In the market, BC is given one of those 'messages' that usually portend trouble of some sort, to the effect that his 'son' has arrived from Luwingu and is waiting for him in Mbala. We end up taking three sick female relatives of BC's, two 'daughters' and a 'sister', plus an unrelated 'nurse' to Mbala for onward transport to Doctor Musukuma, a traditional healer who lives thirty kilometres away, in the bush near the Tanzanian border. One of the sick 'daughters' is Charity Namuyemba, said by BC to be the only one of his children who understands him (he added, wistfully: 'I wish she were male!'), and badly afflicted by what BC says is arthritis, though barely thirty years old. Mr Chisanga pays K20,000 (£10) to a man for transport for these four women, plus a substantial amount for food, all from an advance on his URP salary. We search in vain for the 'son'.

Next morning is the dawning of *Ngulu* Day. It begins inauspiciously: BC says that in the night he dreamed of 'dead snakes' (snakes being the pre-eminent *ngulu* symbol). Prophetic indeed, because in the end the grand *ngulu* festival misfires completely. First Uncle shows up and tells us Robert Simpungwe can't, for unexplained reasons, make it after all. Then Mama Lisita reports having toothache, so she too will not be appearing. In the end only the drummers, together with a patient from their village (Nono), show up. The pressure lamp on which we rely for light to film the nocturnal action inexplicably fails to work. BC spends a maddeningly long time fiddling with the lamp's mechanism, taking it down and reconstructing it over and over again, all to no avail. In the midst of this confusion and frustration, our neighbour Aggrey Sinyangwe arrives with a facial injury caused by stone-throwing fellow villagers with whom he has a long-standing dispute over land. He wants to borrow some petrol so that he can drive to Dr Muziya's clinic in Mpulungu for treatment. I start to say (in halting ciLungu) that of course our neighbour is welcome to the jerrycan of fuel we always keep for emergencies when BC breaks in with the (to me) surprising statement that the petrol was used for cleaning purposes during the recent servicing of the Peugeot at Moto Moto Museum: and, sure enough, the can is almost empty. I feel doubly mortified at not being able to act the generous Big Man and being made to look a fool who doesn't know what's going on in his own house. And behind it all the unpleasant suspicion that BC has been doing something sneaky behind my back. At this point, two more people arrive, the 'brothers' whose hospitality on their splendid estate at Makola we had recently enjoyed and had invited, by way of reciprocity, to experience the big *ngulu* night. More apologies and loss of face. Stay up late making rather laboured conversation with our guests, one of whom is a big wheel hereabouts in the Movement for Multi-Party Democracy (MPD), the currently governing party in Zambia. I tell them the aborted *ngulu* event will be rescheduled for Friday, 1 November. Still in control, but a Diary entry for that day notes a 'sense of navigating uncharted seas, with concealed rocks and lurking serpents everywhere'.

The next morning, still worried over the jerrycan incident, I am even more perturbed to find the damned thing missing. When I ask BC about it, he tells me, surprisingly, that our guests of last night have taken it with the intention of replenishing our supply of petrol. We go into Mpulungu and buy maize meal for Uncle and Sylvia, who seem suitably grateful. On the way back, we encounter our guests of last evening and receive our jerrycan back – but unexpectedly empty. Mr Chisanga also seems disconcerted.

> The jerrycan plot thickens. On the one hand, why they should give us petrol is incomprehensible. On the other, if they hadn't intended doing so, why go off with the jerrycan in the first place? Finally, if they had such an intention why didn't they carry it through, or at least explain to BC why they hadn't: for he was clearly taken aback on finding it empty after all. Now, the tale about the petrol (most of 20 litres!) being used for cleaning purposes in connection with the Peugeot servicing at Moto Moto looks increasingly like a cover story. But why shouldn't BC tell the truth, whatever it was? Why try to fob me off with a tale that was likely to be exposed (since I can easily check it out with Mr Mulengo [at Moto Moto])? Mystery on mystery. (Diary 19.10.96)

17.00 Sylvia has just dropped by, BC having taken off (with my permission) Mbala-wards to see the missing 'son'. Profiting it seems by BC's unusual absence, SN begins by saying that she is 'someone who likes to talk and bring things out'. That, of course, makes me prick up my ears! She then goes on to deliver a long narrative, in the 'total coverage' style familiar in ciLungu (she's talking English), focusing on her relations with BC, who, she alleges, wants to marry her! But instead of the juicy stories of 'sexual harassment', such as we are used to these days in the British media, the scandalous 'incidents' consist entirely of occasions, some of the circumstances of which I recall, when BC has tried, sometimes successfully, to give her various small items, usually food. I find it hard to see anything wrong in all this, with the possible exception of one occasion when, SN alleged, a man briefly stayed in the village who attempted on BC's behalf, apparently unsuccessfully, to initiate marriage negotiations. Concerned to be fair to the absent BC, I remind SN that she owes her job to him, since it was BC who recommended her to me. She concedes the point.

After Sylvia's departure, I spend a long time puzzling over the fact that, although I understood every word of her extended narrative – grammatically it was well ordered and made perfect sense in English – in a deeper sense I understand nothing:

> On the BC–SN relationship. The (naive) idea of a vulnerable young woman being harassed by a predatory older male sits uneasily with my repeated observations of the bold way SN can enter BC's room when he is there and engage him in animated conversation. As with the jerrycan business, am again aware of being peripherally involved in a world of shadowy, shifting meanings. (Diary 19.10.96)

Looking for a way through this maze, I resort to the concepts of semantic anthropology. I doubt whether there is some deep pattern of meaning in SN's words, such as might be revealed by the techniques of structural analysis. I suspect the meaning – since there surely is one – to be entirely concentrated in the surface structure, in these meticulously detailed accounts of a series of apparently trivial transactions. The food items mentioned by SN included sweets, sweet potato leaves (which BC had asked SN, or SN's mother, to prepare in two ways: using oil and using groundnuts; and I do remember BC showing me these leaves and saying they were good); fish and meat, minced and otherwise; rice (which I also remember); and carrots (from Kasama, and which neither SN nor her family liked). If I had asked SN, 'Why are you telling me this?' I doubt if she would have understood the question. Or perhaps one could say that the meaning lies both in the surface detail and in the interconnections, infinite in extent, of these local events with the wider social universe.

Again, having given up on the 'sexual scandal' idea, I begin to wonder if SN was suggesting, or insinuating, that BC was illicitly diverting URP monies to personal ends, but again careful attention to what she was saying fails to substantiate this reading either: the items described were apparently bought with BC's own money.

> So twice today, in different social contexts, I have come up against seemingly impenetrable mystery, consisting in my inability to empathatically fathom the motivations of the social actors concerned. (Diary 19.10.96)

Finally, I seem to understand what happened in the 'mysterious' interview with SN:

> It has just occurred to me that what SN was doing, though the actual content of her narrative seems banal, was making me privy to aspects of BC's social behaviour which she calculated, correctly, I was not aware of. In a way she has established a certain shared intimacy between us, based in our mutual knowledge that BC is unaware of *my* newly acquired knowledge about him and his relationship with SN.
>
> In giving me this information SN has succeeded in *changing* the whole set of relationships between SN and BC, between SN and RW, and between RW and BC. With my tacit agreement (since I allowed SN to tell me her story) she made me complicit in a sharing of knowledge about the absent BC. We both know that BC does *not* know of my new knowledge about his transactions with SN. But SN knows that I know and further that I know that she knows that I know, and so ad infinitum. Moreover she now has a hidden advantage over BC, one of which he is unaware, so in a sense she has

> succeeded in injuring him without his knowledge, a subtle action which has obvious analogies with the secret powers of the *muloozi* [sorcerer]. (Diary 20.10.96)

Night of Dancing

Friday 1 November I've just despatched BC and SN to bring in the Lisita Nakazwe group and our other *ngulu* doctor, Robert Simpungwe. The latter has told us he wants three metres of cloth (any colour except black) and K500 (£2.50) if he has to 'lift' a collapsed patient during the ceremony, which begins this evening.

Dramatis Personae

Lisita Nakazwe, *ngulu* doctor. Born in Kaizya Village near Mpulungu, year unknown. No formal schooling. She married Laurent Kasikila in the early 1960s and they have six surviving children, four female and two male. Lisita became aware of having *ngulu* in the first year of her marriage and was initiated by Chama, now dead, a formerly famous female *ngulu* doctor of Muswilo Village near Isoko. Lisita's mother also had *ngulu*. The leader of Lisita's *ngulu* spirits is called Chama, followed by Kapembwa, Chisya, Nundo, Chakulukunta (the last two said to come from 'far'), Katai, Nonde, Mbita and Mwanzandolo.[12]

Lisita treats people suffering from *vyuuwa* (afflicting spirits of departed relatives), *ngulu* and 'all illnesses connected with *ngulu*'. Fee: maize flour, chicken, K1000 (50p). She first divines, using a rubbing board inherited from her mother.

Lisita insists on being accompanied by her husband, Laurent Kasikila, when doing *ngulu* work. Her *ngulu* spirits have forbidden her to eat pork, elephant or small animals. (Interviewed by KS, SN, 23.10.96.)

Robert Ogeon Matafale Simpungwe, *ngulu* doctor. Born in Kaunda Village near Kasito in the Lunzua valley in 1924. Two years of primary schooling. Married first wife in 1944: no children. Married second wife in 1946 and they have eight children. Became 'very sick' in about 1950 and underwent *-tuntuula* treatment by an *ngulu* doctor called Eliya Chitente. Three *ngulu* revealed themselves in him: Musonda (Bemba), Kapambwe (said by KS to be Tabwa) and Melu (Fipa). He says:

> I have worked with other *ngulu* doctors, including Mama Namwinga Mulipe[13] of Kapoko Village, where I used to live. All *ngulu* doctors are like that. You

> can't work in isolation, just as long as you have your own patients. Drumming and singing are collective.
>
> Each doctor examines his or her own patient. If there are evil spirits, I drive them away with medicines about which the good [*ngulu*] spirits tell me. Some evil spirits even talk like *ngulu* spirits, but I can tell the difference.

Simpungwe's paternal grandmother also had *ngulu* but his parents did not. (Interviewed by KS, 29.10.96.)

Lonia Kasikila Chimbaya, *ngulu* patient. Born Kaizya Village, 1964. Second daughter of Lisita Nakazwe. Five years of primary schooling. Married 1976 and had three daughters, of whom one died. In 1981, after a series of health problems, Lonia's mother took her for divination to Chama, the *ngulu* doctor who had initiated her (Lisita). Chama established that Lonia indeed had *ngulu*, but did not put her through *-tuntuula* initiation. Two years later, she and her husband divorced and Lonia's health deteriorated. She suffered from chronic lack of energy, pains in head, back, chest and abdomen and frequent nose bleeding. Her mother took her to *ngulu* doctor Robert Simpungwe, who found that Lonia had 'misused' her *ngulu*.[14] He promised to 'purify and stabilize' these spirits. Lonia married for the second time in 1993 but the marriage has so far not produced any children. (Interview by SN, 28.10.96.)

Catherine Namwanza, *ngulu* patient. Born Musombizi Village, 1969. No schooling. In 1987 became the second wife of Johnston Sichone, *ngulu* drummer. They have four children. For several years has suffered from backache and chest pains and inability to eat certain foods, including meat and cassava leaves. Says: 'I never know for certain if I have *ngulu* but the symptoms suggest I have. Most people have advised me to see *ngulu* doctors and because I am continually sick I have decided to do so' (interviewed by KS, 31.10.96).

Mevis Kasikila Chimbaya, *Musano*. Born Kaizya Village in 1962, the first daughter of Lisita Nakazwe. She reached the seventh grade in Kaizya Middle School, leaving in 1979. She married the following year and she and her husband have one child, a boy. Mevis acts as *Musano* (or 'manager') for her mother when she does *ngulu* work and does not go into trance.

Johnston Sichone, lead *ngulu* drummer. Born Israel Kasomo Village, 1954. No schooling. Married 1974 and there are six surviving children of the marriage. In 1987 married a second wife, Catherine Namwanza. Johnston's father was a traditional healer (*sing'aanga*), who taught Johnston his craft. Johnston says: 'I have no *ngulu* myself, all the medicine I know is from learning. But my elder brother did have *ngulu* and I used to drum at his ceremonies. I feel very happy when drumming and that is why I have taught the art to my children. If I wasn't so lazy I would be a good doctor, like my father was' (interview by KS, 1.11.96).

A Sense of Flowing

> 17.15 The Nono crowd are already here – must be about 25 including children, drummers, wives, patient, etc . . . Robert Simpungwe has been playing hard to get but Uncle's rhetoric has brought him round: '*yazumila*, *yaomba*' – he agrees, and will work. Madam Lisita is ready to go but there is a problem: two patients but only one *inkoko* [chicken]. Is this acceptable? If not, BC says he is willing to contribute one.[15] (Diary 1.11.96)

After all the hassles of the past few weeks and the fiasco of a fortnight ago, the atmosphere tonight seems something special: almost from the word go, there has been a sense of *flowing*, a camaraderie between doctors, musicians, anthropologist and patients, something quite remarkable. Both BC and KS comment on it.

The ritual begins with the now familiar 'induction' of the two doctors – Robert Simpungwe and Lisita Nakazwe – into the altered state of consciousness where the *ngulu* spirits take over. We use the house where our two domestic staff live. Simpungwe drapes a *citenge* (a patterned cloth normally worn by a woman) over his trousers. The drumming has begun, to continue well into the next day.

I can see why Robert, and Lisita too, talk of this activity as work. They have taken over their respective patients: Robert has Lisita's daughter Lonia, and Lisita has Catherine Namwanza, the drummer's junior wife. Robert seems to be taking charge of the *-tuntuula* preparations, making three chalk marks on the reed mat where the two 'patients' will sit during their ordeal. Lisita is also busy with a charcoal brazier, and it seems that it's her patient, Catherine Namwanza, who will be treated first.

Now the patient is being made ready, sitting upright on the mat where Robert had made the white 'spirit' marks, legs straight before her. What must it feel like? Scary no doubt, but Catherine's face betrays no emotion. Lisita covers her with a *citenge* and then introduces smoking incense from the brazier under the cloth. Sylvia tells me the incense is made from an oil-bearing stone called *ubane*, commonly used here to 'call' the spirits, together with other 'medicines'. Lisita adds a finishing touch, resting her *mupunga* fly-whisk lengthwise on the patient's cloth-covered head, like a lightning conductor. And all the time the drummers build their insistent dah-di-dah-dah beat, working creatively against each other to magnify the throbbing summons to the powerful *ngulu*, drawing them to this specially cleared space in the night. Catherine is alone in there, in the very centre of darkness, under simultaneous assault through several sensory channels. Soon she will have lost her sense of social selfhood, her name, her wifehood and motherhood, her village and tribal identity.

For some minutes the veiled figure is motionless, the drumming and chanting become increasingly urgent; then the first trembling movements signal the onset of spirit action. Everyone's attention is concentrated on what is happening there, on the imminent revelation. The movements become convulsive, the cloth falls away, something is struggling massively in her, urgently seeking to emerge. Those around her stoop to listen, straining to sift intelliigible words from the semi-human babble of glossolalia, to learn the name of the spirit entity stirring in Catherine Namwanza.

'Mbita!' someone cries, triumphantly repeating the newly uttered, newly known name of Catherine's leading *ngulu* spirit and followed by four others: Mwiila, Katende, Chilimanjaro and Meru. Mbita is the spirit of the eastern lake, his shrine on Nkumbula Island off Mpulungu; Mwiila is from Mambwe country; Katende is another name for Katai, the wandering female spirit and estranged wife of the lake god Kapembwa; Chilimanjaro and Meru are from Tanzania, and respectively male and female. So, five in all.

A moment later the spirit-filled body of Catherine Namwanza ceases its convulsive quivering, the wordless cries of pain or ecstasy cease and, amazingly, it rises to its feet, suddenly whole, reborn from suffering and chaos. And now, in its new, changed state and moving with the continuing rhythm of the drums, the spirit dances before us all, visible, revealed.

As the entranced Catherine begins her dance, holding a fly-whisk in her left hand as a sign, it would seem, of her new status as a hostess of the gods, the two doctors and *Musano* join in, all moving together for some minutes before Simpungwe turns to his patient Lonia Kasikila and leads her to a place on the mat, which he first marks with three daubs of white clay. That is where she sits, bolt upright as Catherine had done. He moves swiftly, placing the *citenge* cloth (I think the same one that Catherine had sat beneath) over Lonia's head and shoulders, shutting out the light, and then fetches burning embers from the brazier and places them, sprinkled with 'medicine', under the cloth. Now he stands by, all attention concentrated on her it seems, clapping and chanting in synchrony with the drumbeat.

Everything seems to be proceeding smoothly, as though following an agreed sequence of events, and yet there is no sense of rigid adherence to a 'programme' – when the group danced with Mbita/Catherine, it felt to me like a spontaneous expression of joy at her epiphany.[16] (Only later do I learn from SN, to my astonishment, that she arranged the allocation of patients to doctors before the performance began.) Now Lonia, hidden under the cloth, starts to shake and utter staccato cries – 'Ta ta ta ta ta ta ta ta ta'; the cloth falls, is retrieved by SN and Lonia begins a strange forward movement, shuffling on her backside, head bobbing, again going 'Ta ta ta ta ta ta ta'. Robert Simpungwe now swishes his fly-whisk with great vigour over his patient's head as the cries grow louder and she finally collapses backwards to lie full length and face upwards on the mat, sequences of 'Ta ta ta' climaxing in ejaculatory gurgles, followed by more 'Ta ta ta', and so on. Simpungwe kneels beside his patient, solicitous. He, and a few other witnesses, including SN, hear the *ngulu* declare their names: Jini Bahari, a sea spirit from Tanzania, Kapembwa, the great lake god of Ulungu, and Matipa, the Bisa spirit who had moved in Jenera Nalondwa. Now, slowly, she sits up again. She looks, unsurprisingly, dazed, as if staring at something, or someone, beyond our perception. More words from her, and I'm surprised to see her elder sister Mevis go and sit on her lap, like a child. It seems that Mevis, already *Musano* to her mother, has been 'appointed' by the spirit Jini Bahari to the same office in respect of her sister! The drumming has momentarily stopped and there is only a subdued babble of voices. Do people feel awe? I wonder. Can't think of a word in ciLungu with that meaning. Now, drumming starts again and she rises, spirit-filled, fly-whisk in hand, and everyone dances.

Then I think: what is it that creates this special harmony, this peculiar atmosphere I have called 'flow' (after Csikszentmihalyi 1992)? So many disparate and contrary emotional ingredients: it's frightening and funny, violent and gentle, deadly serious and lightly playful, weird and erotic, all somehow combined in *ngulu* at its best. Lisita Nakazwe sings over and over, all night long, a song in praise of the *ngulu* spirit Kapambwe (said by KS to be of Tabwa provenance); *Musano* seems ecstatic – hard to believe that she too, like her mother and younger sister, is not filled with divinity. Likewise SN, who dances wildly like the two initiated patients, Catherine and Lonia, the spirit in them immune to their mortal hosts' bodily aches and pains, but most astonishing of all is the 'frail' seventy-two-year-old Robert Simpungwe, who, incredibly, is leaping

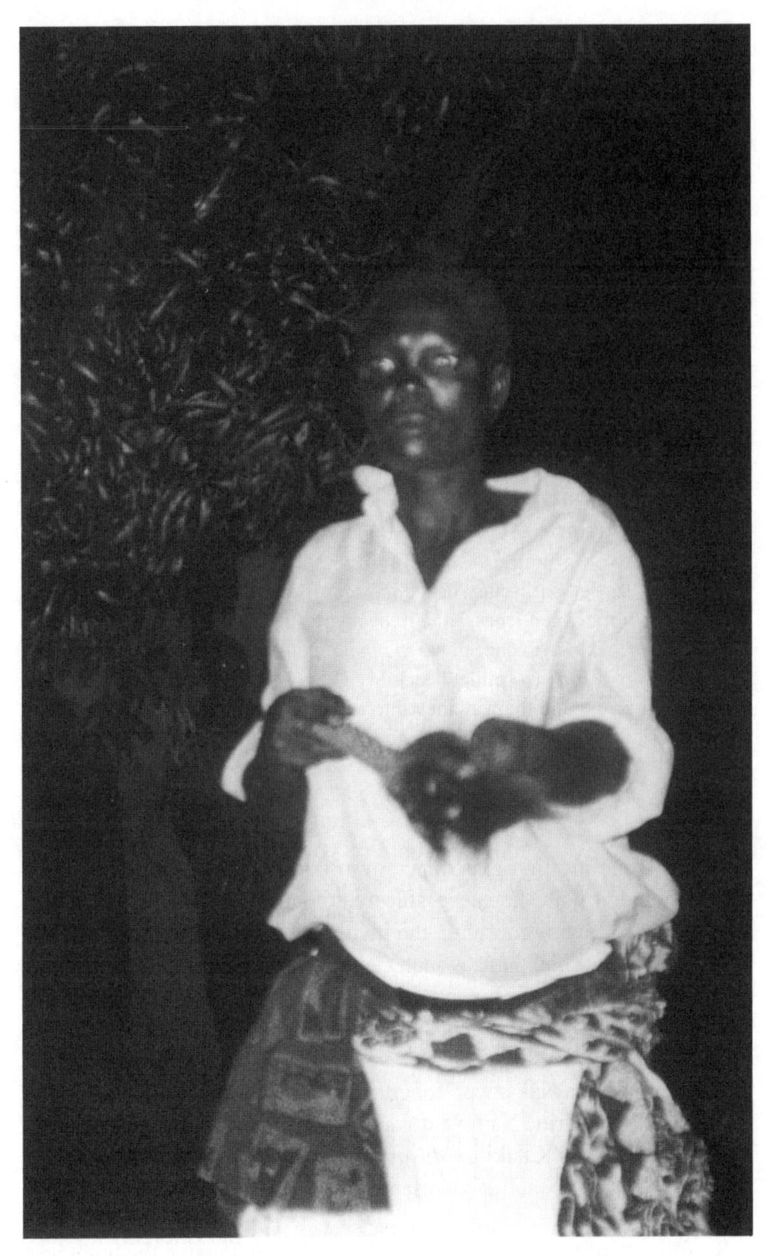

Figure 4. 'Staring at something we can't see': Lonia Kasikila moments after emerging from the revelatory ordeal. (Photo: Roy Willis.)

around like a ballet star. I am dodging about with my camcorder, getting the shots, part, in my own way, of the ritual performance, aware that the drumming and the movement have pleasantly dissolved the boundaries of ordinary selfhood.

Uncle, returning to the scene after an absence of possibly several hours, tells me, in his idiosyncratic fashion that's oddly reminiscent of New Age jargon, that 'the drums activated my non-dancing spirits, and I went away and worked on myself'. In what looks like a state of profound reverie, BC sits immersed in the music and dance. Near dawn, Robert Simpungwe, who's been dancing all night, approaches BC and asks him for permission to leave. Although BC points out that it's still dark, Simpungwe replies, 'No, we're not going anywhere but we'll leave your man here,' whereupon BC realizes that it's not Simpungwe but his spirits that are talking. The 'real' Simpungwe lies down, yawns several times and then gets up and starts talking normally: he is back in ordinary reality but continues none the less to participate in the proceedings.

> Feel in a 'spaced out' state, soaked in impressions from last night. There was a hard-to-define 'gentleness' about the night's performance, notwithstanding the quite shocking violence of the *-tuntuula* inductions. Lisita has just brought me a cup of *uwengwa* [millet beer]. My guess is that the personalities of the principal actors and the way they interact are a significant factor in creating the special 'feel' of each *ngulu* performance. (Diary 1.11.96)

Sacrifice

This was to be my first experience of a 'complete' *ngulu* ceremony, in that it included both the successful treatment/initiation of two patients and, on the following morning, the involvement of Catherine and Lonia in ritual actions which had, as such symbolic proceedings commonly do, the dual effects of confirming their changed social status and establishing their membership in an ancient spiritual lineage.

Present: Lisita Nakazwe, Robert Simpungwe (doctors);
Catherine Namwanza and Lonia Kasikila (initiated patients);
Mevis Kasikila (*Musano*);
KS, SN and RW (research team).

Before the proceedings began, with us all seated inside the hut where the doctors had entered trance the previous evening, Lisita daubed white clay (*mpemba*) liberally on the faces of the two initiates. The rest of us were each given a single mark in the centre of the forehead. Then the two doctors and two patients all joined in the strangulation of the chicken, which was soon accomplished, followed by the removal of all its feathers. The carcass was taken outside by *Musano*, and lightly roasted and then brought back inside. A musician, a brother of Johnston Sichone, joined our small group and started to drum as Robert Simpungwe pulled out the chicken's entrails and placed them with the mass of white feathers in a bowl nearby. He then cut off the bird's legs and beak and put these in the same bowl.

Musano produced a small bag, which appeared to contain a number of cylindrical twigs. Lisita selected two of these and used them to plug the gullet and anus of the chicken carcass. She then, pulling out a wing of the bird with either hand, 'draped' the carcass for a few seconds across the chests of the two initiates, who were seated side by side opposite her. Lisita leaned forward, hands clasped behind her back, and sank her teeth into the chicken, although she didn't appear to eat anything: it seemed a symbolic gesture. The initiates did likewise, also with hands behind their backs.

The whole party, including the drummer, proceeded to the river about 250 metres away, with Lisita carrying the bowl of chicken remains. These she then buried in the river-bed, helped by the initiates.

To the steady beat of the drum the party returned to the dancing ground of the previous night, where, under Lisita's direction, the two initiates carried the mat on which they had undergone their *-tuntuula* ordeal back into the house with their teeth.[17] The trio then danced again, to drumming by the Sichone brothers and Robert Simpungwe.

Order of Precedence

The rest of the chicken carcass was boiled and eaten by the two doctors, *Musano* and the initiates. Lisita began this ceremony by adding medicine to the chicken and *insima* (maize porridge) and to the bowl of water (used for washing hands before the meal). Lisita and the initiates then washed their hands, followed by Simpungwe and Sichone. Lisita prepared a large ball of maize porridge filled with bits of chicken, adding medicine and salt. She daubed *mpemba* (white clay) on the foreheads of the initiates, Simpungwe, RW and *Musano*. She then placed the ball on top of the bowl of maize porridge.

Lisita asks Simpungwe to sing but he declines. *Musano* holds a *citenge* (cloth) over Lisita and the two initiates while they eat from the ball, bending down with hands clasped behind backs. Lisita sings a song to Kapambwe, and *Musano* says that Kapambwe (one of Simpungwe's *ngulu* spirits) is father to Matipa (Lisita's spirit), so Simpungwe has to be served first with chicken. Simpungwe then sings and breaks up the chicken with his hands. Lisita gives a portion to her newly initiated daughter Lonia.

Dismissal of the Spirits

'I am giving to a friend,' Simpungwe says to Lisita as he gives her chicken. He also gives chicken to the other initiate, Catherine Namwanza. He then hands the bowl of chicken to Lisita and she does some more breaking up. She hands a piece to Catherine, another to *Musano* and another to Sichone. She also offers a small piece to SN, who declines politely: this is a meal for those directly involved in the work of *ngulu* initiation.

Afterwards Lisita sings about the *ngulu* Chama in a language said by KS to be ciLuba (language of the Luba people of south-east Congo).[18] I'd been told there was to be a 'ritual' disposal of the chicken bones after the meal, but this doesn't appear to happen.

The final act in this *ngulu* ceremony was the dismissal, *kuziinga* ('driving away') of the spirits animating the two initiates, Catherine and Lonia.

> The two newly initiated patients are standing side by side under the mango tree. Lisita approaches them and puts her right hand on top of her daughter Lonia's head while applying the metallic butt-end of her fly-whisk to the centre of her forehead, while saying something I couldn't catch. After a second or so Lonia collapses as if poleaxed, gibbering in glossolalia.
>
> Lisita does the same to Catherine, with the same spectacular result.
>
> As Lonia continues to shake and babble, Lisita presses the fly-whisk handle against the top of her daughter's spine, twisting her hair with her right hand. She also strikes the soles of her feet with the handle.
>
> Lonia sits up, still gibbering, and Lisita responds by driving the end of her *mupunga* [fly-whisk] into the sensitive area at the base of her nose, forcing her back down, at the same time shouting, angrily, '*Mwapala!*' a word said to mean 'Go away!' in *ngulu* language. I notice Lonia blinking as the pain gets through. A few moments later she and Catherine have returned to normal consciousness. So the return to ordinary reality for *ngulu* initiates has much of the violence of induction into the spirit realm. (Diary 1.11.96)

Mr Chisanga brings all the participants back into the house to, as he puts it, 'disperse' them. The doctors and musicians have to be given their fees. *Musano*, who has quietly assisted her mother back into normal consciousness, is no longer ecstatic but appropriately cool and businesslike in sticking out for her family's cash. Well, they have all given us excellent value and I certainly don't begrudge them their *kwacha* [name of the Zambian currency]. Lisita's husband Laurent Kasikila is completely rat-arsed and unable to contribute to the discussion, but *Musano* concludes agreeably by inviting us, on her mother's behalf, to attend another *ngulu* ceremony at their house in Kaizya in three days' time, an invitation we are delighted to accept.

Out of Space and Time

Kaizya Village, 4.11.96 The URP arrives in strength – BC, Uncle, Sylvia and myself – at Lisita Nakazwe's house. We are greeted with the news that the original patient, a teenage boy suspected of having AIDS, has 'absconded'. The good news is that his place has been taken by the youth's mother, Agrin Mazimba. She tells us she was born in Sondwa Village, near Mpulungu, at an unknown date. She never went to school and could not recall the date of her marriage. She had four children and had been separated from her husband for four years. Agrin, who appeared debilitated and depressed, said she had been sick 'for a long time' and her health had deteriorated further in the previous two months. For this reason she had decided to see a (traditional) doctor. She added: 'I suffer from general pains, especially backache and coughing. People tell me I've been bewitched. I don't know if it's that or *ngulu*.'

Sylvia helps Lisita's daughter Lonia to prepare the patient in the now familiar way, sitting straight-legged under a cloth. Lisita, already in trance as it seems, gives the patient something to smoke (possibly *mpwani*, cannabis), pushes burning incense under the cloth and positions herself at the doorway, *mupunga* in hand, swishing it in the four directions of east, west, north and south, while inviting *ngulu* spirits, including Kapembwa, Mbita, Wamwaka, Mwanzandolwa, Chisya and others, to attend. Three drums begin beating, a colossal din in this confined space. The drummers are Lonia, Mevis and Christopher Silavwe, Lonia's second and present husband. Soon a violent shaking is visible beneath the cloth and the patient emerges and goes into what SN describes, graphically, as a 'rolling dance'.

Lisita dowses the face of the writhing, gibbering figure with medicated water, urging the spirits to name themselves. Some seemingly refuse to do so, a sure sign of their evil nature, and Lisita tells them brusquely to 'Piss off!' ('*Pitanga!*'). She takes over one of the drums and is very much in charge, confident of her control over the spirits, who, she says, will soon be 'dancing'. And, indeed, within a few seconds they are speaking their names: Chanda (the leader), who is said to be Bemba, Kapumpe, from the eastern Lungu plateau, Wamwaka (another name for the wandering goddess Katai) and Kapembwa, lord of the southern lake. These names are greeted with joyful ululations by the women around. Questioned by Lisita, the *ngulu* spirits agree they are indeed four in number.

While Agrin is sitting up, legs outstretched, Lisita instructs Agrin's seven-year-old daughter Sarah Nachula, who is present, to sit on her mother's lap. Sarah has, it seems, been appointed by the *ngulu* Chama to be *Musano* to her mother (as Mevis Kasikila was 'appointed' three days earlier to her sister Lonia). She stands, the newly healed one, and goes outside. She dances to the drum and sings her brief unearthly song.[19] Lisita also dances, Matipa powerful in her, placing her feet with extraordinary precision on and between the huge stones jutting from this barren hillside, moving rhythmically in time with the drum, pausing momentarily at each step to emphasize control, until suddenly she falls, rigid and apparently unconscious, to be caught in falling by her husband and *Musano*, evidently prepared for just such a happening. She lies there motionless for several minutes before slowly 'coming to'.

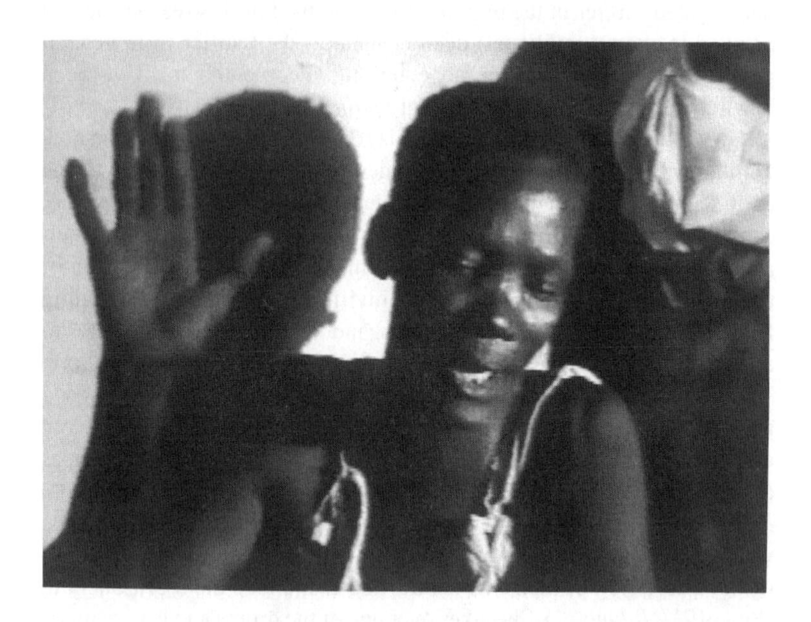

Figure 5. 'Yes, you are going to dance!': *ngulu* doctor Lisita Nakazwe commanding the spirits. (Photo: Roy Willis.)

Aware again, as three days earlier in Mankonga, of being 'lifted' out of normal consciousness into a state where ordinary perceptions of time and space are drastically altered. Absurdly, for a time that could be as long as several hours, I'm convinced that I'm in Britain, and probably not the Britain of today but of several thousand years ago, and I'm among kinsfolk. Yes, I can see that I look different from those around me, and I'm distinctive in possessing this instrument (the camcorder) of magic or sorcery, but the difference seems trivial. We are all related, different versions of each other, but there are no fixed boundaries to selfhood, there is a permeability and flexibility between self and other, an infinite reflexivity, and again this sense of everything flowing within the all-encompassing rhythm of the drum.

Likes her Job

> These women, and a few men, are drawn to divinity as moths to a candle flame. (Diary 4.11.96)

We planned one more *ngulu* ceremony, to be held at our temporary home in Mankonga Village after the arrival in late November of my spouse Mary Taylor Willis (MTW), known locally since 1990 as Mama Mary.

Mankonga, 29 November 1996 One of the doctors, Madalena Mulipe Namwinga, has arrived early with her *Musano* and patient. The doctor is lame and walks with some difficulty, using a stout stick. She tells me she was born in the royal village of Isoko in 1947 and has two children. Both her parents had *ngulu* and she has had them since childhood. Her leading *ngulu* spirit (she has eleven in all), a male called Mukupa, has forbidden her to drink millet beer or to eat barbel fish, hare, pork or zebra. These prohibitions she also applies to patients.

Doctor Namwinga's initial fees are a white cloth, a chicken and K1000 (50p). If successful in revealing a patient's spirits, she receives a further K4000 (£2).

The doctor is accompanied by her *Musano*, Annet Mazimba. Born in Kaizya at an unremembered date, Annet is married with five children and lives, like Namwinga, who is a classificatory younger sister, in the lakeside village of Kapoko. She has never had *ngulu* but became *Musano* after being 'appointed' by Namwinga's spirits. She tells me she enjoys her job but would never want to have spirits herself.

Doctor Namwinga's patient is a young man called Samuel Sichilima, born in Itimbwe, Chief Chungu's royal village, in 1968. His parents moved to Kapoko when he was a boy and he reached the fifth grade in primary school there. In 1993, he married and had two sons, both of whom died in infancy. He explains: 'In 1995 pains began in my head and upper back. I went to Doctor Namwinga and she divined, using a bottle containing liquid medicine. She told me I had *ngulu* and I should come here to undergo *-tuntuula*.'

In late afternoon, Lisita Nakazwe arrives with her usual entourage of husband, *Musano* and daughter Lonia. Shortly afterwards, a middle-aged man I hadn't met before, invited by Uncle, turns up with a younger male companion. The older man turns out to be an *ngulu* doctor called Joseph Simpanje. He was born in 1935 at Landula Village in Senior Chief Tafuna's area and claims to have worked as a primary schoolteacher for eight years, although he himself had only two years of schooling. He is married with, he says, 17 children. His life story is similar to that of other traditional healers I've worked with in Ulungu and elsewhere, in that his healing gift emerged in the wake of a major life crisis:

Figure 6. Patrick Sichilima in process of undergoing the revelatory ordeal. (Photo: Roy Willis.)

> I got sick and was almost blind for a year. I couldn't eat for another year or sleep in the house. I slept outside. Whenever I entered the house the spirits were against me. I went to Masamba where my brother was. There an *ngulu* doctor found I had very strong spirits but could not reveal (*-tuntuula*) them. But he gave me some medicine in which to bathe. After twelve days I started to prophesy (*-sesema*). I was told by the spirits to get *sambwe* [a riverine shrub, the leaves of which are used to make spirit-revealing medicine]. Then in 1962 a doctor called Kabwe showed I had four *ngulu* in me, of which the leader was Chela Muhulu. The others were Mwansa, Chisya and Kaluba. After that I began healing.
>
> I specialize in mental problems, childbearing (*visengo*), fortune-telling and business. I also *-tuntuula* with drums and dancing. I am forbidden to eat *insima* [maize porridge].

The drummers arrive and the ceremony gets under way, beginning as usual with the invitation to the spirits, *kunwama ngulu*. The three doctors – Simpanje, Nakazwe and Namwinga – retire to the small house, together with the master drummer Johnston Sichone and URP members RW, KS, SN and MTW. Drumming begins, weird vocalization from the three recumbent figures signals the advent of the spirits. Simpanje sits up and, grinning broadly, produces a woman's dress, white and woollen, and proceeds to put it on, followed by several strings of beads. He completes the ensemble by draping a *citenge* cloth around his ample waist. We all go out into the central space in front of the main house, where a reed mat is lying. The first patient, Samuel Sichilima, is made ready, sitting in the customary posture with straight back, legs fully extended. His entranced doctor, Madalena Namwinga, places the cloth over him and stands back to watch while Simpanje adjusts the fly-whisk on the patient's head. Now Simpanje, no less entranced, joins Sichone in drumming as the patient begins to sway in time with the beat. Swaying changes to shaking and he falls straight back, still shaking.

A few moments later, the veiling cloth removed, he sits up. What has happened? I could detect nothing, no blurted spirit name, but Namwinga tells me later that her patient has two *ngulu*: Kapembwa and Mbita. A certain disappointing flatness about all this, though: the dramatic intensity of the earlier *-tuntuula* operations in Kafukula, Mankonga and Kaizya seems lacking this time. Mind-stopping revelation has become routine. I feel irritated with the two female doctors for not doing more: they both seem bored, almost lethargic. Only Simpanje, or his spirit, seems to be enjoying himself.

A second patient is being prepared on the same spot on the mat newly vacated by Sichilima and I realize with a shock that it's Sylvia, fulfilling

Figure 7. Entranced *ngulu* doctor Joseph Simpanje wearing female dress and ornaments. (Photo: Roy Willis.)

her declared wish and prearrangement with Lisita to undergo the *-tuntuula* ordeal. Her 'treatment' looks like a cooperative effort, with Lisita Nakazwe and Simpanje working together to prepare her. I feel concern mixed with admiration for Sylvia's courage. The drumming starts again, and soon Sylvia is rolling about, seemingly convulsed with laughter. Now she is emitting what sound like high-pitched barking noises. She is sitting up and shaking her arms about. More yelping noises. There is much laughter among the large crowd of spectators. Kapembwa Sikazwe doubts the authenticity of Sylvia's experience and MTW seems deeply shocked at her behaviour. But I hear someone say 'Katai' and recall that possession by this errant female divinity is commonly associated with hilarity in the possessed and that the goddess can take the form of a bitch.[20] Afterwards, SN tells me she could remember nothing between the onset of drumming and finding herself confronted by a weeping mother and daughter, both devastated by the transformation in her. That, she told me, was when she 'woke up'.

Still this unexpected sense of 'flatness' about this whole performance. When, after another hour or so, the drums fall silent, I realize that this sense is general: the 'vibes' are just not right. Mr Chisanga tells me later that the cause of the problem was what might be called a 'theological' rift between Nakazwe, on the one hand, and Namwinga and Simpanje, on the other. The two latter doctors represented an older, 'classical' tradition in *ngulu* practice, while Lisita belonged to a more recent, 'modern' school.

Testing the Spirit

Morning brought an unexpected demonstration of the 'classical' tradition in action, as Namwinga, assisted and advised by her *Musano*, subjected their newly initiated patient Samuel Sichilima to a series of 'confirmatory' rituals and tests.

It began in the wilderness area behind the house. Wielding a hoe, the initiate clears a space several metres in diameter. A live chicken has been brought to the site by SN. The doctor ties together two small trees called *mufutu*, which bear black edible fruit. The initiate is sent to collect leaves called *masuku* (from the *Uapaca kirkiana* tree, which bears red edible fruit). Cloths (*vitenge*) are draped over these trees to form a small shelter at the back and northern end of the clearing. The patient sits on *mufutu* leaves before the doctor. She takes a five-pronged twig made from the flowering portion of the same tree, dips it in a paste made from white clay and proceeds to mark the face and upper body of the patient with imprints supposed to resemble the footprints of a chicken. The doctor drapes herself in a cloth, lies on her back with her head towards the shelter and holds the chicken against her abdomen. Then, almost completely covered with the cloth, she wriggles towards the initiate, who is sitting in front of the shelter. Evidently, she's miming a snake, probably a python, which has just swallowed its prey. Together, doctor, *Musano* and initiate mime strangulation of the chicken (which is not harmed), while the two women sing a Bemba song 'This is how the lion eats the animal when it catches it' ('*Efyo nkalamo ilya nga yaikata nyama*'). The patient runs and then jumps over the cloth shelter, afterwards prostrating himself twice before the doctor, first to her right side, then to her left. The initiate is sent by the doctor to collect leaves called *cizika* and *katumbi*. He then makes a fire and these leaves are burned on it, together with the *masuku* leaves collected earlier. As the smoke rises, the patient sits by the fire under a cloth, inhaling the smoke. This is to drive 'bad spirits' out of the initiate. While this is happening, the doctor and *Musano*, the initiate joining in, again sing the song about the lion catching and eating its prey.

After that, we all go to the river a few hundred metres distant. The doctor enters the water and swims with remarkable agility about ten metres downstream. There she was supposed to hide a shell called *mpande* (*Conus*) in the river bank, out of sight of the initiate. In fact, according to SN, she uses a small piece of wood as a substitute for this rare item. Shortly thereafter, the initiate swims down the river and, in a matter of seconds, discovers the hidden 'shell', a feat greeted with cries of joy by the two women. This was a 'test' designed to confirm the authenticity of the two spirits (Kapembwa and Mbita) revealed as dwelling in him the previous night.

Later that same day, the initiate went through a further series of symbolic acts, attempting (apparently in vain) to strike a match held between his teeth against a box on the ground, approaching the doctor on his knees with a small cooking pot which the doctor decorated with white spots before returning it to the initiate. He then, with an appearance of reverence, laid the pot, inverted, on the ground. Neither the doctor nor *Musano* offered any interpretation for this latter series of 'ritual' acts, which appeared to refer to the domestic domain of fire and cooking in contrast to the 'bush' symbolism of the earlier ceremonies.

Evening, Friday 29 November Dusk, and it's time for the *ngulu* spirits of our two 'classical' practitioners to depart (Lisita returned to normal consciousness about midday, with a good deal of histrionics, holding the butt of her fly-whisk to the middle of her forehead, and then collapsing, together with recently initiated daughter Lonia). According to KS, 'real' *ngulu* leave in the dark, never during the day! Simpanje has accordingly remained in exuberant trance through the morning, drumming and singing *ngulu* songs in what BC says is Bisa language. Strange words like 'all you people who eat pork are mad', and 'you people with breasts, we shall cut them off' – nonsense rhymes of the gods.

Namwinga has been unable to eat cooked food all day, and neither has Simpanje. In contrast to Lisita and her daughter, these two manage the transition with decorum, almost imperceptibly moving back into ordinary reality. Namwinga, in the obscurity of the small house where her trance began, says she wants to go home. Sichilima is also out of trance, presumably with his doctor's help. He tells me he now wants to be an *ngulu* doctor like her! Within a few minutes, he, Namwinga and *Musano* have left on the return journey to Kapoko. Simpanje, restored to workaday dress, and his companion bid us a cheerful farewell and head back to Muswilo. Lisita's consort Laurent Kasikila is in his customary end-of-session state of amiable stupefaction. I reflect it must be hard for him dealing with a wife who, almost from the beginning of their marriage, has been heavily involved with spirit powers.

Theory and Practice

> BC on Chama of Muswilo, who died *c.* 1980: 'She married my uncle when I was ten [*c.* 1944]. She was a very pure and powerful *ngulu* doctor. And she could dance!'
>
> Diary 3.11.96

> Evidence on Central African religious history is fragmentary and scattered.
>
> Wim van Binsbergen, *Religious Change in Zambia*, 1981

It's time to consider, from the peculiar but sometimes enlightening perspective of social science and anthropology, what *ngulu* is all about. This involves a drastic switch from the 'grass roots' level of first-hand experience to an abstract and impersonal but also much wider view of that experience within a regional and, ultimately, global framework of evidence and theory. As a social institution, the Lungu *ngulu* ritual has obvious affinities with other African 'cults of affliction', as they have been called since Victor Turner's classical work with the Ndembu people of north-west Zambia (Turner 1968). These cults usually involve the use of rhythmic drumming in the driving out or 'domestication' of invasive spirit entities held to be the occult cause of sickness. More recently, Janzen (1992) has sought to reveal the lineaments of what he calls a 'unique historical institution' devoted to the healing of spirit-borne affliction throughout a huge Bantu-speaking region of southern, central and eastern Africa. One of the core features of this institution is the use of percussive instruments, usually but not invariably drums, and singing to effect the therapeutic purpose. Other central features are the progression of the healing events through a day–night–day sequence; the use of white symbolism in initiation; and a spatial movement from profane to sacred space and back again (Janzen 1992: 90). All these features are recognizable in the Lungu *ngulu* ceremonial, suggesting that its ethnic and historical roots extend across vast reaches of space and time, a point I'll return to in a moment when considering the nature of the *ngulu* experience. The broad, comparative perspective also enables us to see, not just the similarities between the *ngulu* phenomenon in Ulungu and similar institutions elsewhere, but also, and just as importantly, what is distinctively different in the Lungu case.

At the organizational level, the *ngulu* cult in Ulungu currently lacks the corporate and hierarchical structure typical of 'cults of affliction' as reported in many other parts of Bantu Africa, where cultists are organized in enduring groups possessing authoritative office-holders. These groups, which are typically named after the spirit entities held to be concerned with particular types of affliction, can be numerous: Turner (1968) lists twenty-three such cults among the Ndembu. Allen Roberts, ethnographer of the Tabwa of Congo (formerly Zaïre), a people closely related ethnically and culturally to the Lungu, has described a corporate Tabwa cult association called *Bulumbu* into which spirit-afflicted persons are initiated (Roberts 1988). To the best of my knowledge, no such associations currently exist in Ulungu, where in 1996, during a discussion with me, Mr Chisanga accurately described relations between *ngulu* cultists as constituting an informal 'network'. There are no named associations and no cultic office-holders.

The amorphous and decentralized quality of *ngulu* 'organization' in Ulungu corresponds in the semantic dimension, the domain of articulated meaning, with a minimal development of symbolic motifs as compared, for example, with the wealth of symbolism deployed in the cult rituals of the Ndembu (Turner, V.W., 1967, 1968, 1969; Turner, E., 1992). Nor was there in the five *ngulu* sessions I attended in 1996 anything like the structured choreography, the 'call and response' singing described by Janzen (1992: 72; 111–16) or the narrative songs recorded in Lusaka by van Binsbergen (1981: 285–6). How to explain these striking cross-cultural differences? The persistent hostility to *ngulu* of the state and church would seem an adequate reason for cultists to prefer the 'low profile' of a loose, acephalous network to a centralized organization which would present an obvious target for repressive action. The lack of an enduring organizational form would then, it seems to me, discourage the elaboration of symbolism. A more positive explanation, one that falls back on an older but still valid theoretical element in anthropology, could point out that the functions of social organization and symbolic structure are fulfilled in Ulungu by the many competing churches, each with its distinctive hierarchic structure, ideology, liturgy and, typically, ceremonial dress.[21] More subtly, the Christian and quasi-Christian churches lack the pejorative 'primitive' and 'pagan' connotations which for many Africans are associated with the *ngulu* cult.[22]

How did *ngulu* originate in Ulungu? The evidence is scanty. Werner suggests that *ngulu* 'was a popular religious movement which was probably known in Ulungu before the beginning of the twentieth century' (1979: 117), although the basis on which he makes this assertion is not clear. If it was indeed a 'popular religious movement' in Ulungu a century or more ago, it is surprising to find no mention of it in the archives of the London Missionary Society (LMS), who were well established in Ulungu from 1884 onwards. In 1905, *ngulu* does not figure in the list of forbidden activities set out by the Society's Tanganyika District Committee, a list that includes 'dancing, public beer drinking and the *Chizungu* [female initiation] ceremony'.[23] The first reference I could find in the Abercorn District Book is in 1950, according to which *ngulu* 'appears to be a secret society based on belief in Mulenga, an ancestral deity of the Bemba, Lungu and kindred tribes'. An unnamed male representative of this society was said to 'eat only uncooked food, go into trance and dance', and then to foretell the future.[24]

This statement by an unnamed colonial official is incorrect in implying that *ngulu* cultic activity was a novelty in Ulungu in 1950, since I have interviewed practitioners who went through *-tuntuula* initiation in the 1930s and 1940s, and met one who claimed to have been initiated in 1915.[25] The cult referred to in this colonial report is likely to have been a specific one classed by Lungu people as a further example of an established cultic phenomenon known by the generic term '*ngulu*'.

Portmanteau Term

The word *ngulu* itself does, however, point to a Bemba origin of the modern cult in Ulungu, as Werner (1979) argues. For, in Bemba usage, this is a term referring to territorial spirits for which the equivalent in the Lungu–Mambwe–Fipa group of languages is *miyaao*. The root meaning of *ngulu*, according to Werner, is 'supernatural being' (1979: 117).[26] In ciLungu, the word *ngulu* refers not only to the local territorial spirits, the traditional *miyaao* deities together with the wandering spirit Katai, but also to a pantheon of introduced divinities, including the territorially proximate spirits of the Mambwe, Fipa, Tabwa and Bemba. Also included in the portmanteau term *ngulu* is the frequently encountered Tanzanian spirit Chilimanjaro (Kilimanjaro in Swahili) and his lesser-known consort Meru, as well as the putatively Bisa spirits Matipa and Chama. The two latter do not appear to be territorial spirits in origin, being the names of two Bisa chiefships (A.D. Roberts 1973: 141). The same goes for Mulenga, a name for the creative aspect of divinity in Bemba theology, whose cult appears to have been introduced into Ulungu at some time during the colonial period,[27] but whose name has come to figure in the heterogeneous pantheon of Lungu *ngulu* spirits. Similarly with two other introduced spirits, Samaliya and Mutumwa, discussed further below, associated with healing and sorcery eradication.[28] What can be said with confidence is that *ngulu* spirits in Ulungu are always thought of as originating outside or beyond the domain of familihood. Further, although they may cause health problems for certain people before being revealed and recognized, they are not intrinsically harmful and can indeed be employed to heal affliction.[29]

The word *ngulu* is also used in an extended sense in ciLungu to refer to the drumming ceremony of revelation in which the spirits are held to announce themselves and to dance in the bodies of their adepts and newly initiated patients. This usage appears to be unusual cross-culturally: throughout most of the vast region covered in Janzen's survey, the drumming 'cult of affliction' is known as *ng'oma*, which in its basic meaning in most Bantu languages, including ciLungu, signifies 'drum'.[30] This difference is consistent with the already noted lack of differentiation of the drumming cult in Ulungu into rituals devoted to specific health problems: there is no need in Ulungu for an overarching generic term.

The Language of *Ngulu*

The meaning of the verb *ku-tuntuula*, used of the psychologically violent process by which *ngulu* spirits are brought to speak their names, is clearly central to an understanding of the Lungu ritual. Its range of meanings includes the ritual or ceremony itself, especially the treatment of *ngulu* patients: in this sense it is a synonym of the word '*ngulu*' when used to refer to the ritual process. I was told that *-tuntuula* also means 'to bring out, cause to appear [referring to the spirits]'. This is similar to the meaning of the word given in Fr. Halemba's Mambwe dictionary as 'to cause to appear, to bring from another place' (1994: 857). According to KS, however, *-tuntuula* has two further important meanings in ciLungu: to communicate with the spirits, and to purify. The latter sense is akin to its meaning in the Bemba language where, according to Fr. Hinfelaar, *ku-tuntula* [thus spelt] means 'to make whole' (1989:95). The obviously cognate Lungu word *ku-tuntuula* embraces a number of superficially disparate meanings which amount to an implicit theory of human selfhood and its potential for limitless expansion. *Ku-tuntuula* is the event and process that brings together doctors, patients and musicians in a working partnership. It is also the locus of a meeting of human and spirit being, which becomes, for the duration of the processual event, an actual fusion of those two orders of life. It's the revelation of indwelling spirithood, followed by the demonstration of cosmic identity in the playful-erotic movement of sacred dance, *ku-cina*, a demonstration that continues through a night and the following day. In taking on spirithood, the human becomes complete and whole, or holy. As Friedson explains regarding the comparable experience of the *nchimi* prophet-healers of northern Malawi, 'the *nchimi* trance is not a loss of self – as these kind of trances are so often described – but an expansion of self' (1996 30). Or as Csordas observes in his study of charismatic healers in the USA, 'healing is the creation of a sacred self' (1994: 276).

In the trance state, *ngulu* practitioners use a special language. An entranced doctor will refer to her or his initiated patient as *kabense,* a word said to mean 'my child' (*umwaanane* in ordinary ciLungu). The same term can be used of the *Musano* (the 'manager') by the spirit speaking through a doctor or inititate. *Fwembe* is the *ngulu* word for 'drum' (*ng'oma*). Maize porridge (*insima*) becomes *wuntopwa* and cassava (*kalya*) becomes *bololeke*. To eat (*ku-lya*) is *ku-nenenkesya*. To go (*ku-pita*) is *ku-pala*.[31] Water *(amanzi*) is *masambacula*, fire (*umooto*) is *cesela*. Man (*umonsi*) is *simukolo* and woman (*umwaanaci*) is *nankolo.* White person (*Muzungu*) is *Cisungunu*. Equipment or tools (*vyombelo*) become *vyombanwa* in *ngulu* parlance.

This peculiar if rudimentary dialect is said by some to be 'ciBisa' and by others to be 'ciLuba'. Whatever the factual status of these assertions,[32] that they are made is interesting in itself, in view of the recognized historical connections between the Luba and Lunda peoples and many ethnicities in northern Zambia, including the Bemba and Lungu.[33] The Bisa themselves, or at least the ruling chiefs, claim Luba origins (Brelsford 1956). It is also known that Bisa, in association with the Lunda king Kazembe, dominated long-distance trade in northern Zambia for a century between 1760 and 1860, when the Bemba became militarily hegemonic in the region (A.D. Roberts 1973: 189). It seems as though the *ngulu* cult in Ulungu has retained in its esoteric lore, including the names of at least two of its major divinities – Matipa and Chama – elements of history going back centuries, possibly to a time before 'Ulungu' itself had emerged as an ethnic and territorial entity.

Symbols of Symbols

We are beginning to get a grip on what *ngulu* is about. Relating to *ngulu* spirits means relating to what is outside or beyond the everyday world, grounded as it is in the complex, conflictual and labyrinthine inter-connections of familihood. Like the Tumbuka *vimbuza* spirits, *ngulu* are 'the quintessential spiritual embodiment of the "other"' (Friedson 1996: 34). For Lungu, relating to *ngulu* spirits means reaching back in time beyond the range of familial or even tribal history to engage with the powers of the wild, the frightening otherness of night and the bush. Exiguous though the symbolic element in Lungu *ngulu* ritual appears to be, the central message is clear: *ngulu* spirits are like predatory wild beasts, seizing and devouring their human prey. We saw this drama enacted in Mankonga when the initiand Samuel Sichilima, symbolically equated with a chicken, was 'eaten' by a python and then by a lion before being immersed in the transforming medium of water and proving his new, spirit-filled identity by finding and retrieving a simulated *Conus* shell, emblem of kingship.

We see here the ritual language of *ngulu* playing with images of violence and transformation – what is devoured 'becomes' the devourer: the human prey 'becomes' the powerful *ngulu* spirit in the ritual of revelation and dance. Other research suggested that the chicken whose sacrificial death was mimed in the Mankonga ritual was itself a substitute for a more ancient animal symbol: the tiny antelope *Cephalopus mergens*, called *pombo* in ciLungu and 'duiker' (originally Afrikaans) in English. An elderly *ngulu* doctor called Elina Nalupya told us:

> I was born in 1932 at Tondokoso in Senior Chief Tafuna's area. *Ngulu* spirits came to me when I was still a child. I stopped eating *insima* [maize flour] and ate only raw maize. When I was older I became very sick and nearly died. An *ngulu* doctor, a woman called Kapumpe, put me through the *-tuntuula* ordeal and they found my spirits were Katende, Chanda, Mulenga, Mangala and Namukale, the last two being prophets (*yakasesema*).[34]

> I was taken into the bush and a duiker was caught with a net. I killed it with an axe and drank blood from its neck. I did the same with a sheep. Then I became an *ngulu* doctor.
>
> Kapumpe gave me my *vyombanwa* [ritual equipment]: an axe, a fly-whisk, ankle bells, a small hoe, beads and two drums.
>
> I charge patients K2000 (£1) and a white cloth.[35]

Nalupya told us that the symptoms of *ngulu* affliction had changed: nowadays patients had continuous illnesses, had weak sight and lost weight but didn't die. Formerly, as in her case, illness caused by *ngulu* spirits was sudden and violent and could lead to death.

The symbolism of *ngulu* ritual in Ulungu images the *ngulu* spirits as predatory beasts, the afflicted patients as their 'prey'. In former times, the possessed patient acted out the overpowering violence of the spirit by drinking the blood of a captured duiker. More recently, it seems, chickens have been substituted for duiker, probably because they are more readily available. Another symbolic motif, the standard refusal of entranced *ngulu* practitioners to eat cooked food, reinforces the image of the *ngulu* spirits as animals of the wild, who eat their food raw, in contrast to humans, whose food is cooked.[36] The association of *ngulu* activity with darkness also evokes the major predators, such as lion and python, who are particularly active at night.

The seizing and eating of a prey animal by a powerful predator is thus the metaphor underlying the ritual symbolism of *ngulu* in Ulungu. Again, in this image of life, death and transformation (the prey animal, in being devoured, 'becomes' the predator), *ngulu* is presented as the realm of the non-human, the alien other.

Nalupya's testimony also offers another piece of what van Binsbergen has called the 'fragmentary and scattered' religious history of East-Central Africa (1981: 29). Her story suggests that not only has the symbolism of the *ngulu* experience been modified in the later twentieth century, but, more significantly, there has been a radical change in the social organization of the cult. Hunting with a net (*nsumbo*) for duiker requires the participation of a sizeable group, suggesting that the *ngulu* cult in Ulungu was formerly a communal institution, as it was among the neighbouring Bemba and Tabwa peoples (Werner 1971; A.F. Roberts 1984). In the Lunzua valley region of eastern Ulungu[37] today, it is a business conducted by competing individual practitioners loosely linked in localized networks.

The Spirit Experience

> I know there's a God and I know there are spirits. I don't listen to preachings.
>
> BC, 15.10.96

> People think they are being civilized when they say spirits don't exist.
>
> KS, 15.10.96

Anthropology has always been fascinated with the weird and dramatic aspects of what is generally called 'spirit possession'. Since for most anthropologists the 'spirit' entities posited by their subjects do not exist in reality (see van Binsbergen 1991: 336; E. Turner 1992), interpreting spirit-orientated behaviour has tended to lead them into explanations which present 'spirit' agencies as colourfully disguised representations of more mundane, 'real' societal forces and phenomena, such as intrusive European political, military and technological powers, or the effects of externally induced economic changes (e.g. Beattie 1969; Colson 1969; van Binsbergen 1981). Alternatively, as with Victor Turner's celebrated studies of Ndembu 'cults of affliction', 'spirit' rituals are explained as ways of managing, and healing, deep-rooted conflicts within the local community (Turner 1962, 1968). Although these theories have undoubtedly contributed much to our understanding of the forms taken by 'spirit possession' in modern Africa and in other parts of the non-Western world, they have also had the effect of diverting attention from the subjective content or experience of 'spirit' agency.

In 1996, I had two experiences during *ngulu* ceremonies in Ulungu which, I now think, came close to being experiences of 'spirit'. On both occasions, at Mankonga on 1 November and at Kaizya three days later, I had the very distinct sense of being in a changed state of consciousness, in which the ordinary-reality parameters of 'time' and 'space' had somehow been dissolved. Of these two *ngulu* experiences, the second (at Kaizya) was the more powerful, but on both occasions I had the strong sensation of being 'lifted' out of normal reality into a condition of pleasurably heightened awareness, which could fairly be called one of mild ecstasy.[38]

How was this remarkable effect, which I feel reasonably certain was shared by my fellows, achieved? It is tempting, in the mechanistic and reductionist fashion traditionally favoured by Western science, to ascribe it, substantially at least, to the mind-altering consequences of percussive rhythm. This is probably the most common, though by no means the only, method of inducing what Ludwig (1969) was the first to call an 'altered state of consciousness'.[39] The experiments of Neher (1962) produced what seemed to be persuasive evidence that a certain type of drumming is capable of fundamentally altering the everyday pattern of electrical activity in the human brain so as to induce what one later source termed 'positive, ineffable affect'.[40]

This blissful state is said to be correlated with a change in relations between the ordinarily dominant left cerebral hemisphere, known to be the source of analytical, linear-logical thinking, and the right hemisphere, associated with holistic, 'timeless' and 'mystical' thought. In the state of 'bliss', both cerebral hemispheres are, in contrast to the asymmetric, left-brain-dominated state of ordinary waking consciousness, at once maximally stimulated and working together in harmony (Lex 1979).[41]

But in my opinion it takes more than percussion to move people into durable trance states. The decisive factor would appear to be the quality of relations between the individuals making up the trancing group. This includes relations between the drummers and between them and other group members. It is this intangible quality that creates the peculiar and specific 'atmosphere' – whether positive or negative – that I noticed at each of the five *ngulu* performances in Ulungu. This 'atmosphere' in turn affects the drummers and other musicians and influences the quality of their performance. On the fifth occasion, at Mankonga on 29 November, the drummers were so disconcerted with the discordant 'vibes' produced by the conflict between representatives of the two 'schools' of *ngulu* practitioners present that they spontaneously abandoned playing until the morning. In contrast, when the 'atmosphere' is positive, the musicians feel able to give of their best, as at the earlier Mankonga and Kaizya performances. Their input in turn enhances the mind-altering effects on participants of the whole occasion. Thus, what could be called the collective will, manifesting itself through the mental and physical actions of the musicians, effects the trance-inducing neurophysical changes in the nervous systems[42] of the participants, including, presumably, the musicians themselves. The ethnomusicologist Gilbert Rouget takes a similar view in his notable study of the relation between music and 'possession' trance. While recognizing the paramount effect of drumming in facilitating entry into trance, Rouget insists that this effect is itself the result of what he calls '*action morale*' (1980: 263–4).[43]

The late Victor Turner was the first British anthropologist to recognize the significance for social science of the American findings on the neurophysiology of ritual trance. Courageously abandoning the deeply ingrained disciplinary dogma that ritual behaviour was entirely cultural in origin, Turner welcomed what he saw as evidence for a universal, genetically transmitted disposition in human beings to enter trance states. For years before he encountered the new discoveries about the human brain, Turner had been developing a theory on ritually induced changes in consciousness associated with climactic moments in what the French anthropologist Arnold van Gennep had much earlier called 'rites of passage' (van Gennep 1909). Beginning with his field experience of Ndembu ritual and broadening his scope to include a vast sweep of history and society from medieval Europe, ancient India and Japan to the 'hippie' cult in mid-twentieth-century America, Turner constructed the concept of what he called *communitas* (Turner 1969). In '*communitas*', ritual participants entered a state of 'anti-structure' in which their ordinarily limited self-perceptions, as moulded by the locally constructed set of hierarchically related statuses and roles, were temporarily dissolved. In this 'liminal' ('threshold') state, participants in ritual *communitas* experienced themselves as unprecedentedly 'whole', relating to other 'whole' persons. Seeking to describe this special state, Turner quotes the theologian Martin Buber's vision of true human community as 'everywhere a turning to, a dynamic facing of, the others, a flowing from *I* to *Thou'* (Turner 1969: 127).

Turner envisioned *communitas* as an institutionalized means by which humans living in specific social and cultural conditions periodically liberated themselves from that conditioning in a state where they were, however briefly, able to 'play' with their experiential knowledge of 'reality' so as to imagine other, and possibly better, ways of constructing that 'reality' (Turner 1985a: 174). Turner's '*communitas*' concept was certainly an improvement on the 'functionalist' theory that long dominated anthropology, according to which all social institutions, including rituals, served to uphold the *status quo*. But it was still Durkheimian in that it saw human reality as contained within an alternation between the limitations of social structure and its libertarian antithesis – the 'anti-structure' of social *communitas*. In this model of '*communitas*', the infra-social world of aliens, beasts and cosmic spirits – especially spirits – would seem to have no part. As Edith Turner has since pointed out, for her late husband Victor the spirit-ridden Ndembu rituals were 'a mixture of moving poetry and undoubted hocus-pocus' (Turner, E., 1992: 8). In similar vein, Devisch argues that in Victor Turner's work 'the religious context appears merely as a surplus-value over and above the social value of ritual action and thought' (1993: 36).[44]

Communitas in Kaizya

Victor Turner tracked the '*communitas*' phenomenon through many and diverse societies and times. We can see why, in spite of its shocking implications for anthropological orthodoxy, near the end of his life he embraced scientific evidence suggesting that ritually induced altered states of 'positive, ineffable affect' were part of the common heritage of the human genetic constitution. Had he lived, he might have been able to resolve the contradiction between his discovery of the social phenomenon of *communitas* – a ritually induced altered state of consciousness in which individuals experience an expanded sense of selfhood in relation to others – and the neurophysiological evidence, which focuses on individual human organisms as isolates. For what is required is to bring together a broader version of his '*communitas*' theory with a broader, group-focused reading of the neurophysiological evidence on ritual trance. For, as it presently stands, that evidence unwarrantably reduces the subjective experience of persons in trance to the behaviour of individual brains. Such an approach excludes the interactive level at which the intangible 'atmosphere' (or Rouget's *action morale*) referred to earlier is generated – the 'atmosphere' which, I suggest on the basis of field evidence, has a decisive effect on the nature of the neurophysiological activity in the brains of group members. Restricting the approach to the level of the individual brain in turn makes it possible for d'Aquili and Laughlin (1979) to suggest, and their mechanical imagery is symptomatic and quoted by Turner with apparent approval, that 'gods, powers, spirits, personified forces, or any other causal ingredients are automatically generated' by a specific cerebral nexus.[45]

In his tireless search for what he seems to have envisaged as the ecstatic essence of '*communitas*', Turner eventually hit on the neurophysiology of ritual trance and the apparent correlation between a certain unusual cerebral activity and subjectively reported 'blissful' states. There is a peculiar irony in the fact that, while Turner was implicitly accepting the materialist and reductionist premises of the proponents of 'biogenetic structuralism', a profound 'paradigm shift' away from this modernist dogma was under way in psychology, partly through the agency of Roger Sperry, prime source of the 'split brain' theory of cerebral hemispheric differentiation, who is cited by Turner in support of his iconoclastic theory (Turner 1985c: 257). 'In the traditional atomistic or micro-deterministic view of science, everything is determined from below upward . . . Brain states determine mental states, but not vice versa. In the new view, however, things are determined reciprocally, not only from lower levels upward, but also from above downward' (Sperry and Henniger 1994).

'Intersubjective Objectivity'

In the experimental evidence on the neurophysiology of ritual trance Turner appears to have seen confirmation from 'hard' science of his insightful conviction that a certain social and ritual state which he called *communitas* was both a source of unique – if ephemeral – individual liberation and wholeness and a potentially universal human capacity. But, in adopting a model of human behaviour located at the level of the concrete organism, together with its reductionist metaphysic, Turner implicitly denied the intersubjective reality that had been the focus of his lifelong search for a 'liberated' anthropology of experience (Turner 1985a: 177).

The new psychological paradigm announced by Sperry and Henniger offers a way of avoiding the reductionist implications of biogenetic structuralism while opening the possibility of reconciliation between the exciting developments in neuroscience and current ethnographic exploration, in the still relatively new climate of post-modern reflexivity, of intersubjective experience. Such experience is most intense, it seems, during moments of communally orchestrated activity of the kind Turner was pointing to with his '*communitas*' concept and which Friedson has wonderfully portrayed in his first-hand account of trance dancing with the Tumbuka prophet-healers. There, the Mzungu stranger was able to verify the human universality of the expansion of selfhood in encounter with what are locally perceived as 'spirit' powers – an experience which, drawing upon the phenomenological philosophy of Husserl and Heidegger, Friedson describes as a knowledge of 'the things in themselves', an intercourse with alien otherness, a liminal space charged with 'the possibility of a communitas that has the potential to release cultural forces of healing' (1996: 126, 164). In this space of *communitas*, Friedson assures us, 'an intersubjective objectivity becomes possible that binds people together in a commonality of experiential space and time' (ibid.: 124). Such was also, I feel certain, the experience of my Lungu associates in the ecstasies of *ngulu* trance.

Triggering Trance Experience

The human propensity to move from ordinary to non-ordinary consciousness can, it appears, be triggered by a large array of external causes, ranging from a variety of psychoactive substances to certain kinds of visual and auditory stimulation. Such effects can be produced in solitary individuals, in couples or in groups.[46] I.M. Lewis has listed a number of methods of trance induction used worldwide:

> trance states can be readily induced in most normal people by a wide range of stimuli, applied either separately or in combination. Time-honoured techniques include the use of alcoholic spirits, hypnotic suggestion, rapid over-breathing, the inhalation of smoke and vapours, music, and dancing; and the ingestion of such drugs as mescaline or lycergic acid and other psychotropic alkaloids. Even without these aids, much the same effect can be produced by such self-inflicted or externally imposed mortifications and privations as fasting and ascetic contemplation (e.g. 'transcendental meditation'). The inspirational effect of sensory deprivation, implied in the stereotyped mystical 'flight' into the wilderness, has also been well documented in recent laboratory experiments (Lewis 1971: 19).

Lewis's inventory reminds us that the term 'trance' is a wide one, covering many qualitatively different kinds of 'altered state' which Western psychology is learning to distinguish: solitary meditation, to take just one example, has its own gradation of states, well documented in Eastern literature, culminating in the ecstasy of *samadhi* or *satori*, supposed union of the meditator with the divine. In the Lungu *ngulu* ritual, initiates were reportedly propelled into a comparably 'ineffable' state by a combination of several of the techniques listed by Lewis: deprivation of visual input, inhalation of smoke and subjection to rhythmic drumming, clapping and chanting. On emerging from trance, the initiates claimed to have no recollection of their altered-state experience: they literally had no words to describe it. The same was true of the *ngulu* doctors, who entered the trance state much more easily, simply lying down in a darkened room, sometimes with and sometimes without rhythmic accompaniment.[47] It seems that, having once 'learned' how to enter the proper state of trance in the violent *-tuntuula* ordeal, practitioners find it relatively easy to repeat the process subsequently without the battery of techniques deployed in their initiation. I'm reminded of the parapsychologist Charles Tart's observation that, once cannabis smokers have learned the initially rather difficult art of getting 'stoned', they require much less of the drug to trigger the desired altered state (Tart 1975: 152–3) . Or, as a more recent commentator summarized the evidence, 'repeated trance experience will alter or "tune" the nervous system in the formation of new, relatively stable neural networks which promote the further experience of trance states' (Castillo 1995: 17).

It may be that I also unconsciously acquired something of their esoteric skill through the series of *ngulu* performances I attended in 1996. Most particularly at Kaizya, I experienced, as well as the sense of being 'lifted' out of ordinary reality I'd felt at Mankonga three days earlier, what I can best describe as the dissolution of the ordinary sense of time and space: the coordinates of ordinary selfhood, the sense that 'I' am a person with a particular inventory of social characteristics, including a 'position' in society, living in a particular time – all these defining and localizing criteria temporarily vanished. I was indeed in Vic Turner's celebrated state of *communitas*, intensely aware of myself in relation to my fellows. Interestingly, I could 'see' myself more clearly than in ordinary reality, when self-perception is typically fragmentary, tied to one or other fleetingly relevant social role. Then, in the moment of *communitas*, I saw myself whole and 'objectively', in that my different skin colour was readily apparent, as was my possession of a peculiar instrument – the camcorder. But these distinguishing attributes in no way detracted from, indeed they seemed to be simply part of, an overall perception that I was 'at home' and among, as it seemed, 'kinsfolk'. I can only assume this surprising information was coming from the holistic right cerebral hemisphere; in that case, the ensuing, apparently absurd conviction that I was in prehistoric Britain could have resulted from the efforts of my logical-linguistic 'left brain', in the absence of the localizing effects of the normal space–time social coordinates, to interpret this information.[48]

Surely also it was temporary liberation from perceived space–time constraints that enabled the extraordinary and highly pleasurable sense of 'flow' I've referred to earlier. Freedom from space–time constraints is also the definitive characteristic of spirit being, as generally understood: spirits can be anywhere, and are unrestricted by the temporal limitations of mortal existence. Though obviously not in the heart of the spirit domain, like the doctors and initiates, or Friedson in his reported experience of the Tumbuka *vimbuza* spirits (1996: 14–20), I was at least somewhere in the suburbs. So, in addition to the fullness of selfhood, the dissolution of social structure emphasized by Vic Turner, the state of *communitas* provides access to those trans-personal entities or forces commonly called 'spirits': the opportunity, indeed, in certain special cases, to enjoy an expansion of selfhood, in temporary fusion with such entities or forces, to limitless dimensions.

Did I then see spirits? No. Although, on further reflection, perhaps I did: a group of them, and prominent in their midst this pale-skinned being with his instrument of magic or sorcery. And I now understand how Sylvia

Nanyangwe could write, in the aftermath of the *ngulu* session at Posa, 'the spirit went outside and danced'.

Several tentative conclusions appear to follow from my material on *ngulu* performances as described in this chapter. One is that group ritual activity accompanied by drumming and other rhythmic actions does have the power, in favourable conditions, to trigger 'altered-state' experiences among participants. The ability to experience such states appears to be a genetically transmitted faculty common to all human beings (see Winkelman 1992: 109), and thus presumably has or had survival value for the species as a whole.[49] In the Lungu *ngulu* performance, some participants enter states of non-ordinary consciousness in which they appear to become aware of forces outside and beyond the worlds of familial and tribal life, forces which in anthropology have been called 'ecological spirits'. As a participant observer from a foreign culture, I was not personally aware of contact with any such entities, but I did experience what I took to be a peripheral form of the altered state apparently accessed by the *ngulu* doctors and initiates. The most salient effect of this personal experience was a dissolution of the ordinary-reality boundaries of selfhood through a transient loss of temporal and spatial coordinates. One consequence was the disappearance of all sense of social structure and hierarchy in relation to my fellows: a pleasurably convivial state of harmony, which Victor Turner has famously called *communitas*. This was also a state in which identification with what might be called 'spirithood', in the sense of liberation from temporal and spatial constraints, was experienced as reality.[50] I am here pointing towards an expanded sense of '*communitas*' from Turner's essentially sociocentric conception of a state of 'anti-structure' (Turner 1969). And when I say 'spirithood' I refer to a ritual experience which, to a Westerner, appears as a strange fusion of the spiritual and the erotic.

I leave to a later chapter the question of why certain members of Lungu society, most of them women, take this particular and perilous path to hidden knowledge. Though capable of causing sickness and distress, the *ngulu* spirits, alien powers beyond familihood and history, are perceived as serving the interests of life and its increase.[51] But in Lungu experience there are also beings – spirits and evilly intentioned people – devoted to destruction and death. It is to this topic that I now turn, before considering the whole range of Lungu healers, *ngulu* doctors among them, and the meaning of their healing work.

Notes

1. In 1956–7, the annual report of St Paul's (Roman Catholic) Mission in Mbala noted that 'a bad pagan practice in many of our villages is"ngulu". By explaining the bad side of it and by Catholic action we overcomed [*sic*] it.' In the 1990s most of the many Christian churches operating in Ulungu outlawed *ngulu*, threatening to expel any of their members implicated in the cult. In 1964, the breakaway Lumpa Church of Alice Lenshina was said, after its bloody suppression by the Zambian Government, to have been heavily involved with *ngulu* practitioners belonging to the neighbouring Bemba people (see van Binsbergen 1981; Hinfelaar 1989).
2. Kapembwa, speaking through Jenera, had told us he approved of our research project.
3. According to BC, this spontaneous crying is the final symptom before the full onset of *ngulu* possession.
4. Justin Chisungu, a sixty-eight-year-old father of ten, acted as *Musano*, or 'manager', of this session. *Musano* literally means 'senior wife' (see above, pp. 93 ff., on this role in *ngulu* ritual).
5. A healing and sorcery-hunting church with a significant following in Ulungu (see Chapters 5 and 6).
6. See below, pp. 82–3.
7. 'Go, sir! Goodbye!'
8. In 1905, a meeting of the Tanganyika District Committee of the London Missionary Society (LMS) decreed that all those who belonged to their church had to 'abstain from all customs contrary to the word of God (i.e. public beer-drinking, native dancing, Chizungu ceremony [female initiation], witchcraft and gambling' (LMS Archives, Box 13, Folder 2, held in the Library of the School of Oriental and African Studies (SOAS), London). The long-standing hostility to *ngulu* of the Roman Catholic missionaries, as well as most of the many indigenous churches, is well documented.
9. This phrase was in English.
10. The Walamo Committee is responsible for planning and executing the first 'swimming' initiatory ordeal for the paramount chief Tafuna. Another *ngulu* session was held in Posa on the same day as the Walamo meeting (see below).
11. Lonia and Mevis (see below, p. 93).
12. Mwanzandolo is the name of a waterfall on the Lunzua river about twenty kilometres inland from Mpulungu. Matipa, said to be the 'father' of Lisita's leading *ngulu* spirit Chama, is said by Lisita to

also 'be there' during *ngulu* ceremonies.

13. On this *ngulu* doctor see below, p. 103 ff.
14. Subsequent enquiries established that Lonia had violated dietary restrictions associated with her *ngulu* spirits.
15. In the end, the patients (and doctors) made do with the single chicken, quite happily it seemed (see below, p. 99).
16. Friedson makes a similar point. Writing of Tumbuka trance dancing and healing sessions, he notes that 'the progression of events surrounding spirit affliction seems to coalesce naturally into dramatic structures' (1996: 194).
17. In *Cisuungu* (female initiation), sacred objects are moved by initiates with their teeth as a sign of respect.
18. See below, p. 112, on '*ngulu* language'.
19. See above, p. 78.
20. In the words of Mr Israel Kasomo in 1990: 'She [Katai] appears in different forms, sometimes as a bitch, sometimes as a pretty girl, sometimes talking like a human being, sometimes people see her shadow.'
21. Apart from the state church, the United Church of Zambia and the Roman Catholics, the following churches were among those active in Ulungu in the 1990s: Seventh Day Adventist, Seventh Day Adventist Reformed, African Methodist Episcopal, New Apostolic, United Pentecostal, Church of Christ, Church of God, Jehovah's Witnesses, Winston Church, Zion Church, Reformed Church of Zambia, Presbyterian, Anglican, Christian Mission in Many Lands, Mulonda, Pentecostal Holiness, Baptist, Zion Simombele, Africa Nation, Sweetheart of Makumbi, Moravian, Mulenga wa Ntambi, Watchtower, Zion Watchtower, Lutheran, Enoch, National.
22. Significantly, perhaps, Mulenga wa Ntambi (God of Tradition), the only church in Ulungu which in 1990 openly advocated and practised a return to pre-European customs and technology, appeared in 1996 to be on the verge of extinction because of a drastic decline in membership.
23. LMS Archives held in the library of SOAS, London (Box 13, Folder 2). See reference on p. 124, n.8, above.
24. Zambia National Archives, Lusaka (KTN 1/1).
25. Emily Nachinsambwe of Isoko (see p. 160 below). See also statement by K.B.S. Chisanga at head of this chapter. Incidentally, Mulenga, creator god of Bemba cosmology, is not an ancestral deity of Ulungu.
26. 'Supernatural' is not a term I personally find attractive in this context, since neither 'natural' nor 'supernatural' translates into ciLungu

conceptual terms. Lienhardt's (1961) usage of 'Powers' in discussing Dinka cosmology seems preferable. Lungu speak of *yamweene* (the 'chiefs' or 'kings') in reference to *ngulu*, a usage which appropriately evokes ideas of hierarchic authority and power.

27. See the 1950 colonial report quoted above.
28. See p. 169.
29. See below, pp. 151 ff.
30. The same appears to be true of the neighbouring Mambwe, whose language is closely akin to ciLungu (Halemba 1994: 551), as well as the more distantly related Bemba language (Hoch 1960: 78).
31. Cf. Lisita Nakazwe's dismissal of the spirits from her entranced daughter Lonia, p. 100.
32. A perusal of van Avermaet and Mbuya's *Dictionnaire kiluba-français* brought scant confirmation of the 'Luba' connection, although *-palakanya* is glossed as 'espacer, disperser' among other and cognate meanings. I have not yet found a Bisa dictionary or word list.
33. See discussion in Chapter 3, pp. 56 ff. One puzzle is the absence from the *ngulu* pantheon of spirits representing the Ngoni, who intruded violently into Lungu territory in the later nineteenth century (see Livingstone 1874, I: 205, 207, where the intruders are called 'Mazitu'; Thomson 1881, I: 317), or the Europeans, who began to appear in the 1870s. In contrast, both these kinds of ethnic stranger figure as Tumbuka *vimbuza* spirits (Friedson 1996: 177–8).
34. Implying that she has the ability to diagnose afflictions and prescribe medicines for patients, with the help of these 'prophet' spirits.
35. Interviewed at Isonkele Village (Zombe's area), 25.11.96.
36. *Ngulu* practitioners are also typically subject to dietary restrictions, supposedly emanating from the spirits and usually imposed on patients by their doctors at the time of initiation. The imposed restrictions are usually those already observed by the doctor. Wild pig, hare, zebra, barbel fish and cassava leaves are among the most frequently prohibited foods.
37. I am uncertain how far the *ngulu* cult I observed in 1996 is operative in other parts of Ulungu. In the fertile but isolated Yendwe valley region of western Ulungu, I was assured in 1990 that *ngulu* ceremonies were not practised, although Werner (1979) says they were 'common' there in the early 1970s. I was told the same in Tanzanian Ulungu and in the plateau chiefdoms of Chinakila and Chungu. It seemed in 1996 that a few female *ngulu* doctors who also worked as general healers, such as Nalupya, were practising in the plateau regions administered by Tafuna and Zombe. Kapembwa Sikazwe also informed me

in 1996 that 'dancing *ngulu*' were not to be found outside the Lunzua valley region – i.e. the fertile hinterland of Mpulungu.

38. Devisch, writing of the Yaka of western Congo, observes that 'for each major cult, there is a type of drumming which summons the spirit to release, to lift one up in the air' (1993: 262).
39. The term was taken up and theorized by Tart (1969).
40. D'Aquili *et al.* (1979), quoted in V.W. Turner (1985c: 262). The drumming capable of achieving this result is said to be in the theta wave frequency range of four to seven cycles per second (Harner 1980: 66). It was Rodney Needham who first drew the attention of anthropologists to the curious connection between, as he put it, 'percussion and transition' (Needham 1967). Neher's methodology is criticized in Rouget (1980).
41. Lex adduces evidence that the state of what she calls 'ritual trance' involves the entire human central nervous system and not merely the brain (Lex 1979). D'Aquili and Laughlin suppose an identification in ordinary consciousness between the subordinate (usually right) hemisphere and the homoeostatic aspects of the nervous system, and between the dominant (usually left) hemisphere and the energy-expending aspects (1979: 175). Neher (1962) had noted that rhythmic auditory stimulation, notably drumming, imposes a synchronous pattern of neuronal firing in the brain which is distinct from the asychronous pattern of normal waking consciousness.
42. More recent work by Goodman and Mueller has noted further unusual physiological phenomena accompanying trance states, including a simultaneous increase in the heart rate and a drop in blood pressure, a combination otherwise recorded only in life-threatening or 'near-death' situations (Goodman 1988: 39).
43. '*Interaction morale*' might seem more accurate. Friedson surprisingly dismisses Rouget's thesis, strangely reading it as purely 'culturalist' and little more than a restatement of an old argument by Rousseau (Friedson 1996:190).
44. Edith Turner in fact presents a much more nuanced evaluation of her late husband's work in *Experiencing Ritual*, seeing his thought. as 'swaying between rationalization and deep understanding' (1992: 29).
45. The 'causal operator' which is said to 'grind out the initial terminus or first cause of any strip of reality [!]' is supposed by d'Aquili and Laughlin to be 'the reciprocal interconnections of the inferior parietal lobule and the anterior convexity of the frontal lobes, particularly on the dominant, usually left side' (quoted in Turner 1985c: 260).

46. On one occasion, while alone in the bush in Tanzania, a sudden close encounter with a beautiful and dangerous snake was sufficient to precipitate me into a state of altered and heightened consciousness, in which I was aware of dialogue between what I assume to have been right and left cerebral hemispheres (Willis 1990: 250–1).
47. Jenera Nalondwa entered apparent trance without drumming at Kafukula on 13 September 1996. So did Lisita Nakazwe and Robert Simpungwe at Mankonga on 1 November.
48. According to the cognitive neuroscientist Michael Gazzaniga, the left cerebral hemisphere contains what he calls an 'interpreter', which constantly operates to construct 'meaning' out of perceived events (1998: 174–5).
49. Lex (1979) suggests, plausibly, that shared trance experience serves to integrate individuals in groups and is thus a 'homoeostatic mechanism'.
50. This is also the Diltheyan concept of *Erlebnis*, or 'lived experience', a structured state transcending ordinary time and space (see Friedson 1996). I assume that it was in some such state that Edith Turner was able to perceive, at the climax of an elaborate Ndembu healing ritual, what she has described as a 'spirit form' (Turner 1992).
51. See Appendix on pp. 200–201 for a summary of follow-up reports on the subsequent conditions of the *ngulu* patients – and doctors – who figure in this chapter.

–5–

Sorcery Attack

You can't see *majini* [evil spirits] but they can see you.

K.B.S. Chisanga (BC), 12.8.96

In the daytime BC drives with skill and reasonable care, but at night, *muloozi* [sorcerer] at the wheel, he drives fast and dangerously on the *wrong* side of the road.

Diary, 4.10.96

A lot of people are mentally disturbed without knowing why. Often they don't have the money to go to a diviner.

BC, 28.8.96

Mbala, Zambia Compound, 1.12.96 Under my hands, gently resting on this young woman's shoulders as she, kneeling, faces away from me, I sense the beginning of a rhythmic movement; then it becomes a definite vibration, increasing in speed and intensity until finally she catapults across the room, rolling around on the floor and gabbling scrambled word-stuff. Spectacular as her behaviour is, I'm not too surprised because Doctor Tembo had described in just such terms how members of his church received the Holy Spirit when we interviewed him in his office at the Education Department a few days earlier.

A second young woman also becomes dissociated but the rest, including half a dozen children, remain calm; altogether I treat about twenty people at this Sunday service in a suburb of Mbala, after being invited to do so by the 'Principal', as he is called. The church is popularly known as *Mutumwa*, a Swahili word meaning 'servant' or 'slave' (i.e. of God), but its official title, emblazoned on the end wall facing us as we entered, is Kasesema Prophet Church.[1] Inside, women sit on the right, men on the left. The women wear white head-dresses and a few also have white tunics; some, evidently of superior rank, carry carved wooden staves. Sylvia says they make these themselves, from trees shown to them 'by spirit'. The men wear ordinary clothing. All of us had to remove our shoes on entering the church.

The service was led by the Principal, Mr E.J. Sefu Siame, assisted by a woman member, who read from the biblical books of John and Corinthians. Mr Siame preached a sermon, warning of the dangers of sorcery, then two women, neither of them a member of the church, came to the front to be 'searched' (for evil entities). The first was a young widow, who said her dead husband was visiting her at night and following her during the day. She was 'healed' with exhortatory prayers and the application of the Bible to her head. The second patient was an old woman, who said she had formerly worked as a *nacimbuuza*, a traditional midwife and expert on sexuality and reproduction. She admitted she had become a sorcerer, using the foetuses of women who miscarried as harmful 'medicine' (*ciziimba*). In this way she had killed a number of people. She had also turned into a dog and this animal had since entered her belly, causing her to suffer from *upunku* (anal ulceration). This woman was also 'treated'. Afterwards, the Principal introduced me, I briefly explained the nature of my gift and made my contribution and the service ended.[2]

On the way home, BC pointed out, only a few hundred metres from the church, the burned-out wreck of a lorry owned by a man from Kasakalawe, who had been stoned to death some months earlier by a mob who accused him of being a *muloozi*, or sorcerer. In such cases, BC said, the police rarely took any action.[3] A few days earlier, Doctor Tembo had shown us a collection of *viwaanga*, or sorcery objects, discovered by members of his church. The haul had followed a visit to the village of Chipando, about twenty kilometres north of Mbala, at the invitation of the village headman. Guided, they said, by the Holy Spirit, church members had found evil instruments of sorcery concealed in the roofs of houses, in gardens and in the banks of the river. Of the dozens of *viwaanga* (a word meaning object of knowledge or craft, *uwaanga*), most were said by Doctor Tembo to be intended to cause sickness and death. Several were used for transport, including a large cow's horn decorated with coloured beads. Doctor Tembo explained that this object could carry up to five sorcerers for long distances such as to the Copperbelt or Lusaka. It was fuelled by the blood of their victims and the leading sorcerer steered it with his penis. A sheep's horn was said to be used for attracting food stores from people's houses or crops from their land. Another cow's horn draped with red cloth had the power, Doctor Tembo said, of going out and attacking people and then returning to report the results to its owner: if it had killed its victim or left him or her seriously ill. A snail shell filled with 'medicines' was used to punish the sorcerer's enemies by making them sick; later the sickness could be increased or reduced at the will of the sorcerer. 'There was a doll's head decorated with hair from a corpse and with its face painted with black and red marks. This is called *jini.* It is a dead person and acts very fast. It doesn't take long to kill' (from SN's diary, 27.9.96).[4]

A small bottle was said to contain part of a human body and to be used by a sorcerer to protect himself (in Ulungu, sorcerers are usually, though not invariably, male) from counter-attacks by those he has wronged. This 'medicine' is called *impimpi* and is installed over the doorway of its owner's house. Another object contained roots uncovered while digging a grave. This 'medicine' caused coughing, malaria and diarrhoea. Another, said by the doctor to contain human excrement mixed with 'medicines', caused children to pass black or green stools.

I asked the doctor, whose authoritative appearance owed something to heavy spectacles secured with a stout 'senility chain', if he wasn't afraid to handle these noxious items. He replied that he was protected by spirit and besides he used a plant called *imboozyo* to 'neutralize' them. Even so, when he picked them up, he sometimes felt what he described as 'a shock like electricity'.

Back home in Mankonga, BC suggested that we contact his relative, the headman of the well-known village of M......, and persuade him to invite Mutumwa to carry out a *viwaanga*-finding operation there, at a particular time when the Ulungu Research Project (URP) team could be on hand to film the event. 'Brilliant', I told him, 'we'll do it!'

Nocturnal Visitation

After the Mutumwa service, we called at Londe Village in connection with an inheritance meeting planned for the end of September.[5] 'Just outside St Paul's, on the way to Londe, we were subjected to abuse from a young fellow who, it being Sunday, was probably drunk. BC immediately stopped the car, got out and slapped the oaf to the ground. He then returned to the car and drove on, without a word. What a man!' (Diary 1.9.96).

Returning, about halfway between Londe and St Paul's Village, BC again stops the car, this time to show me a site of ethnographic interest. It's a large anthill a few yards from the road. Mr Chisanga tells me that some years ago he'd witnessed a traditional healer, who was also his 'mother''s 'brother' (*yama*), treating a man called Mr Chilofya, who'd been attacked by *majini.* Typically, someone attacked by these fearsome entities was unable to speak.[6] The only hope was to force the invasive entities to reveal who had sent them. This was done, BC said, by getting the afflicted person to sit with a blanket over him (or her) and then burning powerful medicine under it. This was done with Mr Chilofya and the *jini* (there was only one in this case) eventually spoke through him, saying it had been sent by a certain man to kill him. 'Mr Chilofya was then sitting by this anthill. I saw my *yama* place seeds of all kinds in this hole here as food for the *jini*, which he then persuaded to go into the hole. It will stay there for 20,000 years'.[7]

The evening of that day was initially peaceful. A pretty young woman from Congo, the wife of our friend Célestin at the fisheries plant in Mpulungu, dropped by and we exchanged pleasantries in French. Later, alone in bed, as I drifted into that liminal state between sleep and waking where there is still consciousness of a 'self' but only a fuzzy awareness of environment, something extremely *un*pleasant happened. I became aware of a vaguely defined 'object' moving towards me, seeming to emerge from somewhere undergound, and landing right beside me in bed, slap against my left flank (I was, I think, lying on my back). Still in that in-between state, I clearly 'saw', although with what 'eyes' I don't know, that the 'object' was cylindrical, about thirty centimetres long and dirty-white in colour. It was unmistakably hostile, and for a long moment I felt paralysed, unable to move. Then I jerked violently awake, and the 'object' vanished.

The next day I told BC and Sylvia of this mysterious and unwelcome nocturnal event, and they seemed appropriately concerned. Remembering a technique practised by Bruce Macmanaway,[8] my teacher in healing, I took out a pendant given me on departure from Britain by my grandson Ryan. As it swung from its chain, I posed several questions.[9] Had the evil object been sent by a sorcerer? – Yes. Was the sorcerer one of the congregation at the Mutumwa church that day? – Yes. Were there more than one of them? – Yes. Was I right in thinking the missile had 'boomeranged' back on the sender? – Yes.[10]

I discussed the results of this little divination session with BC. He was not surprised. Sorcerers, he told me, regularly 'hid' in the churches. They – he also thought there would have been more than one – were undoubtedly inspired by jealous resentment of my attempts to heal people. I asked BC why sorcerers worked in groups. He told me there were two reasons. One was that when they killed they ate: one person made a meal for four or five. The other was that sometimes (as in my case, apparently) the proposed victim was too powerfully protected to be overcome by a lone sorcerer: hence their need to combine. I was not much comforted by these words. 'Thursday, 12 September. Another scary nocturnal experience. This time I was, as before, in bed and half-asleep when I became aware of what seemed like a largish animal resembling an over-sized domestic cat moving about the room. Awoke in terror, to find nothing there' (diary excerpt).

The following night, BC, evidently worried about my predicament, brought me some incense against *majini* spirits he'd obtained from Doctor Muziya (a traditional healer whom we'd interviewed and filmed a few days before). Burning, it produced a pungent, acrid aroma but seemed to do the trick – I slept peacefully until the morning.

> Another *uloozi* [sorcery] attack last night, in the shape of an unseen 'animal' rooting around the bed. Could have been the same evil entity that disturbed me a few nights ago: had the impression of a thickset creature about the size of a beaver or badger and I could hear it snuffling with predatory excitement. Awoke shouting 'Damn you!', and again it disappeared. Went back to sleep and dreamed of being buffeted around by invisible hostile forces, like winds, while managing to remain standing. Is this some kind of initiatory ordeal? (Diary 18.9.96)

As far as I was aware, the first '*majini*' attack in Mankonga during our stay there occurred on 30 August 1996, when a man of about forty years, a distant classificatory cousin of SN, was brought home from his job in Mpulungu in a state of speechless collapse. He had been taken to Dr Muziya's clinic in Mpulungu but nothing seemed to be wrong with him, apart from his apparent inability to speak. According to SN he died the following day, still without having uttered a word. Everyone felt certain the man had been killed by *majini* sent – of course – by a sorcerer.

Friday, 20 September Another busy day for the URP, setting up interviews with traditional healers on the plateau south of Mbala, and then heading north to Chief Zombe's headquarters near the Zambia–Tanzania border, where we collect a list of likely interviewees, including a prophetess. In Mbala, on the way home, BC, who as usual is driving, suddenly complains of a headache, so we stop off at the Ten Kwacha Store, where he gulps down a couple of paracetamol with water. After we've returned to the car and BC has resumed his place behind the wheel, I ask him if he's OK and he assures me he is, so I 'allow' him to continue driving. Inconceivable that this iron man could crack up; none the less, I am aware of a growing sense of unease as we race down the achingly beautiful escarpment in the gathering dusk. Back at our village base, BC, uncharacteristically taciturn, retires to his room. Some while later, Sylvia, perhaps having heard something from our domestic staff, comes in and calls to BC, asking if he's asleep. He denies it, in what seemed to me a pretty feeble voice.

18.45. Chisanga definitely seems ill. Looking through the half-open door of his room, I see him lying face down on the mat beside his bed.

His 'sister' and another young woman, presumably 'tipped off' by SN, are now visiting him, so I presume he is at least sitting up. I have just been reading a worrying report in *The Times of Zambia* about fuel shortages in Lusaka. No explanations offered. Here kerosene is said to be unobtainable at petrol stations and the only source, according to BC and SN this evening, is 'black marketeers' on Ngwenya Beach (Mpulungu).

Has BC been driving himself too hard? Even this evening, in bad shape as – I now see – he was, BC insisted on parking and locking up the car, and then getting the Tilley lamp going, as usual.

1915. Chisanga's female relatives have departed – cheerfully, suggesting it's not a matter of life and death. On the fuel business, one gets used to hearing gloomy prognostications in Africa. Usually things somehow go on: the things that do go wrong, and they are many, typically come as total surprises, unforeseen by the 'experts'.

> Midday in Mbala met 'Andy' the Norwegian anthropologist, just back from research in Kaka (Johan Pottier's stamping ground). Told us he'd had a good time and witnessed an anti-sorcery operation. Two 'witches' had been tried in the local court and found guilty. One, convicted of killing four children, was fined K4000 (£2) by the Chief. (Diary 20.9.96)

20.00. Ventured into BC's room and called gently. No reply, but distinctly heard breathing. He is now lying flat on his back on the same mat.

21.00. Went to bed, and received only a faint response from BC to my bogusly cheery 'Goodnight'.

> On BC: a case for divination? Have suggested taking him to Dr Muziya's clinic but the response was hesitant. Communication is difficult. Last weekend it was the condition of the car that generated so much *angst*: this weekend it looks like being BC himself. His 'mother' and 'sister' are back with him outside, together with his newly arrived 'son'. BC himself is relaxing in the early morning sun in one of our newly acquired deckchairs.

> 08.15. A family conference is going on under a nearby mango tree. Earlier I was surprised to see/hear the 'son' holding forth with remarkable self-confidence in the presence of his 'father'.[11] Now the 'patient' himself is talking, at length, notwithstanding his earlier protestations of infirmity. Sitting in my 'office', I can hear his voice, loud and clear, from fifty metres away. So perhaps his condition is more 'psycho' than 'somatic', though earlier he had indicated his lower back ('*musana*') as a site of pain.
>
> The domestics have just gone off for their weekly prayers [to the local Seventh Day Adventist Church].

08.35. BC now fully in stride, powerful and gesticulating – no longer the pathetic, weak-voiced invalid of an hour ago. SN has just shown up and there seems no reason why he should not be in shape for the scheduled Staff Meeting at 0900.[12] (Diary 21.9.96)

Medical Opinion

Saturday 21 September, afternoon We go into Mpulungu and meet a *sing'aanga* (traditional healer), a nattily dressed gent of middle years, who'd been invited home yesterday by BC. We have a chat session in the rest-house with him, over Cokes. I thought him a rogue, but obviously intelligent. Later, I learn from BC that the good doctor had formed a similar opinion of me.

Then to Dr Muziya's clinic, where BC was found to have abnormally high blood pressure. A three-day course of twice-daily injections is prescribed and I decide, in full managerial/executive mode, to order BC to desist from his arduous round of duties (some of them, like his obsessive tinkering with the car, self-imposed) for a period of three days, to give him a chance to recover. The doctor also suspects him of having malaria.

Sunday, 22 September Waiting, with a tinge of anxiety, for our invalid to emerge from his room. Is he still in the land of the living, or am I to have the melancholy distinction of being the first anthropologist to work his research assistant to death?

Monday, 23 September Head off to the village of M..... with Uncle Kapembwa (KS) and SN to implement BC's splendid plan of organizing a Mutumwa sorcery hunt in collaboration with his relative the headman. Of course, BC remains at home to convalesce. Before setting off, BC magisterially briefs Uncle as follows. Explain to him (the headman) that nowadays we no longer have *Kamcape*,[13] but *Mutumwa* have taken over their task of rooting out *uloozi* [sorcery] and finding *viwaanga*. We travel uncomfortably in the Moto Moto twin-cab Toyota. Once there, we have to walk what seemed to me a great distance, but was probably less than a kilometre. The heat is crushing. Finally, we run our man to earth, only to find him totally incoherent with drink.

Back home, the three of us have a brief consultation with BC on what to do next. We decide to write off M..... village: we can't do business with a pisshead. There are plenty of other villages and headmen. Uncle mentions one called Jacob's Village, not far from our base, and we decide to concentrate our efforts on it.

Wednesday, 25 September 10.20 Waiting for Uncle to return from his assigned interview with Mr Sichone, the *ngulu* drummer. Now apparently fit again, BC has been working industriously on the car. Sylvia is quietly writing up her diary, her daily task.

Yesterday a young woman dropped by who turned out to be Helen, daughter of our late friend Herbie (H.M.K. Sikazwe), accompanied by a young fellow introduced as her husband, and a baby. I remembered Helen as a plump ten-year-old in 1990, and Herbie's vivid account of how, only weeks before our arrival in Ulungu, she'd been attacked by *majini* spirits while walking home from school, and also how it had been only Herbie's prompt and skilful medical intervention which had saved his young daughter's life. Now she looks fine.

A Disc in the Night

One night in mid-October, another disturbing paranormal event occurred. I'd awoken at about three in the morning and gone out for a pee. Heading back, still half-asleep, I happened to glance left in the general direction of Sylvia's house, about a hundred metres distant, and in my somnolent state it took a moment or two before I realized I was looking at something that shouldn't have been there – a whitish disc or sphere at least a metre in diameter, seemingly suspended the same distance above the ground and several metres to the left of the entrance to SN's (and her mother's) house. Suddenly scared, I felt myself a moment later being spun round as if by some external force until I was again facing our front door. Then I was through that door and locking it from the inside, as the saying is, pretty damned quick. Not wishing to alarm Sylvia or her mother I kept this little experience to myself.

> On the way back from talks with members of the Walamo Committee [set up to reactivate the ancient 'swimming ritual', in which the Tafuna submits himself to the authority of the lake god Kapembwa], we were stopped by a woman who told BC an extraordinary story. One of BC's 'nephews' had been bewitched four years ago and, as a consequence, been unable to remove his *shoes* ever since. Then yesterday he was finally 'unbewitched' and succeeded at last in liberating his feet. BC roared with laughter – not, it seemed, because he disbelieved the story, but because of its intrinsic comicality. (Diary 25.9.96)

> On the way back from Moto Moto Museum Uncle [Kapembwa] remarked on the virtues of SN. He (KS) had worked a lot with women and they tended, he said, to be always complaining. SN was not like that: she didn't complain, even behind my back! (Diary 25.10.96)

Isoko, 25 October During our meeting with the Tafuna and the Council of Elders today, a plate of small stones was gravely circulated. Apparently the stones had been found in the faeces of a small boy at Kasakalawe on the lake shore and the consensus was that a sorcerer had introduced these objects into the child's stomach. My suggestion that the boy might have voluntarily eaten the stones was met with utter incredulity.

> URP staff meeting. SN reported that people here in Kafukula wanted a *Mucape* [witchfinder] because of the deaths of a succession of teachers at the primary school.
>
> KS said he had a *Mucape* contact. The Tafuna would never agree because of fear of breaking the law [under Zambian law accusing someone of being a 'witch' is a punishable offence], but said 'Do it without my knowledge.'
>
> KS also reported that a certain Mr Sikazwe in Jacob's Village had a team of Mutumwa people ready to hunt for sorcery objects. (Diary 28.9.96)

Sunday, 6 October We return to the Mutumwa Church in Mbala. Gratified to learn from the Principal, Mr Siame, that with one exception, which he didn't take seriously, all the people I treated five weeks ago have benefited.

Majini Attack

Mankonga, 21 October, 08.20 BC has just been found slumped in his seat at the breakfast table in a comatose condition. Uncle, Sylvia and Friday (Friday Maliawanda, our cook) together carried him to his bed.

08.35 People, mainly relatives of BC, including his 'mother' (maternal aunt), 'sister' and 'son', appear with astonishing speed after BC's collapse. Within half an hour, the house is full of people. What to do? A consensus soon emerges that BC has been attacked by *majini* spirits and that a qualified traditional healer should be brought in to treat him. Only our neighbour Mr Aggrey Sinyangwe suggests, what had been my own first thought, that BC should be taken to Dr Muziya's clinic in Mpulungu.

Swift action is obviously called for. On consideration, I decide to go with the majority and fetch a local healer. Here, after all, is a wonderful ethnographic opportunity – to observe and, if possible, film a Lungu doctor in action. Mr Chisanga himself would appreciate that point. So I take off with SN in the car and in Posa Village we locate a certain Doctor Elias Simwanza, who is said to have the expertise needed to deal with this case.

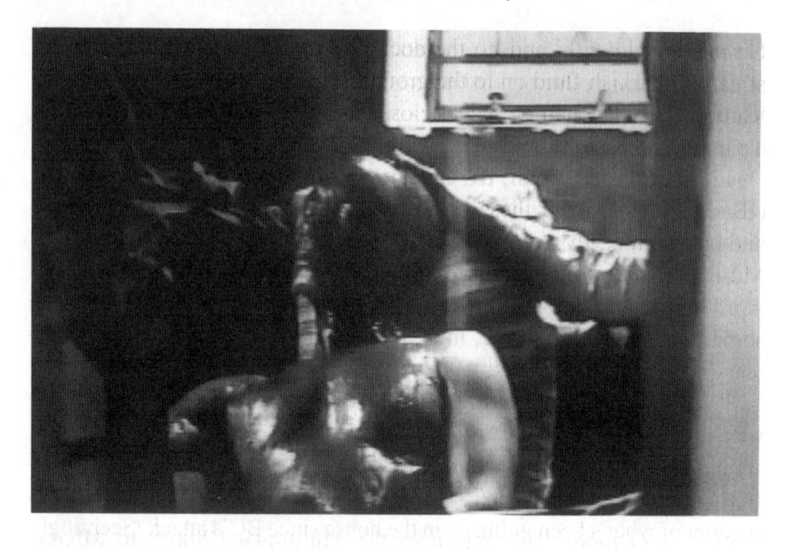

Figure 8. K.B.S. Chisanga under supposed attack from *majini* spirits. (Photo: Roy Willis.)

09.20 Back home with the doctor to find at least thirty people milling around the house and BC still flat out on his bed, seemingly unconscious. The treatment prescribed includes application of moistened river grasses to the patient's nostrils, *inkaalo* (incisions, into which 'medicine' is rubbed) on top of his head, on the upper chest, back and feet, and fumigation, using leaves burned on a nearby brazier. The doctor rubs leaves over BC's body, particularly his feet and lower legs. He is also given oral medicine and splashed with medicated water over his face and trunk (his shirt having been removed earlier). The doctor continually asks him, '*Muli ci? Watumanya*?' ('What's up? Don't you know us?'). No response from BC. His 'mother' bursts into tears. The doctor persists, gently pressing BC's upper chest and asking, 'Is it hurting?' At the fourth such enquiry, the doctor's hand just above his heart, I notice BC give a barely perceptible nod: something is getting through.

In the middle of all this tumult, 'Uncle' goes into trance and his 'healing spirits' make suggestions on what 'medicines' to use. The atmosphere is charged with a degree of intensity that's almost unbearable. I will my hands to stop shaking as I film the action (Willis 1997). This doctor is fighting passionately for BC's life, his struggle with the forces of evil plain to see, right in front of our eyes. After four anguished hours, the doctor at last manages to persuade the patient to get to his feet and he is led outside, into the garden, and given an emetic of salted water to drink.

He retches violently and, to the doctor's evident satisfaction, expels a stream of darkish fluid on to the ground. The bad stuff is out of him, he leans back in the chair with eyes closed and still unspeaking, but there is a palpable sense of relief: we are winning.

12.30 Still in his chair, BC calls me over and whispers, '*Vilooto vipi*' ('Bad dreams'). After these cryptic words, he adds, '*Mupite*!' ('Go!') and I am summarily dismissed. Mr Mulengo, who has just turned up with Museum transport in accordance with our scheduled 'programme' (a vogue word in Zambia) but will not now be needed, kneels beside BC and says something, inaudible to me, in his ear. I am surprised to see two large tears run down BC's cheeks.

17.20 Mr Chisanga is still reclining under the mango tree, thankfully speaking at last, albeit in a feeble voice. I have just returned from a shopping expedition into Mpulungu with SN, during which I managed to find a bottle of brandy. I need a stiff drink, especially after hearing Sylvia's account of what's been going on in the house since BC's attack. Seemingly there are two schools of thought about the cause of BC's affliction. One is that our cook Friday had tried to poison him.[14] The other is that Uncle sent the *majini*, coveting BC's senior post.

Figure 9. Kapembwa Sikazwe entering trance during the *majini* attack on K.B.S. Chisanga. (Photo: Roy Wills.)

18.20 Uncle is going to spend the night with BC, to protect him against the agents of evil (what will the anti-Uncle faction make of *that*?) He (KS) has just gone home to get *umuula* (white clay). A succession of visitors for BC, mostly unknown to me.

When I asked BC how he was this evening he complained of pains in his lower back, throat and intestines *(amaala*). He indicated he'd been given a purgative.

18.45 BC's 'son' has just turned up with a male companion. Four men are now sitting on the floor by his bed. Sylvia is going in and out with cups of water (or other liquid). Am enjoying my brandy, mixed with Coke.

KS brought *umuula* and I applied some to the centre of my forehead, for protection. KS says he will be covering BC, burning herbs and fumigating him – the classic treatment for *majini.* (Diary 21.10.96)

Tuesday, 22 October I awoke from a restless night to the sound of voices. Found BC in his deckchair on the porch and obviously, to my intense relief, much better. *Sing'aanga* Simwanza returned early and went off, accompanied by KS, hoe in hand in search of *milembo* (medicines). They returned after some while and I got a good shot of them approaching the house.

Can now hear BC's voice loud and clear as I write these notes. Have decided to defer going to Moto Moto to get the car's collapsed window fixed and observe the next and, hopefully, final stages of BC's healing here today.

09.15 It's only a quarter past nine and already we've had a major *-tuntuula* session with Doctor Simwanza and Uncle, who in trance produced Chilandu Musi, Kapembwa and Samaliya (who spoke in Swahili). All dispensed advice on healing. Beforehand the doctor sprinkled white powder on KS's head.

A large puff adder (*icipili*) has just been killed in the front garden. (Diary 22.10.96)

'You've Always Wanted to Die – Let's Go!'

Tuesday, 22 October, evening Mr Chisanga is better – thank God. I told him at teatime of our (mine and Mary's) decision to bring him to UK next year in recognition of his tremendous work and he seemed chuffed, in his dignified way.

I asked BC if he remembered anything of yesterday's events. He told me he'd had a bad dream in which someone he couldn't see was forcing him to eat shit. After that, he recalled sitting at the breakfast table and hearing a voice in his right ear – like a telephone, he said – saying, in ciLungu, 'My friend, I know you've always wanted to die – let's go!' Mr

Chisanga said: 'I tried to reply, but my throat seemed to be blocked, as if by cold sweet potatoes.' He remembered nothing after that until he found himself in the garden, being given salted water to drink.

19.45 Sylvia has just dropped round to see our invalid and I hear her giving him a comprehensive report on what happened yesterday, in the usual 'total coverage' style. They are both in his room, and BC is also talking a lot but in a low voice, very hoarse, but I can't make anything out beyond the occasional English phrase, especially 'That's why . . .'.

> SN has been in BC's bedroom (door open) for at least half an hour, conversing earnestly with him in low tones, interspersed with the occasional giggle. It would be almost impossible in Western culture for two unattached and unrelated people of opposite sex to sustain a communication of such intimacy without 'sex' entering into it. Here it's different.
>
> Uncle is spending a second night watching over BC. He told me that the previous night BC had refused fumigation treatment. (Diary 22.10.96)

Wednesday, 23 October Mr Chisanga is much better, apart from a sore throat. He also complains of pain from the incisions made on his body on Monday. He told me this morning of the many rumours going about on the source of his *majini* attack (he seems to accept that that's what it was). Uncle had suspected his (BC's) 'grandfather', the old man who'd been bringing us firewood but been 'laid off' because BC reckoned he was overcharging us. Mr Chisanga admitted his own family 'wanted to attack' our cook, whom they accused of poisoning him. Others suspected Uncle Kapembwa. Mr Chisanga commented that KS was widely regarded as a sorcerer in Isoko, his home village. He (BC) thought, however, that the attack had come from 'outside'. He had told his family not to go for divination, *ku-saapola*. 'Spoke with SN and she told me her conversation with BC last evening had been largely about the sorcery accusations associated with his recent attack and what SN called BC's "business" relations with KS – pretty much what BC told me this morning' (Diary 23.10.96).

Thursday, 24 October More discussions last night between BC and his family, gathered round him on the verandah. His line was magnanimous and politically astute. They shouldn't look among people here for someone to blame: the attack came from outside and was intended precisely to cause conflict and dissension among the URP team. He quoted the Lungu saying, *Kavine aasime*, 'Loud mouth causes bewitchment.' He concluded, sententiously, 'You should all love one another [!].'

I took BC, at his request, to Dr Muziya's clinic, where his blood pressure was checked and found to be abnormally high (140/100). A five-day course of what sounded like 'Procain' injections has begun.

> On the way back from dropping off Chipo and Webster [two members of Moto Moto staff] at the Museum, feeling that *kizungu* rage at BC's staccato driving, stopping every few hundred metres to greet a relative and/or business acquaintance, I was momentarily lifted out of it when we were delayed behind an open lorry (initially more *kizungu* irritation), on finding it full of Mbala Mutumwa people, all singing, then smiling and waving at us (perhaps some were those I had healed). Just felt glad. (Diary 25.10.96)

Sunday, 6 October Uncle back from his expedition to Jacob's Village, full of information and confidence. He met a certain Doctor Gibson Museka, born 1940, eighteen children from two wives, works as a carpenter and bricklayer. The doctor's story:

> In my youth I never went to church – the spirits wouldn't allow it. Then the spirits showed me St Moses Holy Spirit Church, and I joined it.
>
> This church goes back to the time of Moses, when the Holy Spirit came to the Prophets. It was looked upon as a 'primitive' church in colonial days, until the Rev. Moses Siwale returned from South Africa in 1938 and then it spread all over Zambia (then called Northern Rhodesia).
>
> The Bible is our source of inspiration. When in spirit we can spot anything dirty like *uwaanga* [sorcery]. We heal and cleanse people who are poisoned by *aloozi* [sorcerers].

Uncle said he saw people 'in spirits' when he arrived at their church in Jacob's Village. Some girls went into the bush and brought back vegetable medicines while in that state. His report concluded:

> I had to walk for seven miles when the car broke on the way there. This morning, after I had stayed there the night, I had to walk for sixteen kilometres until I got transport at Mwanzandola. The ration money the Director [RW] gave me helped me so much. I bought some scones, two bottles of Fanta, some fish and some sugar for breakfast.
>
> We [the URP team] are invited to visit them [St Moses Church, Jacob's Village] any time on the morning of Sunday, October 27th. There is a nearby village where they will go and search for sorcery objects.

Thursday, 17 October The morning began with an interesting discussion on the scheduled meeting in Kafukula today between Senior Chief Tafuna and residents on the matter of the series of suspicious deaths of members of the teaching staff at the local primary school. Sylvia said the recently appointed new head teacher, who lived at Posa, was refusing to take up his post because of the felt danger of sorcery. Many local people wanted the school closed down. Uncle, who has been instructed to act as our representative at the meeting, said there had been seven sorcery-linked deaths of teachers at the school since 1985, the most recent occurring last month (September).

Uncle said he was going to suggest that they bring in *Mutumwa* sorcery hunters from Jacob's Village.

BC: What about the schoolchildren? Don't they die too? And the villagers?

KS: The (DS) District Secretary will be at the meeting, directing the people on the law relating to witchcraft (sorcery) and witchcraft accusations.

BC: The famous *Kamcape* is dead: it's no longer with us. I also advise them to invite *Mutumwa*, who don't point at people, which is against the law. Schoolteachers should also be searched.

KS: Everybody.

SN: In the 1980s houses were burned down and people beaten in Kafukula.

KS: *Kamcape* was banned in 1991. I was behind that. My nephews in Isoko were sleeping out in the bush because their houses had been burned down.

Later, that evening, KS returns from the meeting to report that, to the disappointment and anger of residents, neither the Tafuna nor the DS had appeared. Uncle said he had suggested bringing *Mutumwa* but the people were 'not interested': they wanted a *Mucape* (a witch-finder who would purport to identify sorcerers). They had appointed a delegation of ten people to complain to the Tafuna and tell him they wanted him to see the DS about their problem as soon as possible.

Sunday, 27 October The day of our projected visit to Jacob's Village to film the *Mutumwa* sorcery-hunters in action. But at the last minute URP's bold initiative is brought to nothing: late last evening BC received a letter from Jacob's Village telling us not to come. The letter is written by the secretary of the *Mutumwa* (St Moses Holy Spirit) church, in ciBemba, advising us 'not to bother' visiting Jacob's Village because their leader had gone to Mporokoso (western Ulungu, Mukupa Kaoma chiefdom) for a church meeting. Clearly this is a diplomatic subterfuge, veiling a decision by someone higher up the organizational ladder in this mysterious 'church' than Uncle's contact in Jacob's Village, Doctor Museka. Suspicion falls on the 'bishop' we met by chance in the road in Mpulungu a few days ago, who made little attempt to hide his hostility towards us.[15]

Monday, 4 November Sylvia has just dropped in and unburdened herself to me on the subject of KS. Seemingly, she and her mother think my appointment of Uncle as a staff member was a grave mistake. In the village, they want to 'chase' him on suspicion of being a sorcerer. Sylvia herself never drinks water in our house, because of Uncle's frequent visits. After we leave, her mother intends to have the house 'medicated'. It seems also that, following our recent team visit to Doctor Musukuma's, where BC's daughter Charity is being treated for rheumatism, Charity suffered a serious relapse. The doctor divined to discover the cause, and the culprit was said to be Uncle. Sylvia also alleged that, although BC denied that KS was a sorcerer to me, he 'admitted' it to others.

07.00 Without mentioning SN, I questioned BC tonight on the rumours about Uncle. He told me that people were suspicious of KS because of 'the way he talked' (so much about spirits, *majini*, sorcery, etc.). As to the accusation about Charity. 'Uncle may have bewitched a few people in the past, but he wouldn't do that to *my* daughter.'

17.55 Sylvia has just returned from her brother-in-law's funeral in Posa. Before dying, he denounced his (male) cousin for bewitching him with the intention of having him work for him post-mortem as an *isea* (zombie)[16] in his (the sorcerer-cousin's) fishing business (Diary 18.11.96).

Monday, 16 December Have just heard that a man has been killed by a mob on Mpulungu beach, accused of sorcery. According to KS, a large nail was hammered into his skull, and then his corpse was burned. This was done to destroy his spirit, which would otherwise seek vengeance on the killers.

Thursday, 21 November Visit to Isoko, the Lungu capital. Am asked to heal, and patients include the *Namweene Tafuna*, the powerful lady to whom I'd been kneeling in customary obeisance only minutes earlier. Much glossolalia, to MTW's consternation.

Thursday, 19 December Our last day in the village. Sylvia has just reported that a member of her *Cisuungu* group[17] was attacked by *majini* and nearly died a few days ago. Then the girl's mother found out who had sent the evil spirits – a young male relative of the girl – and went to him and said that, if her daughter died, so would he. The man called off the *majini* and the young woman is now OK.

09.10 We visit a funeral in the house of our neighbour and old friend Mr K....., whose son has just died, apparently of an AIDS-related and long-drawn-out sickness. Later, we learn that a wealthy Mpulungu businessman is being accused of causing the young man's death. Supposedly, the businessman will turn his victim into an *isea*, a zombie who will work for him. This man is said to have many such unfortunate creatures under his control.

Conclusion

There is none. For all of modernist anthropology's attempts to rationalize sorcery/witchcraft as supposed institutions, phenomena of this sort finally elude analytical closure. As Favret-Saada remarked in connection with her field research in the Bocage region of northern France, 'nothing directly concerning witchcraft lends itself to ethnographic description' (1980: 25). My use of the English word 'sorcery' to render the ciLungu *uloozi* is, of course, a nod to the long-standing convention in Africanist anthropology whereby a supposedly innate capacity to inflict occult harm is labelled 'witchcraft' in contrast to the deliberate use of noxious 'medicines' to achieve the same result.[18] However, the 'fit' between the Zande/English concept 'sorcery' and the Lungu notion of *uloozi* is not demonstrably exact. For there is more to *uloozi*, as we have just seen, than simple manipulation of noxious 'medicines'. There is also the confection by sorcerers of zombie-slaves *(masea)* from the persons of their victims, and the potentially lethal practice of 'sending' evil spirits called *majini* to attack those they wish to kill.

There is evidence that Lungu beliefs in the general area of sorcery have evolved over time. My Lungu sources assured me that the *majini* phenomenon had emerged in Zambian Ulungu in the past thirty years. H.M.K. Sikazwe told me *majini* first appeared just after Zambian independence in 1963 and were a 'more developed' form of malign entities called *mizyuuka.*[19] The idea of the zombie-slaves called *masea* may have spread, like the *mizyuuka* concept, into Ulungu from Ufipa (see Robert 1949: 228–30; Willis 1968b). Mr H.M.K. Sikazwe told me a sorcerer's victim appeared dead and was buried, and then was secretly resurrected by the sorcerer, who turned his victim's head back to front and reduced his[20] body to about sixty centimetres long. It worked at night for its master, either in the fields or fishing. It could also be sent to attack people. I obtained a similar account in Tanzanian Ulungu:

> The *muloozi* bewitches the victim, who goes into a trance state so his kinsfolk think he is dead. The sorcerer substitutes a banana stem for his victim, and this object is buried by his unknowing relatives. The sorcerer takes the body and turns its head back to front. It is now an *isea*, and works for him as a slave.[21]

As to how sorcerers actually go about their malign work, no one I talked to in Ulungu seemed keen to go into details. Even Uncle, with his intellectual's love of abstraction and comparison, made no claim to special knowledge in this area – presumably to avoid arousing suspicion of being himself a *muloozi*.[22] The only generalization Uncle permitted himself on the topic was one which I found to be shared by other Zambian Lungu healers: that the 'medicines' (*milembo)* used in sorcery were of a distinctive and singularly powerful kind called *viziimba*. These are typically substances of animal or even human origin. The word '*viziimba*' (sing., *ciziimba*) comes from a root with connotations of 'delayed action' and 'catalytic' effect. Apart from their supposed employment by sorcerers for evil purposes, *viziimba* are also regularly used by legitimate indigenous doctors in conjunction with another major category of 'medicines' called simply *milembo* or, in Zambian English, 'herbs', and which are always substances of vegetable origin – usually the leaves (*amafwa*), or roots (*misizi*) of trees or shrubs or the bark (*cipaapa*) of trees.[23] A doctor goes out and collects vegetable 'medicines' from the bush as needed, but also keeps a stock of *viziimba* on hand. Mr Herbert Sikazwe listed his collection of some fifty *viziimba* for me in 1990. They included such exotic items as part of a gorilla (*nsoko muntu*), said to have been shipped down the Lake from Ruanda, a piece of elephant's ear (*kantaalala*, lit. 'what does not sleep'), a pangolin scale (*nkaka*) and the claw of an aardvark (*nengo*).[24]

Dangerous Powers

Because of the dual association of *viziimba* with both legitimate medicine and the sinister works of sorcery this category of substances is regarded by many as morally tainted, in contrast with the 'purity' *(uluswepo*) of vegetable medicines, or 'herbs', as they are called in Zambian English. Even Mr Sikazwe, who made lavish use of the supposed powers of *viziimba* in his practice, admitted that two items in his collection were, by reason of their dangerous nature, never kept at his home but lodged instead in the custody of his 'grandfather' Kalupi, a famed doctor, who lived thirty kilometres distant, on the other side of the Zambia–Tanzania border. These items were *mutambalila*, remains of a person who had died in the bush, and *mpulalulilo*, charred fragments of bone from the corpse of an alleged sorcerer which had been ritually disinterred and burned. Because of the morally ambiguous status of *viziimba*, many doctors claim not to use these substances in their work, typically asserting either that the practice is 'unchristian' or, more frequently, that 'the spirits forbid it'.[25]

'Sorcery', says Paul Stoller, 'is a metaphor for the chaos that constitutes social relations . . . we are *all* in sorcery's shadow' (Stoller and Olkes 1987:229). It's a judgement with which most Lungu people would readily concur, and none more than those experts in the treatment of affliction whose lives and work are the subject of the next chapter.

Notes

1. *Kasesema* means 'prophet' in the Bemba, Tabwa and Lungu languages. According to elders of the church interviewed in Mbala in 1996, the origins of the church associate it with the work of the famous Malawian healer Chikanga, the Tumbuka *nchimi ya uchimi* ('prophet of prophecy'). According to Friedson, Chikanga and other Tumbuka healers regularly claim connections with Biblical prophets (1996: 25–7). See also Willis 1968a; Redmayne 1970. This topic merits further research.
2. During an earlier discussion with Doctor Tembo, I had mentioned my healing work in Britain (Willis 1992a) and I assume he passed this information to the Principal, who may well have decided to 'test' my reported abilities.
3. An apparent exception was the case of Davidson Simumba, a hero of the liberation struggle and a friend of BC, who was killed in Mbala Location in 1995 by a mob who accused him of being a sorcerer. Mr Chisanga, who told me this in November 1996, said two people were still being held in Kasama prison on charges arising from this crime.
4. A *jini* (plural, *majini*) is said to be the spirit of a dead person sent by a sorcerer to attack and kill a living human being. The word itself is of Swahili origin and the spirits themselves are often said to come from Tanzania. *Jini* comes from an Arabic term meaning 'nature spirit' (the same Arabic word appears in English as 'genie'). In Tanzania, *majini* are said to come from the sea and can be blamed for causing sickness

(see Singleton 1978) but are not usually attributed with the lethal qualities associated with *majini* spirits in the Lunzua valley and eastern plateau regions of Zambian Ulungu.

5. See account of this meeting on pp. 35–7 above.
6. Cf. Bruce Kapferer's evocation of the 'all-consuming' fear induced by Sri Lankan sorcery, when 'speech becomes silenced' (Kapferer 1995: 140).
7. Statement by K.B.S. Chisanga, 1.9.96.
8. Founder of the Westbank Healing Centre in Fife, Scotland, and for many years a renowned paranormal healer. Bruce died in 1989.
9. A pendulum, which this pendant effectively became, can be made to deliver yes/no answers to questions, depending on whether it rotates clockwise or counter-clockwise. In this respect, it resembles various 'mehanical' methods of divination in use in Ulungu (see below, pp. 170, 176n26).
10. 'Serve the bastards right!' I observed in my diary of 2.9.96.
11. Lungu convention normally requires extreme deference from junior to senior in this relationship.
12. The meeting was duly held, and mainly devoted to the then forthcoming *ngulu* session at Posa.
13. A sorcery-hunting cult, famed throughout a vast region of eastern and central Africa since the 1920s. The word is said to come from a Nyanja (Malawi) word meaning 'to cleanse' (see Willis 1968a).
14. Only later did I learn from Friday Maliawanda that some of BC's relatives had threatened to kill him (Friday). To defuse their anger he had eaten the remains of BC's abandoned breakfast in front of them. Then he had gone down to the river and prayed for help to Jesus, as a devout member of the Seventh Day Adventist Church.
15. Wearing his other 'hat' as a leading member of the Lungu Tribal Council, KS later interviewed this man, who also described himself as 'President of the Mutumwa Church in the southern hemisphere and East Africa'. According to KS, his interviewee 'boasted' of frustrating our plans in Jacob's Village.
16. Certain sorcerers are said to become rich by creating *masea* (the plural form) from the bodies of their victims (see below, p. 145).
17. Sylvia organized a group of young women to 'act out' the ritual of female initiation or *Cisuungu*. An account of this event will be published in another place.
18. The distinction was first made by Evans-Pritchard, who in turn derived it from his Zande sources (1937: 387). Not being students of Evans-Pritchard, English-speaking Lungu regularly translate *uloozi* as

'witchcraft' and *muloozi* ('sorcerer' in my Evans-Pritchardian usage) as 'witch'. However, to the best of my knowledge the concept of innate capacity to inflict occult harm does not exist in indigenous Lungu thought.

19. Literally, 'awakened ones'. Like *majini*, *mizyuuka* have no names (statement by H.M.K. Sikazwe, 23.5.90). Also like *majini*, *mizyuuka* could be of Tanzanian origin: I encountered reports of them in Ufipa, south-west Tanzania, in the early 1960s (Willis 1968b).
20. Like the stereotypical sorcerer in Ulungu, the *isea* always seems to be male.
21. Statement by Mr Teddy Simuzosha, 21.7.90. Similar stories were told to me in Ufipa, twenty-five years earlier (Willis 1968b).
22. Even so, his freely expressed interest in occult matters in general seems to have generated just such suspicions (see p. 144 above).
23. This twofold categorization of 'medicines' into substances of veget-able and animal origin is widespread throughout East-Central Africa. See, for example, Richards on Bemba medicine (1939: 343); Willis (1978) on the Fipa; Davis- Roberts (1981) on the Tabwa; and Morris (1995) on the Cewa.
24. The *viziimba* category can also include mineral products of the earth. Among Mr Sikazwe's inventory was salt from the Lake Rukwa region of Tanzania (called *mkuulwe*) and white clay (*umuula*), and some items identified with humans by contiguity, including a piece of a chief's clothing *(mutotelwa)* and a piece of rope used by a suicide (*mukuliko*). *Nkula*, a powder made from the bark of the red camwood tree (*Pterocarpus* spp.), was included in this collection as a *ciziimba* because, Mr Sikazwe said, it 'stood for' human blood (in ritual symbolism).
25. As reported in the census of indigenous doctors carried out by the research team (see below, pp. 150 ff).

–6–

Dreaming Medicine

> Uncle just dropped by *en route* to Doctor Malonga's. He is in search of 'dream medicine'.
>
> Diary 28.10.96

> BC [K.B.S. Chisanga] stepped out of the car outside the post office and immediately engaged in conversation with a man who, he said, brought him a message from his daughter Charity saying she wanted out from Doctor Musukuma's care at Kanondo. How a message could be sent from such a remote place, and above all how that man 'happened' to be there at that particular time are matters that all but defy rational explanation. Also met Webster [BC's classificatory cousin] in the street and he reported that my young female patient of yesterday was 'much better'. That too, of course, defies rational explanation.
>
> Diary 4.11.96

This chapter is based on personal information obtained from 208 Lungu healers distributed through ninety-three villages: a cross-section of Lungu-speaking society, mainly concentrated in the primary research area of the Lunzua valley but also including representatives from the Yendwe valley in the west and the southern and eastern plateau regions. Analysis of these census data shows that the various categories of healer are not absolute but shade into each other, as shown by numerous personal testimonies. In these biographical accounts, Lungu healers appear as conscious explorers of a reality experienced as a relation between their socially constituted selves and an otherness that includes the non-human world of the bush, source of 'medicines' and revealed for many, along with various 'spirit' beings, in the nocturnal adventure of dreaming.

The healers' life stories suggest that these individuals are distinguished by an acquired ability to alternate between their original familial-ethnic selfhoods and an expanded, 'ecological' selfhood, embracing the para-human, 'spirit' world of the bush. For them, selfhood is paradoxically both plural and integral.[1]

'Spirits are Alive'

In 1990 we interviewed 'Uncle' Kapembwa, then chairman of the *Kamata* or Lungu Tribal Council, on his career as a traditional healer. In 1996 I questioned him again on the same topic, and he responded with a much fuller account of his initiation into the healing role. It's interesting that I found his narrative on this occasion emotionally disturbing, for a Diary entry says: 'felt shattered after hearing these stories (notice the shaky hand above)' (11.10.96).[2]

This is what Uncle said that day in Mankonga:

> It happened in 1985. I met a tall man dressed in rags – I would recognize him now if I met him. He told me in the Mambwe dialect that I would be a *sing'aanga* [traditional healer] and that his name was Chilundu Musi [the name of a territorial or *ngulu* spirit in Mambwe country, to the east of Ulungu].
>
> At that time I was very confused. I was manager of the Government store in Kasama but felt I had to resign. Shortly after doing that I was travelling in Ufipa, Tanzania, and bought an ox for slaughter. I stayed with a man who said he wanted that ox for ploughing, and then used some magic so that I had to leave the ox with him. The next day I was in Mwazye [southern Ufipa], sick and vomiting, and I dreamed I was flying and my dead grandmother told me about that man who had tried to kill me. Then I flew to another village and met my two brothers, who had died young. They showed me a certain tree, crushed the leaves and roots and put them in a bottle. I drank, washed and rubbed it into incisions in my body. When I woke up I was told by those around that I had been prophesying (*ku-sesema*). I told them I remembered everything, which was what I had dreamt. From then on I was healed.
>
> I returned to Isoko and went to a doctor, Rafael Mumba, who told me I had *ngulu*. He referred me to Emily Nachinsambwe.[3] She treated me with *ku-tuntuula* [bringing out the *ngulu* spirits] and from then on I became a doctor myself.

Kapembwa Sikazwe (KS) is here describing his initiation into the healer role: he feels impelled to abandon his prestigious position as manager of the major, Government-owned store in the Northern Province capital of Kasama, he is in danger of death (by sorcery in Ufipa), he is violently sick. He encounters a territorial (*ngulu*) spirit (Chilundu Musi), who informs him of his destiny as a healer. Then, in his sickness he dreams of flying – moving like a spirit, freely, from place to place. He encounters the spirits of dead family members, who introduce him to new knowledge: first his grandmother 'fills in' the background of his recent waking-life experience with the ox; then his dead brothers instruct him how to heal himself, showing him medicine, which he uses in the traditional way – drinking, washing and rubbing into bodily incisions (*inkaalo*). It is significant that the new initiate remembers everything that occurred in his 'spirit' dreams: in contrast with the reported amnesia of *ngulu* adepts about their journeys in the spirit domain.

I ask Uncle to say more about his relations with 'spirits' and he says: 'Spirits are alive. I see them at night, in dreams and also in the daytime, openly, just as I am seeing you . . . Without these spirits, doctor, I would have been dead long ago. My spirits protect me . . . I never keep medicines in the house. I wait for the spirits to show me [them].'

Uncle went on to say that when he was four years old he lost his voice because of sorcery. Even when he grew up, his voice was very 'small', but after the spirits came into him, in 1985, it became 'big', as it was now:[4] 'The spirits opened my voice, which was very tiny. The medicine I was told to use was *Mwivintukila*, a tree parasite. You cut the crossed [overlapping] leaves, put them in water and drink for two days. After a month I woke up and started coughing and vomiting. Then I began speaking with the big voice I have now.'

In 1990 Uncle told me he had various healing spirits 'in my chest',[5] one of them a white man called Dr Jones, who was killed in a plane crash when he came to Zambia. The other spirits were 'doctors from long ago, both women and men, dressed in rags but huge people and very healthy'.

> Yesterday afternoon enjoyed an interesting chat with KS, in BC's temporary absence. His Muzungu 'guide' Dr Jones had reappeared in a dream the previous day, after an absence of almost a year. He told him he had an AIDS treatment involving certain roots, which he [KS] intends to try on a niece with suspected HIV [human immunodeficiency virus] infection. I asked KS what this white doctor looked like and Uncle told me he was 'a stocky man in shorts'. (Diary 23.10.96)

Kapembwa Sikazwe's account includes most of the themes found in the life histories of the most numerous category of healers (105 of a total sample of 208): those claiming to work with the aid of 'spirit' helpers. These themes are a preliminary bout of sickness, which can be prolonged and is sometimes life-threatening, leading to the revelation of a spirit-guided healing vocation; a change in social role, coupled with a sense of changed and expanded selfhood; the appearance in dreams of dead relatives, parents, siblings or grandparents, who typically worked as healers in life; and the incursion of benign and healing spirit entities from the non-human domain, the territorial spirits (*ngulu*).

Not uncommonly, the accounts of initiatory life crises describe near-death experiences and occasionally resurrection from the dead. In Tanzanian Ulungu in 1990, for example, I interviewed Augustino Museka, who was born at Sopa in 1942. He told me:

> I left school in 1959 and joined TANU [the Tanganyika African National Union], which became the governing party of Tanganyika, later Tanzania, under Julius Nyerere in 1962]. I became a regional organizer. I also became a çatechist in the Roman Catholic Church.
>
> In 1968 I became very sick. I was treated at Sumbawanga Hospital but without avail. It felt like a fire inside my head and inside my arms. Then I went to a native doctor and he told me I had bad spirits (*mashetani*) inside me. He took out four of the bad spirits with his medicine, leaving just one, who is called Pungamuza [a local territorial spirit], He comes to me whenever I sit with my rosary round my neck and call on him.[6]

In the same year we interviewed a 'spirit' healer who was then living and practising in Kafukula Village, a few hundred metres from the home of our research assistant Herbert Sikazwe. She was a young married woman called Penka Kalumba and she entered an apparent trance state before the interview, using a rattle and inhalation of smoke from a cigarette containing a sweet-smelling herb, which may have been cannabis. Doctor Kalumba was wearing a flowing white head-dress. ornamented with red, white, green and yellow beads, which, she told us later, represented the Tanzanian spirit Kilimanjaro.

The doctor began by describing her discovery of a healing vocation:

> I became very sick, went to the Government hospital but they could do nothing for me. Just when I had given up hope, I found an African healer, who told me the spirits needed me, he gave me medicines and the spirits took up residence in my chest. From then on I began to heal people, with the help of these spirits.

Later during the same interview, the 'spirits' themselves began to speak through the doctor's mouth, as follows:

> Yes, we came to this lady, we came from our ancestors, we were carried by them and since that man got lost [died?] we had nowhere to stay and by chance we saw this lady here, and we asked ourselves whether she was fit for us to work with. We saw that indeed she was, and that is how we came to live with this lady, to make her know how to heal people.

The 'spirits' went on to describe the genesis of the doctor's awareness of her healing vocation in terms that seemed to confirm and even echo her earlier account:

> But before our person could realize we had come into her we first made her sick, and during those days of sickness she was looking for a cure in hospitals and other places but without success. Then we made her decide to go to African healers and they detected the source of her sickness. They realized she had spirits, and gave treatment accordingly.

The entity who was speaking at this time identified itself as Kabwe, a territorial spirit from Bemba country, adding, 'altogether we are sixteen [spirits]'.

Near-death Experience

During the 1996 census, many doctors also described their initiation into a healing role as a return from near-death. Joseph Katai of Tongwa Village told how he became very sick and collapsed: 'I died for 23 hours and the people were preparing to bury me. While they were digging the grave I "woke up". Doctors took me to be purified (*ku-tuntuulwa*) and found I had the *ngulu* spirits Musonda, Chilimanjaro, Kongolo and Kalema. They help me now to heal most diseases, also to find sorcerers.'

Lare Nakazwe of Isoko Village, aged sixty-seven, said that in 1974 she was in her house when it was struck by lightning.

> I saw two angels who were bleeding. Soon after that I collapsed and lay half dead. Then I found myself in the river. I was taken to hospital but could not speak or see anything. It took me two and a half weeks to open my eyes. I used to see the two angels every night. Then one night I saw an arm stretched over my head and heard a voice commanding me to heal. From then on I became a healer.

Other respondents told of experiences suggestive of religious conversion. Esther Nakatali of Chipote Village on the southern plateau and a Roman Catholic, said she was going to Nsumbu on the western lake when the boat passed Nyundo Cape, traditional home of a noted *ngulu* spirit. 'I was caught by the spirits and started prophesying. I would have jumped out of the boat to go and worship, but other passengers held me back. In 1986, at the age of thirty-five, my spirits were revealed by Doctor Nachula as Chisya, Kapembwa, Kilimanjaro and Chilowela . . . Now I heal other *ngulu* patients.'

James Simumba of Onzye Village in the Lunzua valley was a devout member of the United Church of Zambia (Protestant). But whenever there was a funeral and he went to a graveyard he started crying and speaking in Swahili. He was taken to a 'spirit' doctor and she revealed that he had a number of *ngulu* spirits, of whom the leader was Kilimanjaro. He was then thirty-nine years old. Now he works as a healer and treats most diseases except AIDS.

Paul Simusokwe of Mupata Village in the same region said that, as a young man, he hated *ngulu* and never wanted to hear about them. Then one day his thumb began swelling and it became so bad that it stank. Several doctors he approached about his affliction told him he had *ngulu* but still he refused to believe it. 'Then there was an *ngulu* ceremony nearby and out of curiosity I went there and without knowing I started dancing. A doctor called Kalumba put me through the *-tuntuula* ritual and found my leading spirit was Mulenga. I also had Musonda. That was in 1968, when I was thirty-five. My thumb healed immediately.'

A similar case is that of Peter Chipeta of Chitili Village on the north-eastern plateau:

> I grew up very ignorant of healing, even though my grandmother was an *ngulu* doctor. Then one day, when my grandmother was putting someone through the *-tuntuula* ritual, I went to help with the drumming. Then I found myself running into the bush, where I spent the night. When I returned home the next morning I was unable to speak. My grandmother divined, found I had *ngulu* and I was put through the revelatory ritual. I had Kilimanjaro, the leader, Mbwilo and Chilowela. That was in 1990, when I was thirty-two. Now I treat many diseases under the direction of the spirits.

Mary Chito of John Kansehenga Village was born in 1927. In 1953, when she was a married woman with several children, she took a trip to Luapula province in north-west Zambia and there suddenly found herself 'paying homage' to a large rock, the dwelling place of a spirit. Back home in Ulungu she was taken to a doctor, who found she had several *ngulu* spirits, of which the leader was Chishimba (spirit of the Chishimba Falls in Bemba country). Now, with the help of her spirits, she treats a number of problems, including *majini* and *uvyaazi* (women's reproductive problems).

Pressure from the Church

> Love? You can't love everyone. Why are there so many churches? Because people don't love each other: each church hates the others. You even hate your child sometimes, and your child hates you.
>
> BC, 25.8.96

> One very annoying thing I've been told by a church convert in Mbala is that naming your children after 'dead' ancestors is a 'sin'. These churches are destroying Lungu culture: each is like a tribe of its own.
>
> BC, 26.8.96

Not infrequently the church wins the battle with the *ngulu* for the doctor's allegiance. Belita Nanyangwe of Thom Chomba village, born in 1919, became sick at the age of forty-three and was found to have the *ngulu* spirits Mulenga (the leader) and Katai and for some years they helped her to heal, showing her medicines in dreams. But recently, on instructions from the United Church of Zambia, she has 'withdrawn' from the spirits and works as a herbalist only, using medicines taught to her by experienced healers.

In 1990, we talked with Hilda Nakambale of Katito area on the plateau about her work as a doctor with helping spirits. In 1996, we re-interviewed her and she told us that she had abandoned her *ngulu* work since her admission in 1992 to the Seventh Day Adventist Church.

Royal Nankala of Kapata Village, born in 1929, was married and had two children when things began to go wrong for her. One day she was walking in the bush when she heard a voice saying that, if she didn't surrender to Kapambwe (an *ngulu* spirit), her marriage would break down. She consulted some doctors, who told her she had 'strong spirits'. Jennifer Nanyangwe put her through the *-tuntuula* ordeal in 1964 and found that Kapambwe was one of several spirits in her: the leader was Mitanga. For many years she practised as an *ngulu* doctor but recently abandoned it because of the anti-*ngulu* teachings of the United Church of Zambia, to which she belongs.

'Could You Work with African Spirits?'

Saturday, 17 August 1996 We are visited by Doctor Loret Muziya, a traditional healer from Sondwa, a lakeshore village a few kilometres north of Mpulungu. He is a smallish man with remarkably delicate hands and feet. Born 1960 in Kaizya, he is married with seven children and is a member of the Methodist Church. He tells us he became a healer after falling ill in 1989 and being saved by the spirits. The leader of his six resident spirits is Kapembwa, followed by Samaliya ('who does the work'), Mbwilo (who helps with divination and choice of medicines), Chilingala (also helps with medicines), Kilimanjaro (against sorcery) and Meru (women's reproductive problems). He used to do *ngulu* drumming and dancing, but stopped because of his church's opposition to this practice.

I tell the doctor something of my own experiences in healing and he questions me keenly. How do I heal? Could I treat sorcery? How do I call the spirits? Could I work with African spirits? On the last question I say I'm not sure but would be willing to give it a go. He seems pleased with this response.

The doctor agrees to be filmed doing trance divination, at a date to be decided. All he asks for in return is a mirror, measuring twenty inches by twelve, for use in his divinatory work.

> At Sondwa, Uncle and Doctor Muziya engaged in an earnest discussion on medico-spiritual matters, as between fellow professionals. The house is well constructed and spotlessly clean: an air of prosperity. Then the doctor withdrew and returned wearing the regulation outfit in these parts of white head-dress and robe, a style probably introduced by Swahili-speaking doctors in the nineteenth century. He inhaled *ubane* incense and almost immediately the spirit Kilimanjaro took over, talking loudly and aggressively in Swahili. The sudden change from the mild-mannered, soft-spoken man who'd been conversing with Uncle to this hectoring bully was quite scary. We had a lecture on medical matters then another abrupt switch, though still in Swahili, as the female Tanzanian spirit Meru moved in, dispensing advice in a falsetto voice to one or two of the women present. Some good footage, I think. For good measure, Uncle also had a spell in trance and, at the doctor's suggestion, I treated a number of people. (Diary 10.9.96)

Specialist Healers

The census data showed that nearly all Lungu 'spirit' healers have a number of such resident, helping entities, who specialize in the treatment of different afflictions. The average number of named spirits resident in a single healer was four, but this is certainly an underestimate since many respondents indicated they had additional, unnamed spirits as well. Doctor Rafael Mumba of Posa Village, a man with secondary education, claimed to have as many as fifty-three! There is always a *mukulu*, a senior or 'leader' spirit, which is normally the first to emerge in the revelatory *-tuntuula* ritual. Surprisingly, the 'foreign' spirit Kilimanjaro turned out to be overwhelmingly the single most prominent 'leader', being cited as such by twenty-three healers. The next most prominent were the Bemba spirit Mulenga and the wandering Lungu/Fipa female spirit Katai (seven citations each). Kapembwa, the locally supreme divinity in 'official' Lungu theology, was cited as 'leader' in only five cases.[7] But, among the minority grouping of sixteen healers who exclusively treat *ngulu* affliction, Kilimanjaro ranked equally as 'leader' with Matipa (a Bisa spirit) and Katai.

When it came to conditions treated, only fifteen of the 208 healers claimed competence in dealing with all afflictions and only twenty-six said they treated 'most' problems: the majority of practitioners mentioned between four and five conditions as their specialities. Of these conditions, by far the most frequently cited affliction in the census returns was the supposed effects of attack by *majini* spirits. No less than fifty 'spirit' healers mentioned treatment of *majini* sufferers as one of their specializations.[8]

The next most frequently represented condition is *uvyaazi* (thirty-eight mentions), a category covering a broad range of women's reproductive and sexual problems, from *ceendamongo*, excessive and prolonged menstrual bleeding, to *mwaana-mimba,* said by Sylvia Nanyangwe (SN) to feel 'like a hard thing moving up and down in a woman's belly', and to be 'really painful'. Then comes *iviiwa* or *vyuuwa*, troublesome spirits of deceased family members: in extreme cases, doctors disinter and burn the remains of such malign spirits, together with appropriate 'medicines'. Next are *cipena* (28), 'madness', *ngulu* (23), venereal disease or *kasweende* (18)[9] and *kakozi* (14), 'fits'. Among other disorders customarily treated by healers responding to the census were *ulebe*, 'polio', *mpinzi*, 'pneumonia', *uvimba*, 'swelling of limbs', and pains in the abdomen and back.

Sunday, 15 September Mr Chisanga has finally conceded defeat with the car and headed into town (Mpulungu) for expert assistance. A *sing'aanga* (traditional healer) has just turned up and SN brings him into the house for interview. Name: Simon Edward Mumba, of Simbao 'clan'. It seems he cured our friend and neighbour Aggrey Sinyangwe (uterine brother of Sylvia Nanyangwe) in 1994 when he was very sick and unable to speak. He was taken to Mbala Hospital but showed little improvement until treated by Mumba. Since then, according to SN, he has been overly talkative ('*yalaandikisya sana!*')

Doctor Mumba began 'having spirits' in 1976 when he became very sick. Since then he can't eat barbel fish (*nsinga*) and can't eat maize meal after midday. His helping spirits are Kilimanjaro (the leader) and Nachisitu (Fipa), also Kapembwa. He tells us that if he treats a patient for three to four days without improvement he knows he or she is not going to get better and sends the patient back to his or her relatives. In particular, if the patient has no shadow (*icinziingwa*), he knows that death is not far away. On the other hand, if the patient has two shadows, that means he or she is going to become an evil spirit after death, and to prevent this 'medicine' has to be sprinkled over the corpse before burial.[10] Another of his regular jobs, the doctor tells us, is to disinter and burn the remains of people who return after death as *iviiwa* or *vyuuwa*. After that they can do no more harm.

'The Doctor Can't Heal Himself'

> Some doctors (like myself) heal through spirits who tell them what medicines to use. So I never keep medicines in the house. Others who don't use spirits only guess.
>
> KS, 21.10.96

Tuesday, 17 September We visit Doctor Malonga of Posa Village, as arranged. Of Lungu descent, he was born at Kirando in Ufipa (Tanzania) in 1948. He told us:

> In education I got as far as Njombe Secondary School [Tanzania}, which I left in 1969 and then returned to Kirando, where my father was a [traditional] doctor. His spirits were Kilimanjaro, Mudimo, Kapembwa, Mizawandi (from Zaïre) and Fatuma (a female spirit from Tanzania), among others. In 1972 my father died, after bequeathing his spirits to me.
>
> My mother's brother gave me the name Malonga, meaning I have gathered many people around me. I also went to other doctors in search of knowledge. In 1968 I moved to my present home in Posa. My religion is Islam.
>
> If I am not sure about a patient I call in other doctors. The important thing is not money but healing. If a patient dies I feel bad because a doctor's job is to save life. I specialize in madness (*cipena*), women's reproductive problems (*uvyaazi*), evil family spirits (*vyuuwa*) and *majini*.[11]

The doctor then goes into trance and demonstrates his spirit-inspired skill as a diviner. In accordance with instructions, Uncle whispers his problem to a K500 (25p sterling) banknote, which he then places on the altar, which is draped as usual with the spotted pelts of the wild (serval) cat called *nsongo*. The spirit turns out to be a male Swahili-speaking one. It begins by observing that Uncle is a doctor, to which KS replies with the Lungu proverb *Sing'aanga siulwaazye*, 'the doctor can't heal himself'.

Spirit: Where you are living, there are two other people, one of them being a doctor like yourself.
KS: Yes.
Spirit: That person is jealous of your work. That is the cause of your health problem.

The spirit then turns his attention to SN, describing her domestic situation with surprising accuracy. Both KS and SN, neither of whom have met this man before, are visibly impressed by this performance. Now it's my turn. Apparently I have sixteen powerful protecting spirits, described as 'Egyptian'. The doctor's spirit sees I have healed many people, but says I am too 'movious' for the good of my own spirits. I should avoid eating pork, barbel fish and cassava leaves.

> Yesterday was introduced by BC to an old man he described as his 'elder brother'. This morning BC casually informed me he had met the man in Mpulungu and invited him here to talk, adding that they'd not seen each other since 1944, when BC was nine years old!
>
> What do you say to someone, re-encountered in old age, whom you last met as a child? The mind is numbed: not just by the sheer impossibility of *imagining* what they might have said to each other, but of *asking* BC to discuss what to him was evidently such a *non*-extraordinary experience. Here, one feels up against some kind of ultimate barrier to that empathetic understanding of the Other to which anthropology aspires. (Diary 7.10.96)

Tuesday, 8 October In Isoko today Uncle takes us to visit an old woman called Emily Nachinsambwe, who was the doctor who revealed his (Uncle's) healing spirits. Emily, now eighty-nine years old, tells us *ngulu* spirits came to her in 1913, when she was six. They were revealed two years later. The first, and the leader, is Mulenga. She has twenty all told, including four – Nachisitu, Katai, Chasyanga and Chivuna Matesi – who are prophets (*yakasesema*) and tell her what's going to happen. She tells us she travelled widely in colonial times in what are now Tanzania, Malawi and Zambia but her spirits 'didn't charge a fee, but healed freely'. She claimed to have been 'blessed' by the White Fathers (Roman Catholic missionaries).

Ms Nachinsambwe specializes in treating *uvyaazi*, *vyuuwa*, *majini* and *ngulu*.

Figure 10. Eighty-nine-year-old traditional Lungu healer Emily Nachinsambwe of Isoko, who underwent the revelatory ordeal in 1915. She is still practising. (Photo: Roy Willis.)

Apprenticeship

Forty-seven practitioners interviewed during the census described themselves as 'herbalists'[12]–healers using knowledge acquired from living teachers, who were usually close relatives, such as fathers, mothers, uncles/aunts or grandparents. The great majority in this category (43) were male. An apprentice healer is called *mwaanang'aanga*, 'child of knowledge'. When the novice healer is judged by the teacher as competent to practise in his or her own right, he or she is said to be given *ntangala*. This word literally means a bag or other container of healing medicines (*amaleembo*), traditionally made from the skin of a duiker antelope, but is also used metaphorically to denote the body of knowledge transferred from teacher to apprentice. Many healers describe themselves as continuing to learn after their initial 'graduation'. One such was Linos Kivuku of Monsi Wenga Village near Mpulungu. Born in 1964, he decided to become a doctor after suffering from bouts of abdominal pains which he attributed to sorcery. His father was an established healer and agreed to train him.

> After my father had given me *ntangala*, I started to look for more knowledge from some more advanced doctors. I went to Kirando in Ufipa [Tanzania] where I worked for a Zaïrean [Congolese] doctor called Barnan. That was in 1986. He didn't hide anything and I learned a lot. But still I wanted to know more and went to Tanga [north-east Tanzania] where I worked with five doctors altogether, including Lupesa wa Piwe of Zanzibar. I learned to divine (*-saapola*), using three different methods. I treat pneumonia, *vyuuwa* and *majini*, and *cipena* (madness) in particular. I also know *cilanduzi*, revenge medicine.

A noted female herbalist is Emily Nakazwe of Mwanangwa Village, uterine sister of our former research assistant Herbert Sikazwe, who died in 1993. Like her brother, she learned traditional medicine from their father Kosam Sikazwe. She also learned midwifery and the craft of the *nacimbuuza* from her mother, Jane Nalungwe. When her brother died she inherited his *ntangala*, a collection of medicines in bottles and a book describing their uses, all of which he showed me in 1990.

When we interviewed the veteran healer Emily Nachinsambwe in 1996, she told how she had handed her knowledge, her *ntangala*, to a former patient called Rafael Mumba, who became her adopted son because he had no family of his own. He now practised as a doctor in Posa Village.

> Commenting on Emily Nachinsambwe's account of her relationship with Doctor Mumba, BC said it was not true that Mumba had no family. What happened was that he worked for Emily for a year or more, cultivating her garden, etc., and in return she had trained him as a healer. He also knew of another man, now dead, whom she had trained in similar circumstances. Aspiring but impecunious apprentices often worked for established doctors like that. (Diary 8.10.96)

Many of the herbalists in our sample said they had acquired their knowledge through working for an established practitioner. For example, Frank Mazimba of Kapandila Village described how he was motivated to become a doctor after a number of his children died. He went to Tabwa country near Nsumbu on the south-western lake shore and found a noted doctor there called Mutempe. He asked him how he could become a doctor and was told to pay a fee for training: 'I had no money so the doctor said I could work for him for three years, which I did. I learned how to 'dream medicines'. When I was qualified, Doctor Mutempe gave me *ntangala*. Now I treat most diseases and people flock to me.

Saturday, 5 October To Londe Village with BC and SN and another mind-blowing interview involving a doctor who is the mother of the dead woman whose inheritance was decided at last night's meeting. Apparently the mother wanted to keep control by having her younger daughter appointed *mupyaani* (heir) (and thus wife to the widower). However, under BC the meeting was eventually brought to appoint an old woman, a paternal aunt of the deceased. The decision was influenced by the fact that the younger daughter had said she wouldn't accept anyway.

While we were chatting politely, a strange utterance was heard outside. It was the 'spirits' of the discontented mother speaking in a strange language, said by one man to be 'Latin'. Out of trance later, the woman, called Kristina Mumena, said she had four Hebraic spirits, who came to her when she was young, before her first marriage (which ended in divorce). The spirits' names were Eliya (Elijah), Jeremiah, Abraham and John. In 1984, they came out openly, with the help of a doctor from Tanzania called Kabila Kubwa. The spirits said, 'We are very powerful people, we are *Mulenga.*' 'Then they started helping people, healing. They don't divine, but they prophesy. The spirits began by using medicines but after six months they changed to water only, which is used either to wash or drink, according to the illness.'[13]

Journeys into the Wilderness

Friday, 11 October In Mpulungu early this morning, an old woman in the road is pointed out to me by SN as her 'mother's sister', called Mika. Apparently, some years ago, Mika was living somewhere in Tanzania with her then husband. One evening as they were sitting down to a meal, she heard a voice calling 'Mika! Mika!' She went outside and the voice led her into the bush, where she lived alone for a year and five months, unharmed by snakes and other animals and eating only fruits and vegetables.

Commenting later on this story, BC says he remembers a similar case in Tanzania in the 1950s. A man he knew was accused of selling his wife to '*Wachinjachinja*' (mythical killers) after she had disappeared from their home in the Rukwa valley. Divination revealed that she had been taken by the *ngulu* spirit Kwimba (identified with a mountain east of Lake Rukwa). The diviner could see her clearly, but said it would be very difficult to bring her back and in fact she never reappeared.

The testimonies collected during the census show persistent connections between the experience of dreaming, communication with 'spirit' entities and the uninhabited wilderness or 'bush', *mpanga*. These correlations occur in the majority of cases, although there are some interesting exceptions, such as Stefano Kabusha of Chitinta Village, a herbalist trained by his father and without helping spirits, who 'smokes medicine' and afterwards 'dreams' the remedies his patients need. In the case already referred to of Frank Mazimba, this herbalist learned to 'dream medicines' during his three-year apprenticeship.

Several established practitioners, however, explicitly disclaimed obtaining knowledge of medicines in dreams, among them the veteran doctor Israel Kasomo.[14] Mr Kasomo insisted that his medical knowledge came entirely from those doctors who had taught him in life, 'all famous in their time, but now dead'. His career as a healer began in 1934 at the age of thirty, when he became sick and was successfully treated by a well-known doctor called Siwabalanga, whose apprentice he afterwards became. Later he learned more from others. This nonagenarian practitioner and hero of the anticolonial struggle is a powerful member of the Lungu indigenous 'establishment', and the source of his knowledge, obtained from notable practitioners of the past, reflects as well as it partly creates his privileged status in Lungu society. But for less exalted people the dream state can provide a means of access to special and valuable knowledge that bypasses the hierarchic restrictions of waking reality. As a recent observer has commented, dreaming is a 'democratic' activity in that it appears to be available to all human beings as well as, probably, other primates and a range of other mammals (Bulkeley 1996). The egalitarian status of dreaming seems particularly marked in Lungu culture as compared with many other human cultures, including some in Africa, where more or less elaborate systems of dream symbolism have developed: in such cases, interpretation of the perceived contents of a particular dream may be referred to specialists such as priests or diviners or, in modern Western civilization, psychoanalysts. To the best of my knowledge, no such code of dream symbolism exists in Ulungu. The only general symbol I came across was that of 'snakes', said to represent the actual or imminent invasion of the dreamer's person by *ngulu* spirits.[15] Typically, it seems, a Lungu dream means exactly what it appears to mean: it's an experience of the dreamer requiring attention rather than interpretation. This seems particularly true of the Lungu healers who claim to work with helping spirits. These people, like the Tumbuka of northern Malawi, make no sharp distinction between the reality of waking consciousness and the reality of dreams, events in both realms being considered equally 'real' (see Friedson 1996: 21).

In ciLungu, the act or experience of dreaming is *ku-loota*, while 'dreams', *viloooto* (sing., *cilooto*) is the substantive form of this verb. This noun form, with its *ci-vi* prefix, belongs grammatically to the noun class containing 'things' made by human agency.[16] This suggests that 'dreaming' in Lungu culture is seen as a creative act of a human agent or 'self', rather than as something that 'happens' to a passively experiencing self, which is the way normal dreaming is generally regarded in Western civilization. In a study of dreaming in non-Western cultures, Barbara Tedlock observes that the Western devaluation of dreaming as a form of knowing goes back to Aristotle, for whom the dream was merely an image of a real object (1987: 2). Recently, however, Western parapsychology has discovered the so-called 'lucid dream', in which the dreamer is, contrary to the supposedly passive and non-conscious state of normal dreaming, aware that he or she is dreaming and is even capable of exerting conscious influence on the unfolding of the dream narrative itself (see Green 1968; La Berge and Rheingold 1990). It may well be that many of the Lungu dreams recounted here are examples of this actively creative 'lucid' category.[17] Certainly the Lungu dreamers whose testimonies we recorded appeared in many cases to be learning a particular technique, as in the case of Frank Mazimba, quoted earlier. 'Learning' was also remarked on by Green in her classic study with European subjects (1968: 60). Lungu doctors also spoke of using 'medicine' to induce dreams of the requisite quality. Leaves of the *mutanga* tree [?*Abrusprecatorius*], secreted under the sleeper's pillow at night, were said to be effective, as were fragments of a swallow's nest.[18]

Some respondents said their first intimation of a healing vocation came in childhood when they dreamed of being taken into the bush by strange people and shown 'medicines' in the form of leaves and roots of certain trees and shrubs. Joseph Kapembwa of Chipote Village had this experience, but he was thirty-five before submission to the *-tuntuula* ordeal revealed his five healing spirits, led by Katai. That was in 1987 and he is now an established practitioner. More commonly, those who become 'spirit' healers are introduced to therapeutics by close relatives, established practitioners who may themselves have 'spirit' helpers. An example is Mela Nalopa of Chilwa Village on the north-eastern plateau. A mother of sixteen children, she was introduced to medicine by her grandmother, Faides Nambao, an *ngulu* doctor who worked with drumming and dancing to reveal spirits. She also taught her granddaughter the use of herbal medicines during expeditions into the bush.

> Since I couldn't write I had to memorize all the roots. But in the end I learned to write and wrote them all down in a book. But in most cases now I dream medicines. I don't have *ngulu* myself but since my grandmother died she comes to me in dreams and shows me the medicines I need to treat my patients. Other doctors, also my ancestors, come to advise me in dreams.
>
> I specialize in *majini*, pneumonia, mental cases and fits.

Sometimes the apprentice of a close relative with healing spirits also becomes a 'spirit' healer. Patrick Sichone of Simoche Village was only eight years old when, following prolonged sickness, his spirits were revealed by his father, an established 'spirit' healer, as Kapembwa, Kilimanjaro and Kwimba. Though only twenty years old at the time of the census, Patrick Sichone claims to attract an average of nine patients a week and to treat most conditions.

A long-established doctor who is advised in dreams by a dead relative is eighty-year-old Kelly Sikapundwa of Muswilo Village. Mr Sikapundwa was introduced to the healing craft by his father's sister Silika Nakapundwa, who, he said, 'had spirits but didn't use them, though she used to divine (*ku-saapola*)'. 'My grandfather was a great doctor and he comes in dreams and shows me medicines. With his help I have been practising for 27 years.'

In other cases, the *ngulu* spirits of a close relative can come to a person after that relative's death. Crispin Mbao of Mwela Village on the southern plateau became very sick when his mother's *ngulu* spirits came to him after she died. His maternal aunt performed the *-tuntuula* ritual on him. After that, he began healing, helped by the spirits, who came to him in dreams and showed him medicines. He has one patient a week and specializes in venereal disease, pneumonia and headache.

Peter Silumbwe of Muzangawale Village on the southern plateau was taught by his mother, a noted healer, how to find medicines in the bush. He inherited her *ntangala* after she died and practised as a doctor. 'Then spirits came to me in dreams and told me my mother would continue to instruct me and I would be working for her. Thereupon I went to an *ngulu* doctor and found the names of the spirits. I had four and Katai was the leader. I treat *majini*, madness and *ngulu*.'

Another doctor of Muswilo Village is Rosemary Kapolyo, born in 1950 and the mother of three children.

> In 1960 I was ten years old when I became sick. It lasted for two years. My parents took me to doctors, who found I was not bewitched, as people had said, but had *ngulu*. My parents took me to *ngulu* doctors, who started healing me. When I was better, they put me through *-tuntuula,* forcing me to dance. Until now, when forced I do dance, but I don't reveal spirits in others. Nor do I divine.
>
> One day I was asleep and started talking. People told me afterwards that I'd spoken of herbs. I went back to *ngulu* doctors, who instructed me what to do. From that time, I've been healing. People tell me their problems and during sleep I dream of medicines for those problems.
>
> I like being a doctor and work with other doctors.

Joseph Mwapo of Muzabwela Village in the Lunzua valley region illustrates another variation on the medicines–bush–spirit theme. His father was a skilled herbalist and taught his son to recognize and collect medicines from the bush. After the old man's death, Joseph inherited his father's *ntangala* and set up in practice himself. Then, in 1984, at the age of thirty-one, he became aware in dreams that the healing spirits Kililmanjaro and Kato had taken up residence in his chest. 'I never went through the *-tuntuula* ritual but these spirits speak to me at night through a telephone[19] and the next day I go into the bush and collect the medicines they have told me about.'

In the case of another established practitioner this sequence was reversed: 'spirit' revelation followed by training as a doctor with living teachers. Francis Musenge of Kawama Village, also in the Lunzua valley, became aware of his *ngulu* spirits at the age of twenty and was put through the revelatory ordeal three years later by a well-known female practitioner, Mama Wakapansa. With the help of these spirits he was able to heal but none the less chose to be trained by other, established practitioners and apprenticed himself to several of them. He now has a regular practice.

Another healer whose 'spirit' helpers came to him without the mediation of an *ngulu* doctor is Cosmos Simae, a forty-two-year-old fisherman of the lake village of Mpondela.

> In 1983, when I was twenty-nine, a male 'Arab' calling himself Kasansi appeared to me in a dream. He showed me medicines. Afterwards the *ngulu* spirits Kilimanjaro, Minkola, Namukale and Mbita also appeared and they too help me with medicines, but the leader is Kasansi. The main conditions I treat are *majini*, *iviiwa* and backache and I have about six patients a week.

Often, Lungu healers say, 'I was taken to the bush,' sometimes but not always adding, 'by the spirits'. Sometimes, again, they say simply, 'I found myself in the bush' and there collected the requisite medicines. Or they say, 'the spirits showed me the medicines' – meaning medicines of the bush, particularly leaves *(mafwa)* and roots *(misizi)* of trees and shrubs. Often it's not specified whether the event or events described occurred in waking or in dream consciousness, as in this narrative by Uncle Kapembwa Sikazwe about the healing of his daughter Chilombo: 'Chilombo became sick and she dreamed of finding medicines by the river Kunyika. In the morning the same medicines were found under her pillow. She used them and was healed.'[20] Or this statement by Dinnis Muziya of Mbuzya Village, a forty-year-old 'spirit' healer:

> I never knew what happened. I went unknowingly into the bush with a white plate and spent a month there. I woke up at night in the forest. I don't know what I ate. After a month I came back when I saw a white stone in my plate. I brought it home and in 1979 was told not to put it away. Up to then, I knew nothing of healing. After a time, I was told that spirits would start healing. I refused, saying I was unable to do that job. I then became sick for a week. Then medicines started flowing. I could see them unexpectedly. That was when I began healing.

A similar fusion of waking and dreaming states is evident in the testimony of another practitioner, Lukas Kasitu of Muswilo Village, who was initiated into healing as an unmarried youth. His account said: 'I was dreaming and went out into the bush. For four days my parents were searching for me. Later I could think of nothing but medicines. I used to see three people bringing me patients. I heal through the instructions of my spirits, Kilimanjaro and Kwimba, who show me medicines in the bush.'

The difficulty, for the analyst, of discriminating what refers to waking consciousness and what to the dream state in these narratives is again reminiscent of similar problems in parapsychology. I've already suggested the relevance of recent work in Britain and the USA on lucid dreaming, the condition in which the subject typically reports a high degree of self-awareness not easily distinguishable from that of waking consciousness. Also relevant here is the close affinity, remarked by Green, between lucid dreaming and so-called 'out-of-body' experiences (1968: 20–22).[21] Here we should recall the marginal status of parapsychological research in relation to mainstream Western science, for which all these reported experiences, together with reported encounters with 'spirit' entities, are in principle defined as hallucinatory.

What is clear in the accounts of so many Lungu healers is the high, even privileged, status accorded by them to dream experience and the information obtained thereby. The dreaming self and the waking self are, it seems, extended or alternative forms of each other, equally engaged in a search for therapeutic knowledge. In the words of Kapembwa Sikazwe: 'I see medicines sometimes in dreams and sometimes in a waking state. I hear a change in my brain, I pause, and then I hear what medicines to get.'[22]

For those who have acquired this special ability, the dreamscape, the territory inhabited by their nocturnal selves, appears identical with the 'bush' or wilderness, *mpanga*. It is here that they meet, and are instructed by, helping 'spirit' entities. These, as we have seen, are often dead, close relatives from whom the dreamer received instruction in healing during life. That is, they are the spirits of people who, as established doctors, were 'at home' in the bush, the source of healing medicines. The same 'bush' is, of course, also the 'home' of the healing *ngulu* spirits of the wild. The category '*ngulu*', as we have already seen, is a wide one that takes in all kinds of spiritual powers beyond the familial universe.[23] It includes 'spirits' associated with sorcery-hunting and healing 'Christian' churches which have been introduced into Zambia by African evangelists. These 'Christian' *ngulu* spirits are sometimes called *Ncimya* or *Samaliya*, or *Mutumwa*.[24] The last-named is a popular church in eastern Ulungu and 'spirits' associated with it sometimes bear Biblical names, such as Yakobo (Jacob), Moses, and Maria. Eight of the census respondents reported themselves as hosts to a mixture of *Samaliya/Mutumwa* spirits with 'traditional' *ngulu* spirits, such as Kilimanjaro, Kapembwa and Mbita. A typical example is Cecilia Nayame of Katoto Village, a member of the Roman Catholic Church, whose four *ngulu* spirits were revealed at the age of fifteen. They are led by the 'Christian' *Samaliya* and the other three are Mulenga, Kapembwa and Chanda.

Fuzzy Roles

Early during the 1996 research, I discussed the various kinds of indigenous Lungu healer with Kapembwa Sikazwe. He told me they fell into six categories: herbalists; 'spirit' healers; *Ncimya*; *Kamcape* (traditional sorcery hunters, not associated with Christianity); *ngulu* doctors; and *yanacimbuuza*, female specialists in reproduction and sexuality. This classification is useful; indeed, I have adopted it here. The categories correspond to recognized social roles in present-day Ulungu. But it is also misleading, in so far as the life histories collected during the research show numerous instances of individual healers going beyond, transcending, the definitions and boundaries prescribed by social convention. Indeed, to become a healer in the first place requires of a man or a woman an active determination to move, at least partially, out of the highly structured and predictable world of familial relations and village society into the initially strange world of the bush, with its unknown, para-human powers. Even the boundaries between the different kinds of socially recognized healer are far from impermeable. Of the twenty-six *yanacimbuuza* recorded in the census, four also worked as *ngulu* doctors, revealing 'spirits' in afflicted patients. An example is Esmat Mazimba of Thom Chomba Village, who was born in 1914 and as a young woman learned from her mother the craft of *nacimbuuza*.

> At the age of twenty-six I began dreaming of drums and dancing, even seeing these figures during the day when no one else saw them. Then at a village *ngulu* ceremony I danced and sang and even spoke a foreign language. I was taken to an *ngulu* doctor, Mangeni Nalwamba, the following year, which was 1937. She revealed my spirits, with Kapambwe as leader. Since then I have worked as *ngulu* doctor as well as *nacimbuuza*.

Of the forty-seven recognized 'herbalists' in the census, more than a third (nineteen) practised some form of divination (*kusaapola*), a practice based, explicitly or implicitly, on appeal to invisible powers beyond ordinary sensation. Seven used a mirror (*icilole*) to reveal hidden agents affecting their patients,[25] three received information in dreams, one depended on the 'spirit' powers of his wife, and the rest used a device delivering positive or negative answers to the doctor's questions.[26] Of the fourteen describing themselves as '*ngulu* doctors', six also treated other conditions, as well as revealing *ngulu* spirits in their patients.

> I got permission from the Director [RW] to go and see Doctor Malonga of Posa Village. With the aid of his spirits he examined me and found a long-standing sickness of *majini*. He took me to the stream to clear away these evil spirits.
>
> From my observations he [Malonga] is cheaper than other doctors. He asked me to buy relish (fish, chicken), maize meal, beer, cooking oil, salt, *kapenta* [sardines], tomatoes, onions, sugar, sugar cane, bananas, groundnuts and cassava.
>
> Doctor Malonga tells me that he regularly works with Madam Lisita Nakazwe.[27] He says she can only reveal (*ku-tuntuula*), anything else is too much for her. (Report by KS, 24.9.96)

Tuesday, 24 September Uncle Kapembwa told me over breakfast that he wanted to see Doctor Malonga in Posa for treatment of a *jini lya nzoka* (snakelike evil spirit) which is affecting his shoulders and threatening to paralyse his left arm. I gave him K1500 (75p sterling) for the journey and the morning off.

12.00 Sylvia has also taken off 'to be seen' (as she put it) at the funeral in Kaizya of her classificatory cousin *uku musana* (on her mother's side).

17.00 Gave Lisita Nakazwe a lift home from Mpulungu and listened to an interesting conversation in the back of the car between her and KS. Apparently she also, like KS, is able to 'dream medicines'. She also mentioned, *contra* Malonga,[28] that she was able to divine, using a rubbing board *(kakumbi*). A case of professional jealousy by Malonga?

'I Am Not the Doctor'

Attaining the status of doctor (*sing'aanga*) is obviously a big deal for a Lungu person. How aware are such people of being 'different' from their earlier, unqualified selves? The evidence is that they do indeed 'feel' importantly changed. Remember Kapembwa Sikazwe's statement, in our first conversation in 1990, that before his life crisis and emergence as a 'spirit' healer in 1985 he had been just 'an ordinary man'.[29] Adam Kaumbi, who described finding himself at the bottom of a river and emerging after five hours,[30] commented that from then on 'my thoughts were changed'. The incursion of 'spirits' typically coincides, as in Kapembwa Sikazwe's case, with the transition from 'ordinary' personhood to an awareness of 'non-ordinariness', of being suddenly gifted with unusual powers. This narrative by John Mulenga of Kaizya Village typifies the experience of many 'spirit' healers:

> I was born in 1957 and reached grade seven in primary school. I am married with five children and work as a farmer and businessman. My father was a well-known doctor and he advised me to write down everything I saw him doing. I did this, and gave the book to my mother to look after.
>
> The first in our family to have *ngulu* was my young brother Musili Katai, whose spirits were showing him medicines. I still had to go to the bush to collect medicines, as my father had shown me. Then, in 1978, when I was twenty-one years old, the *ngulu* spirits came to me as well. It got to be that when someone was sick I could go to that person and say whether he or she was going to live or die.
>
> I knew I needed more knowledge so I went to Luba country in Zaïre [Congo] and trained for two months with a woman doctor called Chisela, who had only one breast. With her, I learned how to find stolen property and to detect sorcery objects. Now I am home again, my spirits help me both to heal, *ku-lwazya*, and to find *viwaanga*, sorcery objects.

Sometimes the sense of radical change can lead a person to make a sharp distinction between two versions of his own selfhood, as in this comment on his healing powers by Dinnis Muziya, whose initiatory ordeal in the bush was described earlier:[31] 'I get told through dreams. In fact I see the patient and someone healing him or her. Then I get told what to do. I never attempt healing except when told. *I am not the doctor*[32] and don't know how to do this work.'

The general sense, here given extreme expression, that to become a healer is to be a different person is recognized in a conventional practice by which the practitioner assumes a distinctive 'healing name' (*izina lya using'aanga*). In the case of 'spirit' healers, this name is often that of the healer's leading invisible helper. For instance, Kapembwa Sikazwe's *izina lya using'aanga* is Chilundu Musi, the *ngulu* spirit from Mambwe country, who, according to Doctor Sikazwe's own testimony, first informed him in 1985 of his destiny as a healer. But, besides advertising an individual's new social persona,[33] the 'healing name' can also indicate the practitioner's own perception of the essential nature of her or his 'expanded self'. Lisita Nakazwe, a woman whose practice in Kaizya embraces the treatment of malign familial spirits *(iviiwa)*, madness (*cipena*) and reproductive problems (*uvyaazi*), as well as *ngulu* patients, calls herself *Sikangulu*, a name that translates as 'male master of *ngulu* spirits'. Madalena Namwinga, also female, who specializes solely in treatment of *ngulu* patients,[34] is known professionally as *Katuntuula*, 'master of revelation'.

> Lisita Nakazwe showed up here as expected, together with daughters Lonia and Mevis. She then surprised me (remembering Doctor Malonga's disparaging comment) by producing a rubbing board and stick and doing a divination job on *me*. She laughed merrily when the oracle returned a positive answer to the question whether I 'had spirits'. Apparently, not only do I 'have spirits' but I've acquired a few more since arriving here, including the renowned Matipa. She commented that I could as well be doing *her* job (of divination).
>
> While Lisita was doing this work her daughters silently observed, *Musano* [Mevis] coolly elegant in a blue dress.
>
> Hearing I was leaving shortly for Lusaka, Madam Lisita suggested after the session that I buy a cassette player for her there. This she would pay for on the instalment plan by inviting the URP [Ulungu Research Project] team to attend a series of *ngulu* rituals at her home in Kaizya. Smart lady! (Diary 9.11.96)

Explorers of Consciousness

> My spirits show me medicines. In dreams I used to see Europeans, some birds, Africans in white robes with Bibles. Now they come in the daytime. I've been healing for twenty-seven years.
>
> John Chifunda, doctor of Katumba Village

These people who work as 'spirit' healers in Ulungu are, it seems to me, all venturing from a secure and familiar home base in family and village life *i*nto the perilous unknown. This movement from known to unknown embraces three experiential dimensions which are separate in ordinary life and for ordinary people but which become equivalent and integrated with each other in the lives of these extraordinary explorers of consciousness who are the 'spirit' healers of Ulungu. These three exploratory movements are from village to wilderness, from social to ecological relationships and from waking to dreaming consciousness. Of course, contrary movements in all three dimensions are implicit in the work of healing itself, which is concerned with action relating to their fellows as patients (*alwale*) in the daytime village and domestic setting. What distinguishes healers, and most particularly the 'spirit' healers, from the laity, is that for them these apparent contraries of village and bush, human and non-human life, waking and dreaming, though of course distinguishable, are also unusually integrated in a way that provides these practitioners with special powers. Their privileged access to a range of knowledge not available to the narrowly focused and compartmentalized consciousness of ordinary people is the source of those powers.

We repeatedly find in the testimonies of these 'spirit' healers awareness of movement from the ordinary into the extraordinary; often this movement is precipitated by a catastrophic event, a near-fatal illness or accident; or, less frequently, a person reports being born with intimations of the alien 'bush' spirits, the *ngulu*,[35] but sooner or later they have to be fully revealed, named, in the *-tuntuula* ordeal. The result of this irrevocable change of consciousness in the fully qualified healer is, as I have suggested, a sense of expanded but also internally differentiated selfhood. 'I am not the doctor' (*'Inene si sing'aanga'*) says one, a variant of Kapembwa Sikazwe's assertion that 'I never keep medicines in the house: I wait for the spirits to show me [them]'.[36] The healer is both the social being, with his or her well-defined roles in domestic, familial, and village society, and the ecological being, with access, mediated by the 'spirits' of healer ancestors, *ngulu*, or both, to the non-human powers of the bush. The selfhood of the healer encompasses all these domains of consciousness, spanning village and bush, waking and sleeping, human and para-human. This extraordinary selfhood is characterized by diversity and multiplicity, combined with an acquired ability to shift at will from one aspect of this multiple and diverse identity to another.

I see the apparent 'fuzziness' in Ulungu of social roles associated with a healing vocation, a characteristic remarked on earlier in this chapter, as a symptom of this intrinsic tendency for healers to 'go beyond' their social identities into an 'expanded' and 'ecological' selfhood. The implications of this finding for our understanding of human selfhood and the 'spirit' phenomenon will be explored in the final chapter of this book.

Notes

1. The census schedule called for information on an interviewee's name, healing name (*iziina lya using'aanga*), gender, address, place of birth, year of birth, education, religious affiliation, employment history, marriage(s), number and sex of children, whether able to divine, method of divination used, whether the interviewee has *ngulu* spirits and, if so, when he/she first became aware of them, if and when he/she underwent the revelatory (*-tuntuula*) ordeal and who performed it, names of *ngulu* spirits, name of the leading spirit, what conditions or afflictions the interviewee treats, whether 'herbal' medicines are used, how the interviewee knows which medicines to use, whether taught by another doctor or doctors and, if so, who, whether or not *viziimba* substances are used and, if not, why not, whether he/she works with other doctors and, if so, who, and how many patients are treated on average per week.
2. I now feel certain, although at the time I seemed unconscious of it, that the cause of this disturbance was a deep resonance between Uncle's narrative sequence of life crisis, paranormal events and discovery of a healing gift, and my own experiences in the early 1980s, as briefly described in the Introduction.
3. Doctor Mumba was himself initiated by Doctor Nachinsambwe (see below, p. 162).
4. Others, including Mr Chisanga, confirmed that, around 1985, Uncle's voice had surprisingly changed from being faint and squeaky to being powerful.
5. In Ulungu, healing spirits are supposed to dwell in the chest (*cifuwa*) of the person who works with them.
6. Interviewed at Tatanda Village, 27.8.90.
7. See Chapter 3, 'Managing Time and Space'. One of the five cases was that pillar of the indigenous Lungu establishment Mr Paul Kaongela, priest of Kapembwa. Mr Kaongela assured me in 1996 that when it came to *ngulu* spirits he had *Kapembwa sile*, 'Kapembwa only'.
8. There is a probable connection between the prevalence of *majini*, evil spirits said to originate in Tanzania, and the prominence in a healing role of the spirit Kilimanjaro, which also comes from Tanzania.
9. Literally, 'syphilis'.
10. As in the case of Dorothy Nanyangwe, p. 32.
11. Statement by Mikidadi Seba Malonga, 17.9.96.

12. In a recent publication, Brian Morris (1998) attacks what he sees as the unwarranted prominence given to 'spirit' healers in Janzen's study of Ng'oma (Janzen 1992), to the detriment of herbalists, who, he says, constitute the majority of indigenous healers in Malawi. It seems to me that not only are there local differences as between the respective proportions of 'spiritist' and 'herbalist' healers in Southern and East-Central Africa, but that the situation in the same locality can also change significantly over time. In 1960s Ufipa, for example, my impression was that the overwhelming majority of indigenous healers were herbalists. My friend and informant Matiya Msangawale, who healed with 'spirit' help (see Willis 1972), was a notable and rare exception. However, during the 1996 research in Ulungu, I obtained evidence suggestive of a current renaissance in Fipa traditional religion and a re-emergence of Fipa territorial spirits in therapy. A further complication in defining the relative statuses of herbalist and spiritist healers in Ulungu (and conceivably elsewhere) is the 'fuzziness' of distinctions between these two ostensible therapeutic roles – as discussed later in this chapter.
13. Statement by Kristina Mumena, 5.10.96.
14. The historian and court elder cited in Chapter 3 above.
15. As in the case of Mary Nakazwe (p. 79). The symbol may also be negative, as when Mr Chisanga dreamed of dead snakes the night before a scheduled *ngulu* ceremony turned into a fiasco (p. 89). Mundkur (1983), drawing on a wide range of scientific evidence, argues powerfully for the serpent as the primordial symbol of human religious experience.
16. In all Bantu languages, including ciLungu, nouns fall into distinctive categories, which govern the form of other parts of speech within a sentence. The categories seem to derive from a primordial classific-ation of objects according to their state of being.
17. See also below, pp. 165–9. The dream quests of Lungu doctors searching for 'medicine' appear to be related to, or are perhaps versions of, the spirit-world 'journeys' of Asiatic and New World shamans, a matter I return to in the final chapter.
18. According to Emily Nachinsambwe, and confirmed as common usage by KS.
19. An actual instrument which he places by his ear at night.
20. Statement by KS,11.10.96.
21. Cf. Kapembwa Sikazwe's account on p. 151 above of 'flying', a frequent element in lucid dreams according to Green (1968: 55).
22. Statement by KS,11.10.96.

23. See Chapter 4.
24. '*Samaliya*' is said to be a version of 'Samaritans', which according to KS is the name of a church in South Africa. I have not been able to verify this statement. '*Ncimya*' is defined in Fr. Halemba's *Mambwe–English Dictionary* as 'a legally approved congregation involved in witch-hunting ceremonies using traditional methods and Christian prayers' (1994: 538). According to the Principal of the Kasesema Prophet Church in Mbala, popularly known as '*Mutumwa*', '*Samaliya*' is the name adopted by his church in Tanzania.
25. A technique called 'scrying' in the Western magical tradition.
26. Two of these devices are in wide use: a friction oracle (*kakumbi*), which can consist of two pieces of wood or an axe-head, which is rubbed on the skin of a duiker or other animal of the bush; and leaves of the strychnine-bearing *mwavi* tree (*Erythrophloeum guineense*), which are placed inside a ball of maize meal, which is then dunked in a bowl of water; if the 'medicine' remains dry during immersion the answer to the doctor's question is 'yes', but if it is found to be wet the answer is 'no'. In precolonial times, *mwavi* was used in the poison ordeal customarily administered to suspected sorcerers. In such cases, vomiting the poison was regarded as proof of innocence (see p. 26 above).
27. Noted *ngulu* doctor (see Chapter 4).
28. According to Doctor Malonga, Lisita Nakazwe was unable to divine (see p. 170 above).
29. See Chapter 1, p. 17.
30. Statement in Sondwa Village, 4.12.96.
31. See above, p. 168.
32. Emphasis added.
33. I am here distinguishing between the social 'person' and the inner 'self' (see discussion in Chapter 8).
34. For a description of this practitioner see Chapter 4, pp. 103–104.
35. In a study of a group of twenty established 'paranormal' healers in Scotland, nineteen had discovered their healing gifts after a life-threatening illness or accident. The exception was a woman who claimed to have had her powers from birth (Willis 1992c).
36. See p. 152 above.

–7–

Dispossession

On way back from Mpulungu met a large crowd in the road outside Paul Nielsen's service station. A man explained that a schoolgirl had just been knocked down and killed by a hit-and-run driver. While I made the Euro-conventional 'shock horror' noises, BC [K.B.S. Chisanga] railed about how 'very cheek' [cheeky] pedestrians were in Mpulungu, with no respect for the power of the motorcar.

Diary, 15.10.96

'I don't like his [BC's] attitude.'

Sylvia Nanyangwe, 20.11.96

Monday, 28 October, 21.00 A disturbing incident this evening: on the front step after dinner I shared a modest glass of Afrikoko (a locally produced sweet liqueur) with BC. After a while he called Maliawanda (the cook) over and suggested he try it. Friday (Maliawanda) took a sip and a moment later violently spat it out, no doubt sensing its alcoholic content. Afterwards he protested to me that alcohol was absolutely forbidden to him as a member of the Seventh Day Adventist Church, something BC must have known when he played this stupid prank on him. Fired with righteous anger, I go to upbraid BC, but no sooner have I begun to raise the issue with him than my *kizungu* (white) certainties dissolve in a fuzzy mist and can find nothing coherent to say to him.

Tuesday, 19 November Last evening I announced that, now, Mary Taylor Willis (MTW)[1] was here, she would be in charge of domestic arrangements, so releasing BC and SN to concentrate on research – their 'real work'. This evening Mary has received two splendid gifts from Kapembwa Sikazwe (KS) and BC: a beautifully carved staff and a handsome black billy-goat. The latter is being quartered somewhere in the rear, reportedly in the bedroom of two young boys.

17.00 Mary's goat has done a runner. Mr Chisanga has advertised a reward of K5000 (£2.50) for anyone bringing in the fugitive beast.

Wednesday, 20 November The goat has been recovered. We went to Katito in the Moto Moto vehicle and filmed and interviewed Rhodson Sichilima, the famed 'television doctor'.[2]

After that, we go to Kanondo and retrieve BC's daughter Charity, who is in a parlous state, with badly swollen arms and legs, hobbling along with a stick in obvious pain. Apparently, she had to sell her watch to avoid starvation. Mary rages against 'these quack doctors'. Charity is now in Mbala Hospital, receiving Western medical care. I'd told SN to accompany BC and his 'sister' into the hospital with poor Charity and to stay there to help while we collected the Peugeot from where we'd left it at the Museum. Was quite nonplussed to find, when we arrived there, that SN was still in the Moto Moto vehicle with MTW, Mr Mulengo (the driver) and myself. I drive back to the hospital and 'pick' (Zambian English for 'pick up') BC there. He seems overwhelmed with gratitude towards MTW and myself for rescuing Charity.

Later, sitting out in the garden under the stars, BC speaks of his daughter and her suffering and weeps. Both he and MTW are indignant about SN's apparent insubordination, MTW describing her as 'too big for her boots'.

Friday, 22 November 'Carpeted' SN today over the hospital incident. All she could say was that she 'didn't like his [BC's] attitude', and hence, apparently, her blatant disobedience of my explicit instructions. Feeling puzzled and irritated. Left BC and two 'sons' in Mbala to look after Charity.

Wednesday, 27 November Signs of bolshie behaviour by BC. Or, rather, behavioural signs of inner bolshieness, like his gratuitous rudeness today to MTW, when he treated her with patronizing condescension. Seems he's finding the discovery that he's not indispensable, consequent on MTW's domestic enterprise here,[3] hard to handle.

Thursday, 28 November Mr Chisanga has made an abject apology to MTW for his rudery of yesterday. I then sent him off on a census mission in the village, from which he has yet to return.

Friday, 29 November, 17.40 Came down real heavy on BC this morning, threatening the ultimate sanction (dismissal) if he has not mended his ways by 8 December or indeed in the week from today to that date.

Saturday, 30 November Visit to Mpulungu with MTW and BC, the latter in docile, even servile, mode in the wake of his blasting yesterday.

Sunday, 1 December Beginning of the final month of this astonishing research period. Astonishing indeed are the kaleidoscopic shifts in relations within this mini-society, the Ulungu Research Project (URP). For instance, Mary began with the highest opinion of Sylvia; then she decided she wasn't so smart, and was deceitful to boot; now she's back again in the sunlight, highly intelligent and admirable in every way. Mr Chisanga has gone from superman to arrogant and bullying object of dislike; now seemingly on his way back to favour, with MTW deliberately introducing into conversation yesterday evening the sensitive topic of his trip to Scotland, earlier held by her to be out of the question. As for RW, he continues to be amazed at his good fortune in somehow bringing about this fruitful situation, which can lead in so many directions, all rich in potential.

On BC: but for his problems, which drive him to be creative and go beyond the limits of his cultural background, he would be just an ordinary Lungu man, retired on his farm amidst his extensive family.

Tuesday, 3 December Mary said SN had 'cheekily' asked her if she was going to Mbala to work, or 'just' to accompany me!

Thursday, 5 December. In Mbala today BC was nobbled by one of his creditors outside the Finance Bank and had to cough up K60,000 (£30 sterling) – advance by RW against his pay this month. Mr Chisanga explained it was a debt of the defunct Northern Beekeepers' Association. He said he was 'embarrassed' by the incident.

Another mystery this evening. Mary told me that Friday (Maliawanda, the cook) had told her that BC had told him (Maliawanda) to tell the Director (RW) he was going to the next village but actually he was going to Mpulungu. BC disappeared while MTW and I were having a stroll along the main road at about 16.00 hours and by 18.00 he was back. Had he been to Mpulungu in that relatively short space of time and, if so, why? Had he indeed told Friday what MTW reported to me and what could have been his motive in thus handing Friday a gift on a plate? If it wasn't true, what could Friday's motive have been?

Sunday, 8 December Uncle Kapembwa has just returned from his mammoth census tour. He's had a successful trip, with about twenty- five interviews. He has some interesting comments on BC, who, he says, 'is never wrong'! Also: 'he [BC] has many different projects, but no direction'. And explaining why he and his wife had agreed BC was no suitable candidate as husband for their divorced daughter: 'He would make her a slave, she would rebel and leave and that would be that.'

Monday, 9 December Another restless night, listening to the persistent rain, wondering what has happened to BC (who is still absent).[4]

15.35 Been going through KS's rich material from his 'doctor' interviews. Been to Mbala and made an appointment to see Mr Sefu, Principal of the local *Mutumwa* church, on Thursday. Still no sign of BC.

Tuesday, 10 December Terrific storm in the night. Just as it was beginning, about 21.00, BC returned with some feeble story of a puncture in Senga Hill. Feel angry and disgusted, but decide to deal with him in the morning. What I see and learn then is worse. The few census forms he's brought back have been hurriedly scribbled and the work is immensely inferior to what Uncle has achieved at far less expense. For good (or rather bad) measure, the borrowed motorbike has been damaged and is leaking oil. Mr Chisanga's whole story seems like a fabrication. And this after I'd warned him in the clearest terms to mend his ways! Decided on dismissal but MTW, to my surprise, takes BC's part and persuades me against this extreme course. In the end, I settle on withdrawal of privileges, including bonus and UK visit.

14.35 Another emotionally bruising interview with BC this morning. He, of course, denies everything. Just no idea how things will go from here. Myself, I'm going to concentrate on getting the work done.

15.50 Mary just looked in while I was going through Vol. I of this diary. She's had a long talk with SN, who's told her of BC's greed and conniving, his purloining of food, etc. The 'other side of the coin' indeed!

Mary says she will not have someone who bullies women like BC in 'her' house. Moreover, she adds, 'He's defying you.' Probably she regrets dissuading me from sacking him this morning.

Wednesday, 11 December Spent long time during night thinking what to tell the troops at tomorrow's staff meeting. In brief: this research period has been a brilliant success. If I am the driver, BC has been the engine powering this effort (for most of the time until recently, that is). He has contributed more than energy and local knowledge: he has also had some great ideas. So, of course, have KS and SN. Funny, it's as though the whole recent crisis about BC is suddenly no longer real, a passing nightmare.

Friday, 13 December Notable softening of MTW's attitude to BC perceptible last evening. Instead of being banished to the dining-room alone, he was sat down between us in the front room for dinner. Explaining the proposed share-out of URP loot,[5] Mary said he (BC) would get 'slightly more' (in value) than the others. Will his sins be washed away. We shall see.

20.15 Mr Chisanga apparently suffering bodily pains. His 'mother' (maternal aunt) was round early this morning and they had a lengthy conversation while sitting on the front doorstep, both staring straight ahead the while, as if the matters were weighty.

Saturday, 14 December The long-prepared *matanga* (commemorative meeting) for Herbert Sikazwe[6] was held today in Mwanangwa Village. Mr Chisanga described the decision to wait for the arrival of Mama Mary (MTW) before holding the event. Uncle Kapembwa described his long illness and Mary spoke of her friendship with 'Herbie' and the work they had done together, the warm hospitality of Herbert and his family and his devotion to his work as a healer. I played a 1990 tape-recording of Herbie describing this work. Hearing her late brother's voice, his sister wept piteously. A self-important local political figure was neatly deflated by BC, who was in his most commanding and charismatic mode.

Prayers and hymn-singing followed and a generous lunch was enjoyed by about fifty guests. Mary commented with distaste on the greedy way BC 'gulped down' his chicken.

We've no sooner returned home than BC is besieged by another creditor, a carpenter called Siame, who says he's owed K140,000 (£70 sterling).

Sylvia has reportedly told MTW that 'undesirable' visitors to our premises have diminished in number since MTW came here. Am sceptical on this one. Mary also thinks I 'haven't noticed them'. On the contrary, I've been carefully noting these visitors (and questioning BC about them) in pursuit of my thesis on the 'enveloping family'. The difference is that, as anthropologist, I make no value judgements. Mr Chisanga says his creditor is a 'fool' but it sounds like bluster. Mary is again excoriating BC. He has fallen like Lucifer.

Sunday, 15 December This afternoon's (farewell) party went off splendidly. Mary and her 'staff' did tremendous work and the atmosphere was friendly and not too nostalgic. Speeches by RW, our venerable neighbour Mr Kazimoto, Israel Kasomo, the grand old man of Ulungu, Paul Kaongela, the redoubtable priest of Kapembwa, our gracious landlady Madam Rides Nakazwe, and BC (whose typically orotund contribution MTW described as 'sanctimonious'). Apparently BC took advantage of the occasion to propose marriage to Uncle's daughter. Reportedly she told him he was a fool.

The day ended with a surprisingly agreeable sitting-room discussion between BC and MTW on Lungu history, while a tired and rather confused RW drifted in and out of sleep.

Monday, 16 December Another incident involving BC in Mbala this morning. He's arrested by a rifle-toting policeman in the high street in connection with his debt to Mr Siame, who is also present. The cop is grinning all over his face, clearly delighted that the Big Man has finally got his comeuppance. Though tempted in my growing irritation and embarrassment at all this to let him stew in jail for a day or two, concern for the URP's public image causes me to finish up bailing him out again to the tune of K90,000 (£45 sterling). Back in Mankonga after his narrow escape from prison, BC is astonishingly as cocky as ever, striding about giving orders to those family members who always seem to be hanging around. Hearing his loudly confident voice outside, MTW comments: 'He thinks he's won again!'

Then further revelations from SN and Friday about BC's high-handed and corrupt dealings with them. It seems that suddenly everyone is turning against him. On the face of it, the things they're complaining about are almost unbelievably petty. Like how he'd tried, unsuccessfully it seems, to pressure the cook into letting him eat *kapenta* (dried sardines) bought for the aborted *ngulu* session on 19 October, instead of keeping them for the rescheduled performance a fortnight later, as SN had – quite properly – told the cook should be done; and SN's account of a prolonged battle of wills between her and him over BC's attempt to purloin a miserable amount of change from SN's purchase for the Project, in an Mbala store, of batteries for the tape-recorder. Utterly trivial matters on the face of it, but the passion in their voices tells me the real issue here is power, and BC's seemingly compulsive misuse of it to browbeat those below him in the Project hierarchy. So this is the man I'd invested with such a mantle of nobility, suddenly revealed as a petty manipulator, a schoolyard bully! If only he'd done something really bad, like killing someone or robbing a bank, I'd have found it easier to forgive.

Finally, KS (?Brutus) informs me – what I'd suspected all along – that, instead of working in Senga Hill over the weekend, BC had been on his farm. He has lied as well as cheated! Again disbelief, remembering the man who'd worked all the hours God sent for the Project, declining to take any time off. And thinking how hard it must now be for MTW to credit that story of mine! Buoyed by a sudden surge of anger over this final betrayal of trust, feeling the tension in myself and in this house to be unbearable, I tell BC I'm finished with him. Yet even as I do so I'm uncomfortably aware how easily he could even now, and given half a chance, persuade me that black's white and *vice versa*, that things are totally otherwise than what I devastatingly know them to be. *Why* is the question I can't even begin to answer. Why, after the tremendous work he did, BC has turned against me, against us. As if sensing my desperation, BC agrees to go. I watch him, he whom I'd loved like a brother, pass through the door, and feel relief, mixed with confusion and pain.

Tuesday, 17 December Another restless night. Healed Sylvia's Mum this morning. She 'felt the power (*amaaka*) moving' in her head.

Mr Chisanga is here again after a night's absence and is at present in his room, apparently preparing to move out his belongings.

09.40 Mr Chisanga has been given until 09.45 to finish his packing. Return authorized at 16.00[7] but has to be out before 18.00. He appears calm, even dignified, this man who has lost everything – bonus, trip to Scotland and, above all, respect (as SN observed last evening).

Apart from the betrayal of trust, the awareness of having been made a fool of, the most disturbing aspect of this business is the sheer irrationality of it. What he managed to embezzle in the way of food, paraffin, etc. could have been worth in all no more than a fraction of what he could have earned as a bonus. On top of that, he has thrown away the prospect of realizing his heart's desire: to visit the UK. Nothing makes any sense. Or could it simply be that he has wearied of his messiah-hood?

Mr Chisanga brought a troop of boys round this afternoon and, with James's[8] help, they made short work of clearing his room. He (BC) was accompanied by a 'brother' from Isoko.

The atmosphere in the house is noticeably cheerful and relaxed, 'liberated', one might say.

Wednesday, 18 December It's ironic that I came here to investigate 'spirit possession' and became myself possessed by a particularly oppressive entity.

Heard that BC is going round telling people that Uncle, Sylvia and Friday together bewitched me into firing him!

The day concludes with an informal party with SN, KS and our domestic staff. Uncle made a rather moving reference to 'our friend', meaning BC, almost as though he had died – which in a sense I suppose he has. There is spontaneous, light-hearted joking and chat, suggesting collective recovery from the trauma and crises of recent days, all focused on the person of the absent senior research assistant.

Thursday, 19 December Left bright and early on the long journey back to Lusaka, the goodbyes thankfully not too tearful. On our way out of the village, MTW thought she glimpsed BC 'in a tatty jacket', standing and watching us depart. What could have been his emotions at that moment? In Mbala we 'pick' Mr Mulengo, Moto Moto's indefatigable mechanic, who is to chauffeur us back to the Zambian capital. Learn that my dismissal of BC has surprised and, it seems, impressed the Museum authorities, who apparently thought I 'didn't have it in me'! Seems BC had been telling the Moto Moto people that he was the real boss of URP. Feel a little better.

Notes

1. The anthropologist's wife. She arrived in Zambia on 14.11.96.
2. So called because he uses a psychotropic 'medicine', which he gives to his clients. They reportedly then 'see' before them, as on a television screen, the thieves, sorcerers or adulterers who have secretly caused them damage. One other doctor in the 1996 census reported using 'television' as a divinatory technique.
3. Mainly affecting the cook, Mr Maliawanda, who was given new reponsibilities for buying foodstuffs in the market and encouraged to try out variations to the daily menu, innovations which he appeared to enjoy.
4. He left on Friday, 6 December, ostensibly with the intention of doing census work in villages around Mbala, using a motorcycle rented from his cousin Mr Webster Walker. He should have returned to Mankonga the same evening, but failed to appear as arranged.
5. Household and office furniture.
6. Ulungu Research Project research assistant in 1990, who died in 1993.
7. To receive what remained of his month's pay.
8. Mr James Bwalya, the house-cleaner.

–8–

Afterthoughts: Selfhood in the Global Village

> The confrontation and the dialogue continue long after our return to the academic home world.
>
> Kirsten Hastrup

Memories of Mankonga. The defining moment when *Kapyaana*, the chosen heir, dons the pink-striped shirt of the recently dead Lwamfwe Arnold and, in so doing, takes on a double identity: that of the deceased and his own. Or rather, and simultaneously with this dual identity, becomes a third, intermediate social entity, with qualities of both living and dead, a newly emergent, composite persona.

This moment of multiple vision, so eerily suggestive of 'spirit' imaginings, disembodied presences spanning past and future, melds in recollection with the passionate local discourse of funerary celebration and sorcery suspicions; a universe of familial relations, all-enveloping and endlessly ramifying recognitions, dependencies, dominations. The Lungu *ulupwa*, the concrete grouping of kinsfolk, is the matrix from which Cohenesque 'selves' emerge, in their necessary clothing of social roles, and this familial universe remains, in its structured complexity, the primary exemplification of human living.

Part of this primordial and enduring social envelope, pervading it but also extending beyond and outside it in different and more abstract orders of time and space, celebrated in traditional history and image, is what I've described earlier in this book (Chapter 3) as the fabric of Lungu ethnic identity, a collective, transfamilial selfhood.

All this is but the prologue to the story I'm particularly concerned with here, the cosmic drama of selfhood's abrupt awakening from the hypnotic familiarity of the quotidian life-world in its Lungu instance to engage with the utterly strange; and the meaning of that drama. But first a step back to consider anthropology's theoretical approach to the general topic of the human individual and society.

In one of his most brilliant – and enigmatic – essays, Marcel Mauss addressed this question with reference to the evolution of ideas of 'the person' *(la personne)* and 'the self' (*le moi*) in Western civilization (Mauss 1938). What Mauss tries to do is show how, from 'primitive' beginnings as abstract representations of social or clan identity (often concretely modelled as masks), the persona evolved into the quasi-sacred 'person' of Western modernity, indistinguishable from the spiritualized and objectively unknowable 'self' of Cartesian and Kantian philosophy. This conclusion raises obvious problems for the Durkheimian tradition of sociological reductionism, of which Mauss himself had been a prime exponent, and it's hardly surprising that a recent volume of essays by some distinguished anthropologists and philosophers who collectively focus on Mauss's argument fail to reach any coherent conclusion (Carrithers *et al.* 1985).[1]

I suggest, however, with Cohen (1994: 55–79), that it's useful to distinguish between 'the self' as the experiencing human agent and 'the person' as the socially constructed (and culturally relative) concept of such agency. If you like, the distinction is between the 'inner' or subjective, 'an essential and continuous core of experience' (Cohen 1994: 68), and the 'outer', objective aspects of human selfhood, as embodied in a repertoire of social roles.

Hobbes and Rousseau

In its engagement with other embodied, role-enacting individuals the self typically engages in an array of situationally changing relations with social others. These range from, at one extreme, total identification with the social whole or what Rousseau called the general will, to, at the other extreme, the self concerned only with calculating and achieving advantage over others, as in Hobbes's famous 'war of all against all'. The latter possibility is represented in anthropology in the theory of transactionalism and 'strategizing man'. Between these extremes, the individual is more usually involved in a set of supra-individual identifications, some ephemeral, others long-lasting, at various levels of collective selfhood, from local-group faction to tribe or nation (see Cohen 1994: Chapter 4, 'Social Transformations of the Self').

Field experience suggests, unsurprisingly, that Lungu folk resemble the rest of us in exhibiting a mix of egoistic and altruistic behaviour in relation to their fellows. Often, conflicting motivations lead individuals to express themselves in revealingly contradictory ways. Take, for example, the Lungu doctor Robert Simpungwe's statement before his masterful performance in the *ngulu* ritual at Mankonga on 1 November 1996, extolling the value of working with other doctors and the impossibility of doing so in isolation, given that drumming and singing were collective activities.[2] However, it's also recorded that immediately before the ritual began the same Robert Simpungwe was saying that he couldn't perform in a group 'because I don't want the other doctors to see how I work', provoking the scornful comment from Sylvia Nanyangwe (SN) that 'they [healers] are always like that' . Eventually, and fortunately, he was persuaded to take part (Diary 30.10.96, 1.11.96).[3]

The simple point I'm making, which is also Cohen's, is that in all societies the human self is characterized both by its moral plasticity and by its ability to assume a potentially infinite variety of social roles. As Cohen succinctly expresses it, 'I am simultaneously an individual, and yet part of relationships; unique, but conventional; the product of my genetic endowment, but also of society' (1994: 153).

Can this primordially unique self ever transcend its embodiment in social convention? For Cohen, apparently not. Whether strategizing or collective, the Cohenesqe 'authorial self' behaves rationally in a social context: little room here for self-transcendence in altered states of consciousness, the type of experience first importantly signalled in anthropology in Victor Turner's concept of astructural *communitas*. Cohen, indeed, sees this controversial state as 'an ideal which is the object of . . . aspiration but rarely, if ever, of achievement' (1994: 126).

This, of course, is where the present account parts company with Cohen's version of human selfhood. For the Lungu spirit-powered healers I'm concerned with here, selfhood is a tale of expansion into realms beyond the customary world of social convention and transaction, even while retaining ascribed and achieved roles in the local community. In the case of his Tumbuka healers, Friedson speaks of a *communitas* 'that is transitory, repeatable, and deep in its affect. In the community of Tumbuka healers people regularly transform their consciousness, by their own account, through musical means' (1996: 164). Likewise, we have Edith Turner's first-hand description of entering a dramatically altered state of consciousness during an Ndembu healing ritual in 1985 (Turner 1992).

The Shaman in Africa

There is also evidence that, in many non-Western societies, including, I suspect, a fair number of those whose ethnographic credentials are examined in Cohen's book, certain individuals experience culturally sanctioned changes in self-consciousness in the directions of expansion and plurality. In his discussion of selfhood in India and Japan, the American psychoanalyst Alan Roland contrasts the restricted and isolated self-concept of North American society with the extended familial and 'spiritual' self hoods available to individuals in the Indian and Japanese traditions (Roland 1988).[4] Speaking particularly of India, the field of his major foreign experience, Roland emphasizes that, although the spiritual goal is common to most, if not all, individuals, comparatively few advance far down that road: 'only the extremely rare person has attained a high degree of self-realization [but] . . . in the Indian cultural context, it is that person, or ones actively engaged in the search, who are profoundly respected at all levels of society' (1988: 291).[5]

So also in Ulungu: those who succeed in becoming doctors, typically through arduous and sometimes terrifying travails and ordeals, are a minority which I would estimate as less than one per cent of the population. As Roland observes, the rational-scientific culture of the West tends to ignore or denigrate the Indian search for 'spiritual' realization (1988: 289). Doubtless, also, there are, among those purporting to have achieved the goal, numerous charlatans seeking to profit from the high status culturally accorded to the spiritually enlightened. Lungu people, too, are aware, as we also are in modern society, that some 'doctors' are frauds.[6]

Another, more subtle interpretation of the behaviour of indigenous doctors purporting to work with the aid of 'spirits' is that these practitioners are subject to hallucinations and are mentally deranged. Earlier this century, anthropologists equated such practitioners with epileptics and hysterics and, in 1967, Silverman argued that such behaviour, long labelled 'shamanic' by anthropologists after the shamans or spirit-aided doctors of north-east Siberia, was equivalent to the Western-recognized psychiatric disorder of schizophrenia (Silverman 1967). In the same year, however, Handelman advanced a contrary view, which has since become substantially accepted in anthropology: that 'shamans', far from being psychically or mentally unsound, manifest an unusually strong sense of selfhood, proved by their ability to control and sustain drastic changes in consciousness (Handelman 1967).

In that context, one further and unnecessary problem which anthropology has created for itself is through its largely uncritical acceptance of Mircea Eliade's mystifying decision, in his classic account of the worldwide phenomenon of tribal shamanism, to exclude Africa from its scope (Eliade 1951). Eliade's decision, justified only in a laconic footnote, has led in its turn to a misleading identification of particular 'mystical' experiences with specific societies and culture regions. Thus, according to some authorities, shamanic 'journeying' or 'soul travel' is found only in Siberia and possibly (through ancient diffusion?) in native America, while black Africa, Brazil and the Caribbean are the domain of 'spirit possession' or mediumship.[7] In fact, as I.M. Lewis has cogently argued, these simplistic anthropological schemas 'by no means do justice to the multi-layered, multi-textured complexity of religion and religious experience. In reality, even within a single culture, the spectrum of religious experience is likely to embrace all those states so far distinguished' (Lewis 1997:125).

The nocturnal 'journeys' into the bush reported by many Lungu doctors, and which appear to resemble 'lucid' or 'conscious' dreams, readily evoke the reports of shamanic journeys into the 'spirit realm', as recounted by tribal and latter-day, urban shamans (see Harner 1980). Like shamans, these Lungu doctors regularly traverse the divide between the manifest world of ordinary reality and the hidden domain of 'spirit'.

A Short Cut to Charisma

Another misunderstanding of the significance of 'spirit' healers in Africa and elsewhere stems from an uncritical application of I.M. Lewis's seminal thesis postulating a causal connection between certain forms of 'spirit possession' and social deprivation or oppression, particularly of women by men (Lewis 1971). While Lewis's thesis has important explanatory value in many ethnographic instances, notably where there is an explicit ideology of male social dominance, even then it is typically far from being the whole story (see Boddy 1989). It makes little sense in the case of Ulungu, where no such ideology exists. It's true that women are prominent in the *ngulu* cult, though less so than I had initially supposed.[8] As I see it, the prime reason for the predominance of women in this cult is that these people belong to a social category whose members, by reason of their socially ascribed child-rearing and domestic duties, generally have little time in their earlier adult life for lengthy apprenticeships. *Ngulu* ritual is the fast track to doctoral status. As van Binsbergen notes, 'ecstasy offers a *shortcut to charisma*' (1991: 335, emphasis in original), and as such is tailor-made for those women who, like their male counterparts, constitute a small minority of their kind, but none the less find themselves impelled towards the life of spirit-aided healing.[9] And, as Lambek observes in Mayotte, possession is a means to a valued source of power and knowledge, and the possessed 'can gain compelling and authoritative voices' (1993: 322).

Whence comes this unusual impulsion? What is it that motivates these 'exceptional individuals', as Peek (1991: 13) describes those Africans 'called' to the path of divination and healing? Explanation has, it seems, to begin by positing an internal division in human 'being' between an innate and primal consciousness of selfhood and that selfhood's projection or objectification in the life-world of social relations.

Csordas, for instance, tells us that 'the self is objectified, most often as a "person" with a cultural identity or set of identities' (1994: 5), a definition echoed in Cohen's picture of the human individual as polarized between the innate and unique and the social and conventional (1994: 153). Jackson and Karp similarly juxtapose cultural concepts of personhood with 'the less explicit, more elusive experiences of self and other' (1990: 15). Sometimes this kind of internal opposition seems to be recognized in indigenous thought, as in Turnbull's account of Mbuti (pygmy) selfhood analysed by Cohen (1994: 29–35) and Jacobson-Widding's (1990) discussion of the shadow as an image of individuality among the peoples of the Lower Congo.

This 'elusive' quality of human selfhood, the fact that it's 'methodologically out of reach' (Cohen 1994: 179), has not deterred Cohen from developing a powerful thesis on the topic, basing his argument for the existential reality of the 'authorial self' on a combination of ethnographic testimonies, some arresting examples of the novelistic imagination and appeals to the reader's subjective sensibility. Victor Turner's 'anthropology of experience', of 'man and woman alive', philosophically grounded, as it is, in the work of Dilthey, invites consideration of human experience as 'a journey, a test (of self, of suppositions about others), a ritual passage, an exposure to peril, and an exposure to fear' (Turner 1985b: 226).

Another branch of human knowledge which offers tantalizing clues to the hidden nature of the human self is infant psychology. In a recent and important paper criticizing some influential suppositions by the phenomenological philosopher Maurice Merleau-Ponty, Gallagher and Meltzoff point to experimental evidence suggesting that the human newborn emerges into the world with an innate sense of the self–other relation, a sense based in a similarly innate concept of body schema (Gallagher and Meltzoff 1996). These findings bear out earlier work by Bower, according to which 'the data indicates that the newborn thinks he is a human being and has a great many social responses directed towards other human beings' (1977: 27–8). Another authority, Colwyn Trevarthen, has similarly informed us that human intersubjectivity is 'innate' (1993: 159).

These conclusions, which are completely contrary to the earlier, *tabula rasa* model of neonate consciousness,[10] are based on observation of the astonishing mimetic abilities of the newborn. A typical experiment, quoted by Gallagher and Meltzoff (1996), reports that an infant only forty-two minutes old exhibited 'strong imitation effects', opening its mouth and protruding its tongue in apparent response to similar gestures by an adult.[11]

This evidence from infant psychology of the existence in the human newborn of an innate, prelinguistic sociality is, I suggest, important confirming evidence for the thesis advanced in this book on the capacity of the human self to expand beyond the confines of the social to embrace para-social and para-human otherness. It's as if this innate – and thus universal – impulsion in the human organism to identify situationally with the other[12] not only enables that organism to engage in its adult work of creating and maintaining intersubjective reality; the same innate impulsion remains as a potential ability to reach experientially beyond the social and human.

In the Lungu instance, I've tried to show how, in the case of indigenous healers, use of this potential is often precipitated by a perilous life crisis; and also that this unusual ability arises out of a culturally general experience of mobile, transpersonal selfhood in the familial context, typified by the ambiguous identity of the heir as he/she goes through the inheritance ritual. I've also sought to show how, in the revelatory ordeal at the heart of the *ngulu* cult of the 'spirit' powers of the bush, adepts and initiates experience an expansion of selfhood beyond the collective boundaries embodied in Lungu social history.

The outcome of this process of expansion, as noted earlier (in Chapter 6), is an apparent paradox: the self-identity of these Lungu healers is both divided and plural, and integrated. The practising healer is, it seems, aware of having both a social self and an ecological or 'spiritual' self: the first focused in village and household and in therapeutic clientele, the second in the powers of the para-social and para-human powers of the bush. The practising healer oscillates between these opposed and yet complementary worlds, these divided and yet reciprocally empowering sites of selfhood.

Though locally exceptional, it appears that cross-culturally this situation is not so unusual. Roland, in his insightful account of a comparable process in Hindu Indian culture, the inner transformation of the seeker after enlightenment, seems to be describing a formally similar outcome when he makes what he describes as a 'paradoxical assertion' that 'the [Indian] spiritual self is simultaneously on a continuum with the familial self and in counterpoint to it' (Roland 1988: 294).

It thus seems that, notwithstanding the blatant cultural differences between Hindu India and Lungu Africa, a similar developmental process affecting the 'self' is at work in both ethnographic instances. It's a process that, though experienced directly by only a small minority of individuals, is yet, it would appear, universally human.

'Equiprimordiality of Human Being and World'

Returning from the general to the ethnographic particular, Friedson's account of his participatory experience of trance dancing during a healing ritual of the Tumbuka of northern Malawi is of special relevance to our theme. As Friedson describes it, the result was a dream in which 'the whisperings of the invisible *vimbuza* [spirits] caused my "self" to expand, creating a space within me, an opening, a clearing . . . the phenomenon of spirit possession is an opening of interior space' (1996: 21–2). In the light of this crucial subjective experience, Friedson proceeds to interpret the *vimbuza* healing rituals as examples of *Erlebnisse*, structured units of experience that are 'timeless' in that they unreflectively contain the past and envision the future. 'Repeated encounters with the music and dance of Tumbuka healing similarly coalesce into a rich lived experience, one that is manifest in its entirety immediately' (1996: 6). Friedson also draws on the radical thinking of Martin Heidegger to convey the way ordinary perception of space and subject-object relation is transformed in the *vimbuza* ritual, when participants experience 'an equiprimordiality of human Being and world' (ibid.: 7).

Friedson's testimony brings together the two topics whose relation provided the initial impetus for this ethnographic enquiry: the self and 'spirit'. And it portrays both entities at a privileged moment of mutual revelation: the 'self' moving outwards, 'expanding', the 'spirit' coming in, engaging with the self, entering in and being known.

Lungu healers' experience of commerce with 'spirits' is more diversely structured than that reported of their Tumbuka confrères, although the component elements are similar. As Friedman describes it, access to the *vimbuza*, who resemble *ngulu* in being spirits of the wild and foreign,[13] is invariably and necessarily mediated through the ancestral spirits, the *mizimu*, who establish communications with the *vimbuza* during the healing trance (1996: 64–5). In contrast, while some Lungu healers are introduced to the *ngulu* spirits of the bush by familial spirits, others (notably those known as '*ngulu* doctors') attain their healing powers through direct contact with *ngulu*. Moreover, the familial spirits reported as helping Lungu doctors are invariably those of recently dead relatives known to the practitioner in life, and who were usually doctors themselves (see Chapter 6). These differences presumably relate to differences in the reckoning of descent in these two societies, particularly the absence of a lineage system among the Zambian Lungu compared with the patrilineal communities of the Tumbuka (Friedson 1996: 53). Similarly, where Tumbuka 'spirit' healing operates through a single institution, that of the 'dancing prophets' who perceive – and recall – the diagnoses and treatments needed for their clients while in a trance state (Friedson 1996: 29), Lungu 'spirit' healers work in two modes: as *ngulu* doctors, who dance but do not speak after their spirits have announced their names in the revelatory ordeal and typically profess amnesia about their trance experiences, and doctor-diviners, whose helping spirits speak through them during consultations with clients. In both cultures, dreaming is salient as a mode of divination and discovery regularly used by healers (Chapter 6; Friedson 1996: 24, 28).

These cultural variations and parallels are the very stuff of old-style anthropology, predicated on an assumption of cognitive superiority *vis-à-vis* the 'anthropologized'. In that context, Friedson pointedly informs us that Tumbuka healing 'is not merely the eccentricity of a specific cultural style informed by a system of religious beliefs . . . all to be explained away as differences typically uncovered by ethnographers or ethnomusicologists' (1996: 36). It's interesting in several ways that, in explaining (as opposed to 'explaining away') Tumbuka healing, Friedson has turned to the philosophical language of Heidegger, the most radical questioner of the world-view of Western civilization, a thinker whose work has been described as obscure and even mystifying by some distinguished Western academic commentators, and to Dilthey, Heidegger's intellectual predecessor and progenitor. It's even more interesting and relevant to our purpose that, in the process of his participatory investigation of Tumbuka musical therapeutics, Friedson found himself doing phenomenology (1996: xvi, 168) in the Heideggerian mode, as, indeed, in the course of his work with Lungu healers, though more modestly, did Willis (Chapters 5 and 6).

The question that supremely concerned Heidegger, one that he claimed had been neglected and obscured through two and a half millennia of Western intellectual evolution, was that of the nature of being (*Dasein*). Reading Friedson, reading Edith Turner's pioneering account of transcendent experience during an Ndembu healing ritual (Turner 1992),[13] reliving the field research days in Mankonga, Kafukula and Kaizya, it seems to me this very question is raised and answered in the African therapeutic experience, in the healing encounter between self and spirit, those problematic entities whose hypothesized relation inspired the enquiry chronicled in this book.

Marriage of the radical thought of Heidegger with the experiential anthropology of Victor and Edith Turner has created a new beginning in ethnographic research, one that I now see as calling for a new language of its own, one apt to convey the verities of a technology wherein human selfhood opens to knowledge of its beingness in a world of objects likewise endowed with being. Such a project forces a fundamental reconsideration of traditional categories in Western thought, particularly 'selfhood' and 'spirit', of Western psychologies that 'tend to presuppose an intrinsic essence of the person which then "grows", "develops", "unfolds" or "matures" as it is "socialized" into the company of others' (Vitebsky 1993: 46).

High Technology and Selfhood

> What kinds of personae do we make? What relation do these have to what we have traditionally thought of as the 'whole' person? Are they experienced as an expanded self or as separate from the self?
>
> Sherry Turkle, *Life on the Screen: Identity in the Age of the Internet*

Before the oddly vacuous term 'post-modern' became current in anthropology, the prescient Marshall McLuhan described how the very nature of high-tech communications media was transforming our consciousness and sense of selfhood, quite irrespective of the actual content of the information transmitted: the medium was the message. Writing before the advent of the Internet and the Worldwide Web, McLuhan coined the pregnant phrase 'global village' to describe the dissolution of traditional boundaries between nation-states, ethnicities and cultures (McLuhan 1964). In this situation, we are told by a more recent authority, 'Computers don't just do things for us, they do things to us, including to our ways of thinking about ourselves and other people . . . The Internet has become a significant social laboratory for experimenting with the constructions and reconstructions of self that characterise postmodern life' (Turkle 1995: 26, 180). Turkle argues that the technology-driven culture of 'post-modernity' is dissolving the long-held conception of self-identity in modern Western civilization, one enunciated most persuasively by Descartes and according to which the self is unitary, isolated and enduring. The emergent new self, Turkle says, is multiple, flexible but – ideally – integrated, with open access between its differing but component aspects (ibid.: 178–80).[15]

Again, Heidegger offers a disturbingly radical 'take' on this issue. Seemingly, Western man fails to understand the meaning and potential of his own technology. Blinded by an ideology of instrumentality in which all nature and even humankind itself become an ordered 'standing reserve' awaiting exploitation, he fails to see the same technology's potentiality to reveal the truly new (Heidegger 1978: 307–9). Heidegger takes us back to the pre-Socratic Greek concept of *techne*, a word that does much more than combine what has since become the separate and opposed ideas of 'art' and 'technology': it also, and crucially, means to bring into radiant presence the dialogue of human and divine (ibid.: 316).

The trance experience of the Tumbuka 'dancing prophets', Friedson tells us, is the product of an indigenous technology, a pre-Socratic *techne* that has the power to bring forth human and spirit being in an encounter wherein quotidian reality is raised to a level of supernormal intensity (1996: 164). So also, I am certain, with the Lungu *ngulu*, and with the Ndembu *ihamba* ritual, we are enjoying what Edith Turner has well called 'a human birthright' (1992: xiii) – albeit one the civilization of the West has almost forgotten. Given that state of affairs, there is a special poignancy in the way Western 'high technology' in its current phase is, according to Heidegger (and Friedson), concealing beneath the appearance of instrumentality an epochal transformation in the Western sense of individual identity, moving it from the isolation and fixity of its Cartesian epiphany towards a fluidity, spontaneity, multiplicity and expansiveness (see Lifton 1993) surprisingly cognate with the nature of spirit being as apprehended in ancient text and 'primitive' culture.[16]

Language and the Matter of Spirits

> there is something beyond the social context . . . a matter of spirits.
>
> Edith Turner, *Experiencing Ritual*

> during *ngulu* . . . was aware of a powerful longing to be in that place where the spirits are.
>
> Diary 5.11.96

> But what do we make of worlds possessed by spirits, spirits moved by music? How do we interpret a world that is neither given nor experienced in Cartesian duality?
>
> Steven Friedson, *Dancing Prophets*

Exactly how do we speak of non-duality within a millennial scholarly tradition predicated on a division between observer and observed, mind and matter? The question becomes urgent with the advent of an anthropology committed to what William James (1977) originally named as radical empiricism. Applied to ethnography, as explained by Michael Jackson (1989), such an approach focuses on the field interaction between observer and observed as the very source of knowledge (see Friedson 1996: 167). Fortunately, we have in the nineteenth-century emergence of phenomenological philosophies a 'native' tradition of Western thought explicitly committed to overcoming the limitations of dualism. It's hardly surprising, therefore, that anthropologists striving to render their experience of cultures with non-dualist modes of being have seized on the ideas of Dilthey, Husserl, Schutz, Merleau-Ponty and Heidegger. What is radically new is the experiential verification of those ideas by Western ethnographers working in non-Western cultures (see Weiner 1991).

At the Edge

> The dialectical drama between the possessed and his spirit, between (human) self and (spirit) other, may well provide an allegory for the confrontation between the ethnographer and his people, between modern man and the primitive.
>
> Vincent Crapanzano, Introduction to *Case Studies in Spirit Possession* (1977)

Writing an ethnographic monograph under the sign of post-modern reflexivity is also an *Erlebnis* or lived experience in the Diltheyan sense; or, rather, it's a continuation, as Hastrup has suggested, of the fieldwork dialogue (or multilogue). In this situation, time expands, as in the passion of *ngulu*, to touch the distant past; for the participants, each performance is interconnected, as Friedson puts it, with previous such experiences (1996: 6). For the anthropologist, the connection, the temporal expansion, points the other way, towards the future, in his awareness that the memory of this experience is destined to grow into a book, this book.

But 'writing up', the post-research conversion of remembered experience into statement, partially creates what it brings into public presence. Return from the insulated universe of the 'field' forces re-engagement in the arena of social-scientific discourse, compelling recognition that this seemingly special *Erlebnis* is cognate with the 'lived experiences' of others and relates to their endeavours to speak what they know. This recognition brings clarification and surprise, taking the form, in my own case, of an unexpected coming-to-terms with the well-nigh shocking aptness of the most iconoclastic current in European thought to mapping the contours of extreme experience in seemingly alien African cultures.

I end with a paradox. The ethnographic data from the Lungu research appear to confirm the hypothesis with which I began: that human selfhood and the otherness of spirit being are intimately related; but true understanding of this 'equiprimordial' relationship, as realized in the ecstasy of the healing encounter, would seem to require a conceptual language that refuses any concession to dualism, particularly the notions of 'selfhood' and 'spirit' as these have evolved in our Western philosophical tradition.[17] Our own exploration as anthropologists of ways of knowing and being developed and perfected in foreign cultures has brought us to the 'edge' of a new territory (see Prattis 1997) for which as yet we have only the sketchiest of maps.

Notes

1. Mauss's equation of 'person' and 'self' seems clear in the title of his essay: 'Une catégorie de l'esprit humain: la notion de personne, celle de "moi"'. Another recent, multidisciplinary study of human selfhood avoids the definitionary issue by treating 'person' and 'self' as synonymous (Stevens 1996).
2. See above, pp. 92–3.
3. Similarly, in the course of work with 'alternative' healers in Scotland, I've more than once been brought up short by manifestations of jealousy and fear in relation to perceived rivals – sentiments far removed from the lofty ideals of New Age rhetoric.
4. Roland suggests that Indian perceptions of time and space are closely related to a sense of involvement in a complex web of extended-familial relationships (1988: 272–4), an argument similar to that advanced in respect of Lungu experience of time and space in Chapter 3 of this book.
5. Brian Morris, in his scholarly cross-cultural survey of concepts of personhood and selfhood, notes that 'the development of the self in India is quintessentially a quest for religious salvation' (1994: 194).
6. To guard against trickery, in serious cases Lungu travel long distances to find doctors they can be sure know nothing about them. The doctor's ability to intuit his or her patient's problems then becomes a test of the practitioner's *bona fides*. In 1990 our then research assistant Herbert Sikazwe crossed the border into Tanzanian Ulungu to find a doctor who could advise on the cause of the recent sudden death of his (Herbert's) elder brother Joseph. Mr Sikazwe told me later: 'The doctor,

whom I had never seen before, amazed me by describing my home and neighbourhood in great detail. Then I knew he was a good doctor.'

7. The threefold distinction between shamanism, spirit possession and spirit mediumship was first proposed by Raymond Firth (1959). Since then, Bourguignon, on the basis of a world-ranging statistical study covering 700 cultural groups, has suggested correlations between various forms of 'dissociational states' and discrete territorially based ethnicities (Bourguignon 1976). Lewis (1986, 1997), however, finds Bourguignon's conclusions in need of qualification.
8. The census of healers suggested that women constituted two-thirds of practising *ngulu* doctors. However, as I explain in Chapter 6 above, the distinction between *ngulu* doctors and other categories of healer is by no means always clear. Incidentally, I could find no evidence that the male *ngulu* cultists were in any sense socially inferior or deprived, as another element of Lewis's thesis would suppose (Lewis 1971).
9. As so often, there are both 'push' and 'pull' forces at work here, or what Schutz distinguished as 'because' and 'in order to' motivations (1972: 86–96). People undergo *ngulu* ritual in hopes of freeing themselves of unpleasant psychosomatic symptoms (the 'because' motive) but also in the expectation of status enhancement (the 'in order to') motive (see p. 189 above). The 'presenting symptoms' mentioned by the *ngulu* patients in Chapter 4 are conditions commonly treated by indigenous herbalists, but only a small minority of sufferers elect to seek relief through the *-tuntuula* ordeal.
10. The formerly unquestioned *tabula rasa* theory of neonate consciousness has been rendered untenable by experimental findings since the 1960s (see Bower 1977).
11. A further example of the mimetic powers of the human newborn, one that Bower found 'truly astonishing', is their ability to engage in what psychologists call 'interactional synchrony'. As Bower explains it, when a person speaks, he or she makes minute bodily movements, usually unconscious, which are synchronized with the meaningful units of speech peculiar to the speaker's language. Infants only twelve hours old, exposed to a stream of spoken language, have been experimentally shown to make corresponding bodily movements, 'a kind of dance' (Bower 1977: 30–2).
12. Another, fascinating insight into the primordial power of the human mimetic faculty is afforded by ethnographic evidence marshalled by Taussig (1993). In *Mimesis and Alterity*, the author brilliantly evokes historic encounters between the self-consciously 'civilized' and

perceived 'primitives', beginning with the dealings of Darwin and his companions on HMS *Beagle* with the aboriginal inhabitants of Patagonia, dubbed 'Fuegians'. What particularly exercised the father of modern evolutionary theory and his fellows was the seemingly compulsive need of the 'Fuegians' to imitate the appearance and behaviour of their alien visitors. Taussig comments, 'It's as if the Fuegians can't help themselves, that their mimetic flow is more like an *instinctual reflex* than a faculty' (1993: 81: emphasis added).

13. On 'foreign' incursions into Ulungu, see p. 126, n.33.
14. Curiously, Friedson neglects to mention Edith Turner's landmark contribution.
15. There is, as Turkle acknowledges, a down side to the post-modern metamorphosis of Western selfhood, in the psychic disintegration termed multiple personality disorder (MPD). The current epidemic of MPD in the USA is described in Littlewood (1996).
16. Despite local, 'cultural' differences, there is an unmistakable affinity between all scholarly accounts of selfhood and personhood under post-modernity, from California (Jameson 1984) to England (Strathern 1992): all emphasize fluidity and multiplicity, and the corresponding absence of the 'traditional' characteristics of 'depth' and permanence in self-identity.
17. Friedson seems to be reaching for such a language when he asserts that '[p]henomenologically, the *vimbuza* [spirits] are *the things themselves*' (1996: 164, emphasis in original).

Appendix: Follow-up Reports on *Ngulu* Patients and Doctors

Eighteen months on from the *ngulu* rituals described in Chapter 4, I asked 'Uncle' Kapembwa to interview the major participants – especially the patients but also the doctors – and report on their condition. He contacted all of them except Agrin Mazimba, whom he was unable to reach because her home in Sondwa Village was cut off by floods caused by unusually heavy rains in March 1998. The substance of 'Uncle''s reported findings was as follows.

All but one of the patients treated in the five *ngulu* rituals in 1996 was said to be in good health. The exception was Mary Nakazwe, who was said by Doctor Kapembwa to be 'worse than before':

> I examined her and found that she had no *ngulu* spirits. Instead she had *vyuuwa* [malign familial spirits] who were causing the trouble. It was unfortunate that the *ngulu* doctor who treated her [Jenera Nalondwa[1]] was not good at divining: if she had been a good diviner she would first have driven out the evil spirits, then discovered whether or not she had *ngulu*.

In contrast, Catherine Namwanza, who, before her treatment in 1996, was said to be suffering from 'eating disorders', is now said to be looking 'fat and happy'. She is currently working as a *mwaanang'aanga* (apprentice) under the supervision of her *ngulu* doctor, Lisita Nakazwe. She is hoping to receive *ntangala* from Doctor Nakazwe (authority to practise on her own with the title of *sing'aaanga* ('doctor')). In fact, according to 'Uncle', Catherine is already treating patients for problems other than *ngulu*, using *viziimba* (medicines made from animal substances), which she obtains from Doctor Nakazwe, and is becoming 'popular' in her neighbourhood.

Lonia Kasikila, daughter of Lisita Nakazwe, is said to have recovered fully from the various afflictions which led to her *ngulu* treatment. Although, like Catherine Namwanza, she has not yet received authority to set up as a doctor in her own right, Lonia is helping her mother in the treatment of *ngulu* patients and expects eventually to practise on her own.

Samuel Sichilima is also working as an apprentice (*mwaanang'aanga*), for his *ngulu* doctor Maddalena Namwinga. He is said to be free of health problems and has learned to 'dream medicines'.

Maddalena Namwinga is also in good health and travelling along the southern lake shore as far as Kapembwa (fifty kilometres from her home in Kapoko) to treat *ngulu* patients, accompanied by her apprentice Mr Sichilima.

Robert Simpungwe's health has improved 'tremendously' since 1996, according to 'Uncle'.

> He is now travelling about treating *ngulu* patients. When I called on him he was engaged in treating one, a woman called Richa Mwambozi, who is married to the local headman. Doctor Simpungwe was able to bring out (*-tuntuula*) her spirits, which included Mbita, Kapembwa, Mulenga and Chibawa (from Tabwa country). Richa is now working with Doctor Simpungwe as his apprentice.

Lisita Nakazwe is also said to be in 'excellent' health and continues to develop her clientele as an *ngulu* doctor, assisted by her daughters Lonia and her elder daughter Mevis (her *Musano,* or 'manager').

Joseph Simpanje has moved from Muswilo to Musipazi Village on the north-eastern plateau in Chief Zombe's area. He is said to be 'doing fine' and is attracting patients from many villages, some coming from across the border in Tanzania.

Note

1. This practitioner moved from Ulungu to Mufulira on the Zambian Copperbelt, a distance of several hundred kilometres, soon after performing the *ngulu* ritual described in Chapter 4.

Glossary of Lungu Terms

Azao, name of ethnic group led by Mwenya Mukulu (*q.v.*) who supposedly migrated into Ulungu and founded royal line of chiefs; also called *Azabu*. Their country of origin, *Uzao* (or *Uzabu*) is said to lie to the north-west of Ulungu in what is now the Democratic Republic of Congo (formerly Zaïre).

amaaka, power.

Chamukoleci, title of a sister of Mwenya Mukulu who traditionally bore the senior chiefs of Ulungu. Her descendant and present owner of the title is said to live at Kilambo in Tanzanian Ulungu.

Cipaapa, hereditary title of a man with the duty of carrying the pre-pubertal wife of Kapembwa, a girl who bears the title *Mwenya Mukulu*, to the shrine of Kapembwa (*q.v.*) during the annual ritual pilgrimage called *Mapepo* (*q.v.*)

Chinakila, Lungu chiefdom on the south-eastern plateau.

Chisya, guardian ecological spirit of the Chinakila chiefdom; said to be a father-in-law of Kapembwa.

Chitimbwa, Lungu chiefdom including part of the southern plateau, lakeshore and Yendwe valley. The chief Chitimbwa is the deputy (*musika wa kalamba*) of Senior Chief Tafuna and plays a major role in the *Mapepo* ritual.

Chungu, Lungu chiefdom on southern plateau.

cikolwe , forefather; anonymous male ancestor.

ciliimba, royal stool of office; kept in special round hut called *muntaalala* (see *miziingwa*, below).

Cisuungu, ritual of female initiation.

Cizaka, elder female in charge of relics at Chitimbwa's royal village; also title of senior wife of Senior Chief Tafuna.

ciziimba, catalytic or activating medicine made from animal or, occasionally, human substance; often associated with *uloozi,* sorcery.

Chilimanjaro (Kilimanjaro), popular *ngulu* (*q.v.*) spirit of Tanzanian origin.

cuuwa, malign spirit of departed relative; pl.: *vyuuwa* or *iviiwa.*

-ezy' uwiinga ('testing of the wedding'), ritual copulation of betrothed pair, to prove their suitability for marriage.

Fwema, chief of Tanzanian Ulungu, based at Kilambo.

ileembo, 'medicine', especially of vegetable origin.

Isoko ('the place of men'), royal capital of Ulungu and seat of Senior Chief Tafuna.

Kamata, Lungu Tribal Council, a body of senior elders charged with advising Senior Chief Tafuna on policy.

Kapembwa, principal ecological or *ngulu* spirit of Ulungu; the shrine of Kapembwa is located at the summit of the Polombwe promontory at the head of the Yendwe valley, overlooking Lake Tanganyika in western Ulungu.

kasesema, prophet; also used of the spirit thought to be gifting a person with predictive powers.

Kwalama, initiatory ritual undergone by a Lungu chief in which he submits himself to 'spirit' power. The greatest of these rituals (also called *Walamo*) requires Senior Chief Tafuna to submit himself to the lake spirit Kapembwa by 'swimming' the half-kilometre strait between Mpulungu and Nkumbula Island.

luumbwe, male consort of queen mother.

majini, anonymous evil spirits said to come from Tanzania, and to be sent by sorcerers to attack their victims.

-lwazya, to heal a sick person.

Mapepo ('Prayers'), traditional annual pilgrimage of Mwenya Mukulu, child incarnation of the founding ancestress of Lungu royalty, to the shrine of Kapembwa.

masiizo, licensed public comments made to an heir *(mupyaani*).

masuunde, instructions given in private to someone taking on an important new social role, such as a bridegroom.

matanga, commemorative meeting for a recently dead person.

Mbete, name of royal burial grove (*musitu*) on lakeshore near Mpulungu.

Mbita, name of spirit of eastern lake; Mbita's shrine is on Nkumbula Island opposite Mpulungu.

miziingwa, hut used to contain priestly or royal sacred objects; the objects themselves; the hut is sometimes also called *muntaalala*, ('doesn't sleep'), because it has to be built in a single day.

mpanga, the bush; non-human environment.

mpango, bridewealth.

mucinzi, respect; honour.

mucisi, ecological (or territorial) spirit shrine.

Mulenga, popular *ngulu* spirit, originally a creator divinity of the neighbouring Bemba people.

mupyaani, familial heir; also *kapyaana*.

musana, lit. 'loins' or 'lower back'; figuratively, *musana* denotes the side of the family (*ulupwa*) consisting of or descended from incoming females.

Musano, 'manager' of a healer with a particular relationship with *ngulu* spirits; the term is said to come from a Bemba word meaning 'head wife'.

Musika, principal executive of the Senior Chief Tafuna; the term is also applied to Songola, the 'killer' spirit guarding Kapembwa.

muzi'mu, ancestor spirit; pl., *mizimu*.

musuumba, royal village; also used of a chief's residence or 'palace'.

Mutumwa, popular name of Kasesema Prophet Church, devoted to healing and eradication of sorcery; has historical connections with the Malawian cult of *Chikanga* (on which see Redmayne 1970 and Friedson 1996).

mutwe, lit., 'head'; figuratively, *mutwe* denotes the side of the family (*ulupwa*) consisting of or descended from resident males.

muvyaala, cross-cousin (mother's brother's child or father's sister's child).[1]

Muwalanzi ('Person of the Sun'), primal male being and father of humanity in Lungu cosmogony.

Muzombwe, chiefling of Mbete (*q.v.*) who was, according to myth, humbled by Mwenya Mukulu (*q.v.*) and reduced to commoner status.

Mwenyami, primal female being and mother of humanity in Lungu cosmogony.

Mwenya Mukulu, female leader of Azao people who migrated into Ulungu and began the royal line of chiefs.

myaala, white cloth sent as tribute to Kapembwa or other divinity.

Namukale, ecological spirit of the 230-metre Kalambo Falls; the original Namukale is said to have been a woman of the Azao group of immigrant royals who killed herself by jumping over the falls to 'ransom' her brothers, who were being given insufficient respect by the indigenous people.

Namukolo, hereditary priest in charge of Mbita shrine and responsible for the *Walamo* (*q.v.*) ritual of chiefly initiation.

Ncimya, generic term for anti-sorcery and healing cult or church using Christian and Biblical traditions.

ndoosya, familial funeral ceremony.

ngulu, ecological spirit of non-human environment; ritual involving revelation of, and ecstatic union with, *ngulu* spirits.

Nondo, Lungu chiefdom of eastern plateau, bordering Bemba territory.

nsuumba, labour service performed by aspirant groom for prospective father-in-law.

Samaliya, name of Christian anti-sorcery and healing church; also name of spirit, classified as *ngulu*.
simapepo ('master of prayers'), priest of indigenous Lungu religion.
sing'aanga ('master of knowledge'), title of a recognized indigenous doctor or healer.
Tafuna, title of senior or paramount chief of Ulungu; the word literally means 'Chewer', and is a reference to a traditional story in which the first title-holder 'chewed' a certain tree before taking the poison ordeal, vomiting , and being found innocent of offending against his mother's brother.
Tunkulungu ('Short People'), name of aboriginal inhabitants of Ulungu.
-tuntuula, process of revealing *ngulu* spirits in afflicted person; to purify, make whole or holy.
uloozi, sorcery; use of noxious 'medicines' to harm or kill others.
ulupwa, collectivity of persons related by common descent or affinity and recognizing mutual rights and obligations; extended family; pl.: *ndupwa*.
umwaao, ancient term for ecological or territorial spirit; pl.: *imyaao*.
uwaanga, lit.: 'knowledge', a euphemism for *uloozi*, sorcery. Also *ciwaanga*, 'sorcery object' (pl.: *viwaanga*).
uwiinga, marriage ceremony; wedding.
viziimba, reinforcing and catalytic 'medicines' (*maleembo*) of animal – sometimes human – origin, often associated with sorcery; sing.: *ciziimba*.
Walamo, initiatory ritual of paramount Lungu chief *Tafuna*.
yama, mother's brother, actual or classificatory; reciprocal: *umwiipwa*, nephew or niece.
Zombe, Lungu chiefdom of north-eastern plateau and lakeshore.

Note

1. See Chapter 1 for a holistic account of Lungu familial organization and a survey of kin terms.

Bibliography

van Avermaet. E., and Mbuya, B. (1954), *Dictionnaire kiluba- français*, Tervuren: Musée Royale de l'Afrique Centrale.

Beattie, J.H.M. (1969),'Spirit mediumship in Bunyoro', in Beattie, J.H.M. and Middleton, J. (eds), *Spirit Mediumship and Society in Africa*, London: Routledge and Kegan Paul: 159–70.

de Boeck, F. (1992), 'Of healers, trees and kings', paper presented to Eighth Satterthwaite Colloquium on African Religion and Ritual, April 11–14.

Boddy, J. (1989), *Wombs and Alien Spirits: Women, Men, and the Zar Cult in Northern Sudan*, Madison: University of Wisconsin Press.

Bourguignon, E. (1976), *Possession*, San Francisco: Chandler and Sharp.

Bower, T.G.R. (1977), *A Primer of Infant Development*, San Francisco: Freeman.

Brelsford, W.V. (1956), *The Tribes of Northern Rhodesia*, Lusaka: Government Printer.

Bulkeley, K. (1996), 'Dreaming as spiritual practice', *Anthropology of Consciousness*, 7 (2): 1–15.

Capra, F. (1982), *The Turning Point: Science, Society, and the Rising Culture*, New York: Simon and Schuster.

Carrithers, M., Collins, S. and Lukes, S. (eds) (1985), *The Category of the Person: Anthropology, Philosophy, History,* Cambridge: Cambridge University Press.

Castaneda, C. (1968), *The Teachings of Don Juan: a Yaqui Way of Knowledge*, Berkeley: University of California Press.

—— (1971), *A Separate Reality*, New York: Simon and Schuster.

Castillo, R. (1995), 'Culture, trance, and the mind-brain', *Anthropology of Consciousness*, 6 (1): 17–34.

Clifford, J. and Marcus, G. (eds) (1986), *Writing Culture: the Poetics and Politics of Ethnography*, Berkeley: University of California Press.

Cohen, A.P. (1994), *Self Consciousness: an Alternative Anthropology of Identity*, London: Routledge.

Colson, E. (1969), 'Spirit possession among the Tonga of Zambia', in Beattie, J.H.M., and Middleton, J. (eds), *Spirit Mediumship and Society in Africa*, London: Routledge and Kegan Paul: 69–103.

Crapanzano, V. (1977), Introduction, in *Case Studies in Spirit Possession*, Crapanzano, V., and Garrison, V. (eds), New York, Wiley: 1–34.

Crick, M. (1992), 'Ali and me: an essay in street-corner anthropology', in Okely, J., and Callaway, H. (eds), *Anthropology and Autobiography*, London: Routledge: 175–92.

Csikszentmihalyi, M. (1992), *Flow: the Psychology of Happiness*, London: Rider Press.

Csordas, T.J. (1994), *The Sacred Self: a Cultural Phenomenology of Charismatic Healing*, Berkeley: University of California Press.

d'Aquili, E., Laughlin, C.D. and McManus, J. (1979), *The Spectrum of Ritual*, New York: Columbia University Press.

d'Aquili, E. and Laughlin, C.D. (1979), 'Neurobiology of myth and ritual', in d'Aquili *et al.* (1979), *The Spectrum of Ritual*, New York, Columbia University Press: 152–82.

Davis-Roberts, C. (1981), 'Kutumbuwa ugonjwa: illness and transformation among the Tabwa of Zaïre', *Social Science and Medicine*: 15B, 309–16.

Devisch, R. (1993), *Weaving the Threads of Life: the Khita Gyn-Ecological Healing Cult among the Yaka*, Chicago: Chicago University Press.

Doke, C.M. (1945), *Bantu*, London: International African Institute.

Durkheim, E. (1912), *Les Formes élémentaires de la vie religieuse,* Paris: Alcan.

Eliade, M. (1951), *Le Chamanisme et les techniques archaïques de l'extase,* Paris: Payot.

Evans-Pritchard, E.E. (1937), *Witchcraft, Oracles and Magic among the Azande*, Oxford: Clarendon Press.

Fabian, J. (1983), *Time and the Other*, New York: Columbia University Press.

Fagan, B. (ed.) (1966), *A Short History of Zambia*, London: Oxford University Press.

Favret-Saada, J. (1980, 1977), *Deadly Words: Witchcraft in the Bocage*, Cambridge, Cambridge University Press.

Firth, R. (1959), 'Problems and assumptions in the anthropological study of religion', *Journal of the Royal Anthropological Institute*, 89 (2): 129–48.

Forster, E.M. (1922), *Alexandria: a History and a Guide*, Alexandria: Whitehead Morris.

Friedson, S.M. (1996), *Dancing Prophets: Musical Experience in Tumbuka Healing*, Chicago: Chicago University Press.

Gallagher, S. and Meltzoff, A. (1996), 'The earliest sense of self and

others: Merleau-Ponty and recent developmental studies', *Philosophical Psychology*, 9 (2): 213–36.
Gazzaniga, M. (1998), *The Mind's Past*, Berkeley: University of California Press.
Goodman, F. (1988), *Ecstasy, Ritual, and Alternate Reality*, Bloomington: Indiana University Press.
Goulet, J.-G. (1994), 'Dreams and visions in other lifeworlds', in Young, D.E. and Gourlet, J.-G. (eds), *Being Changed: the Anthropology of Extraordinary Experience*: Peterborough: Broadview Press: 16–38.
Green, C. (1968), *Lucid Dreams*, Oxford: Institute of Psychophysical Research.
Griaule, M. (1951), *Conversations with Ogotemmêli*, London: Oxford University Press.
Guthrie, M. (1971), *Comparative Bantu*, Farnborough: Gregg International.
Halemba, A. (1994), *Mambwe–English Dictionary*, Ndola: Franciscan Mission Press.
Handelman, D. (1967), 'Development of the Washoe shaman', *Ethnology*, 6: 444–64.
Harner, M. (1980), *The Way of the Shaman*, New York: Bantam.
Hastrup, K. (1992), 'Writing ethnography: state of the art', in Okely, J. and Callaway, H. (eds), *Anthropology and Autobiography*, London: Routledge: 116–33.
Hayes, E.N. and Hayes, T. (eds) (1970), *Claude Lévi-Strauss: the Anthropologist as Hero*, Cambridge: M.I.T. Press.
Heidegger, M. (1978), *Basic Writings*, London: Routledge and Kegan Paul.
Hinfelaar, H.F. (1989), Religious change among Bemba-speaking women of Zambia, PhD Thesis, London: University of London.
Hoch, E. (1960), *A Pocket Bemba Dictionary*, Abercorn: White Fathers.
Jackson, M. (1989), *Paths Towards a Clearing: Radical Empiricism and Ethnographic Inquiry*, Bloomington: Indiana University Press.
—— and Karp, I. (1990), 'Introduction', in Jackson, M. and Karp, I. (eds), *Personhood and Agency: the Experience of Self and Other in African Cultures*, Uppsala: Acta Universitatis Upsaliensis: 15–30.
Jacobson-Widding, A. (1990), 'The shadow as an expression of individuality in Congolese conceptions of personhood', in Jackson, M. and Karp, I. (eds), *Personhood and Agency: the Experience of Self and Other in African Cultures*, Uppsala: Acta Universitatis Upsaliensis: 31–58.
James, W. (1977), *The Writings of William James*, Chicago: University of Chicago Press.

Jameson, F. (1984), 'Postmodernism, or the cultural logic of late capitalism', *New Left Review*, 146: 53–92.

Janzen, J. (1992), *Ngoma: Discourses of Healing in Central and Southern Africa*, Berkeley: University of California Press.

Kagaya, R. (1987), *A Classified Vocabulary of the Lungu Language,* Tokyo: Institute for the Study of the Languages and Culture of Asia and Africa.

Kapferer, B. (1995), 'From the edge of death: sorcery and the motion of consciousness', in Cohen, A.P. and Rapport, N. (eds), *Questions of Consciousness*, London: Routledge: 134–52.

LaBerge, S. and Rheingold, H. (1990), *Exploring the World of Lucid Dreaming,* New York: Ballantyne Books.

Lambek, M. (1993), *Knowledge and Practice in Mayotte: Local Discourses of Islam, Sorcery, and Spirit Possession,* Buffalo: University of Toronto Press.

Lan, D. (1985), *Guns and Rain: Guerrillas and Spirit Mediums in Zimbabwe*, London: James Currey.

Lévi-Strauss, C. (1955), *Tristes Tropiques*, Paris: Plon.

Lewis, I.M. (1971), *Ecstatic Religion: an Anthropological Study of Spirit Possession*, Baltimore: Penguin Books.

—— (1986), *Religion in Context: Cults and Charisma*, Cambridge: Cambridge University Press.

—— (1997), 'The shaman's quest in Africa', *Cahiers d'études africaines*, 145 (XXXVII-1): 119–35.

Lex, B. (1979), 'The neurobiology of ritual trance', in d'Aquili, E., Laughlin, C.D. and McManus, J. (eds), *The Spectrum of Ritual*, New York: Columbia University Press: 117–51.

Lienhardt, R.G. (1961), *Divinity and Experience: the Religion of the Dinka*, London: Oxford University Press.

Lifton, R.J. (1993), *The Protean Self: Human Resilience in an Age of Fragmentation*, New York: Basic Books.

Littlewood, R. (1996), *Reason and Necessity in the Specification of the Multiple Self*, London: Royal Anthropological Institute.

Livingstone, D. (1874), *The Last Journals of David Livingstone,* London: John Murray.

Long, A. (1992), *In a Chariot Drawn by Lions: the Search for the Female in Deity*, London: Women's Press.

Ludwig, A. (1969), 'Altered states of consciousness', in Tart, C. (ed.), *Altered States of Consciousness*, New York: Wiley: 9–22.

McLuhan, M. (1964), *Understanding Media*, London: Routledge and Kegan Paul.

Macrae, J. (1963), 'Kapembwa', *Northern Rhodesia Journal,* 5: 246–50.

Mauss, M. (1938), 'Une catégorie de l'esprit humain: la notion de personne, celle de "moi"', *Journal of the Royal Anthropological Institute*, 68: 263–81.

Mitchell, J.C. (1956), *The Yao Village*, Manchester: Manchester University Press.

Moody, R.A. (1975), *Life After Life*, New York: Bantam Books.

Moore, H. and Vaughan, M. (1994), *Cutting Down Trees: Gender, Nutrition, and Agricultural Change in the Northern Province of Zambia, 1890–1990,* London: James Currey.

Morris, B. (1994), *Anthropology of the Self*, London: Pluto Press.

—— (1995), 'Woodland and village: reflections on the "animal estate" in rural Malawi', *Journal of the Royal Anthropological Institute, n.s.*, 1, 301–15.

—— (1998), 'The powers of nature', *Anthropology and Medicine*, 5 (1): 81–101.

Mundkur, B. (1983), *The Cult of the Serpent*, Albany: State University of New York Press.

Needham, R. (1967), 'Percussion and transition', *Man, n.s.*, 2: 606–14.

Neher, A. (1962), 'A physiological explanation of unusual behavior in ceremonies involving drums', *Human Biology,* 4: 151–60.

Okely, J. (1992), 'Participatory experience and embodied knowledge', in Okely, J. and Callaway, H. (eds), *Anthropology and Autobiography*, London: Routledge: 1–28.

Pagels, E. (1979), *The Gnostic Gospels*, London: Penguin.

Parkin, D.J. (1978), *The Cultural Definition of Political Response: Lineal Destiny among the Luo*, London: Academic Press.

Peek, P.M. (ed.) (1991), *African Divination Systems: Ways of Knowing*, Bloomington: Indiana University Press.

Pottier, J. (1988), *Migrants No More: Settlement and Survival in Mambwe Villages, Zambia,* Bloomington: Indiana University Press.

Prattis, J.I. (1997), *Anthropology at the Edge: Essays on Culture, Symbol, and Consciousness,* Lanham: University Press of America.

Ranger, T.O. (1973), 'Territorial cults in the history of Central Africa', *Journal of African History,* 14 (4): 581–97.

Redmayne, A. (1970), 'Chikanga: an African diviner with an international reputation', in Douglas, M. (ed.), *Witchcraft Confessions and Accusations*, London: Tavistock.

Richards, A.I. (1937), 'Reciprocal clan relationships among the Bemba of N.E. Rhodesia', *Man*, 37 (222): 188–93.

—— (1939), *Land, Labour and Diet in Northern Rhodesia: an Economic Study of the Bemba Tribe,* London: Oxford University Press.
Robert, J.M. (1949), *Croyances et coutumes magico-religieuses des Wafipa paiëns*, Tabora: Tanganyika Mission Press.
Roberts, A.D. (1973), *A History of the Bemba,* London: Longman.
—— (1976), *A History of Zambia*, London: Heinemann.
Roberts, A.F. (1984), 'Fishers of men: religion and political economy among colonized Tabwa', *Africa*, 54 (2): 49–70.
—— (1988), 'Through the bamboo thicket: the social process of Tabwa ritual performance', *The Drama Review*, 32 (2): 123–38.
Roberts, M. (1984), *The Wild Girl,* London: Minerva.
Roland, A. (1988), *In Search of Self in India and Japan: Towards a Cross-cultural Psychology*, Princeton: Princeton University Press.
Rouget, G. (1980), *La musique et la transe: esquisse d'une théorie générale de la possession*, Paris: Gallimard.
Schoffeleers, J.M. (ed.) (1979), *Guardians of the Land,* Gwelo: Mambo Press.
Schutz, A. (1972), *The Phenomenology of the Social World,* London: Heinemann.
Shorter, A. (1972), *Chiefship in Western Tanzania*, London: Oxford University Press.
Silverman, J. (1967), 'Shamans and acute schizophrenia', *American Anthropologist*, 69, 21–31.
Singleton, M. (1978), 'Spirits and "spiritual direction": the pastoral counselling of the possessed', in Fashole-Luke, E., Gray, R., Hastings, A. and Tasie, G. (eds), *Christianity in Independent Africa*: London: Rex Collings: 471–8.
Southall, A. (1972), 'Twinship and symbolic structure', in La Fontaine, J. (ed.), *The Interpretation of Ritual*, London: Tavistock: 73–114.
Sperry, R.W. and Henniger, P. (1994), 'Consciousness and the cognitive revolution: a true worldview paradigm shift', *Anthropology of Consciousness*, 5 (3): 3–7.
Stevens, R. (ed.) (1996), *Understanding the Self*, London: Sage.
Stoller, P. and Olkes, C. (1987), *In Sorcery's Shadow*, Chicago: University of Chicago Press.
Strathern, M. (1992), *After Nature: English Kinship in the Late Twentieth Century*, Cambridge: Cambridge University Press.
Tart, C. (ed.) (1969), *Altered States of Consciousness,* New York: Wiley.
—— (1975), *States of Consciousness*, New York: Dutton.
Taussig, M. (1993), *Mimesis and Alterity*, London: Routledge.
Temple, R.K.G. (1976), *The Sirius Mystery*, Rochester: Destiny Books.

Tedlock, B. (1987), *Dreaming: Anthropological and Psychological Interpretations*, Cambridge: Cambridge University Press.

Thomson, J. (1881), *To the Central African Lakes and Back*, London: Cass.

Trevarthen, C. (1993), 'The self born in intersubjectivity: the psychology of an infant communicating', in Neisse, U. (ed.), *The Perceived Self: Ecological and Interpersonal Sources of Self-knowledge*, Cambridge: Cambridge University Press.

Turkle, S. (1995), *Life on the Screen: Identity in the Age of the Internet*, London: Phoenix.

Turner, E. (1992), *Experiencing Ritual: a New Interpretation of African Healing*, Philadelphia: University of Pennsylvania Press.

—— (1993), 'The reality of spirits: a tabooed or permitted field of study?', *Anthropology of Consciousness*, March: 9–12.

Turner, V.W. (1962), *Chihamba, the White Spirit: a Ritual Drama of the Ndembu*, Manchester: Manchester University Press.

—— (1967), *The Forest of Symbols: Aspects of Ndembu Ritual,* Ithaca: Cornell University Press.

—— (1968), *The Drums of Affliction: a Study of Religious Processes among the Ndembu of Zambia*, Oxford: Clarendon.

—— (1969), *The Ritual Process: Structure and Anti-structure*, Chicago: Aldine.

—— (1985a), 'The anthropology of performance', in Turner, E. (ed.), *On the Edge of the Bush: Anthropology as Experience',* Tucson: University of Arizona Press: 177–204.

—— (1985b), 'Towards a new processual anthropology', in Turner, E. (ed.), *On the Edge of the Bush: Anthropology as Experience,* Tucson: University of Arizona Press: 205–26.

—— (1985c), 'Body, brain, and culture', in Turner, E. (ed.), *On the Edge of the Bush: Anthropology as Experience,* Tucson: University of Arizona Press: 249–73.

van Binsbergen, W. (1979), *Religious Change in Zambia*, London: Kegan Paul.

—— (1991), 'Becoming a sangoma: religious anthropological field-work in Francistown, Botswana', *Journal of Religion in Africa*, 309–43.

van Gennep, A. (1909), *Les Rites de passage*, Paris: Librairie Critique.

Vitebsky, P. (1993), *Dialogues With the Dead: the Discussion of Mortality among the Sora of Eastern India,* Cambridge: Cambridge University Press.

Wagner, R. (1975), *The Invention of Culture*, Chicago: University of Chicago Press.

Watson, W. (1958), *Tribal Cohension in a Money Economy,* Manchester: Manchester University Press.

Weiner, J.F. (1991), *The Empty Place: Poetry, Space, and Being among the Foi of Papua New Guinea,* Bloomington: Indiana University Press.

Werbner, R. (ed) (1977), *Regional Cults*, London: Academic Press.

—— (1989), *Ritual Passage, Sacred Journey: the Process and Organization of Religious Movement,* Manchester: Manchester University Press.

Werner, D. (1971), 'Some developments in Bemba religious history', *Journal of Religion in Africa*, 4: 1–24.

—— (1979), 'Miao spirit shrines in the religious history of the southern Lake Tanganyika region: the case of Kapembwa', in Schoffeleers, J.M. (ed.), *Guardians of the Land*, Gwelo: Mambo Press: 89–129.

Whiteley, W. (1964), 'Suggestions for recording a Bantu language in the field', *Tanganyika Notes and Records*, 62: 1–19.

Willis, R.G. (1964), 'Traditional history and social structure in Ufipa', *Africa*, 34 (4): 340–52.

—— (1966), *The Fipa and Related Peoples of South-west Tanzania and North-east Zambia*, London: International African Institute.

—— (1968a), 'Kamcape: an anti-sorcery movement in south-west Tanzania', *Africa,* 38 (1), 1–15.

—— (1968b), 'Changes in mystical concepts and practices among the Fipa', *Ethnology*, 7 (2): 139–57.

—— (1972), 'Pollution and paradigms', *Man*, 7 (3): 369–78.

—— (1975), 'Is the anthropologist human?', *New Society*, 31 (651): 778–9.

—— (1978), '"Magic" and "medicine" in Ufipa', in Wallis, R. and Morley, P. (eds), *Culture and Curing, Anthropological Perspectives on Traditional Medical Beliefs and Practices*, London: Peter Owen: 139–51.

—— (1981), *A State in the Making: Myth, History, and Social Transformation in Precolonial Ufipa,* Bloomington: Indiana University Press.

—— (1990), 'The meaning of the snake', in Willis, R. (ed.), *Signifying Animals*, London: Unwin Hyman: 246–52.

—— (1991a), *Social and Political Organization of the Lungu People of Zambia and Tanzania: End of Award Report to the ESRC*, London: British Library.

—— (1991b), 'The Great Mother and the God of the Lake: royal and priestly power in Ulungu', *Zambian Journal of History*, 4: 21–9.

—— (1992a), 'Encounter with healing', *Journal of Alternative and Complementary Medicine*, April: 14–15.

—— (1992b), 'Triality, duality and unity in Lungu cosmology', *Shadow*, 9: 42–8.
—— (1992c), 'What makes a healer?', *Journal of Alternative and Complementary Medicine,* November: 11.
—— (1994), 'New shamanism', *Anthropology Today*, December: 16–18.
—— (1997), *Some Spirits Heal, Others Only Dance.* Film produced in association with the Audio-Visual Department, University of Edinburgh.
Winkelman, M.J. (1992), *Shamans, Priests and Witches: a Cross-cultural Study of Magico-religious Practitioners,* Tucson: Arizona State University.

Archival Sources

Abercorn District Notebook (ref. KTN 1/1), Zambia National Archives, Lusaka.
London Missionary Society, correspondence from missionaries in Ulungu, 1883–1939. Held in library of the School of Oriental and African Studies, University of London, Church Missionary Society Archives, Central Africa.
Rhodes House, Oxford, East African Colonial Archives: Ufipa District Notebook.

Index